The Future of the Accounting Profession

The Future
of the Accounting
Profession

A GLOBAL PERSPECTIVE

Kenneth S. Most

Quorum Books
WESTPORT, CONNECTICUT • LONDON

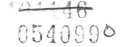

Library of Congress Cataloging-in-Publication Data

Most, Kenneth S.
 The future of the accounting profession : a global perspective /
Kenneth S. Most.
   p.   cm.
 Includes bibliographical references and index.
 ISBN 0–89930–726–4 (alk. paper)
 1. Accounting. 2. Financial statements. 3. Auditing.
 4. Accounting—Standards. 5. Auditing—Standards.   I. Title.
 HF5635.M8758   1993
 657—dc20   92–34945

British Library Cataloguing in Publication Data is available.

Library of Congress Catalog Card Number: 92–34945
ISBN: 0–89930–726–4

First published in 1993

Quorum Books, 88 Post Road West, Westport, CT 06881
An imprint of Greenwood Publishing Group, Inc.

Printed in the United States of America

The paper used in this book complies with the
Permanent Paper Standard issued by the National
Information Standards Organization (Z39.48–1984).

10 9 8 7 6 5 4 3 2 1

Copyright Acknowledgment

Permission is gratefully acknowledged to reproduce pages 5–10 of *Accounting Theory* by Kenneth
S. Most (Toronto: Holt, Rinehart and Winston of Canada, Limited, 1986).

CONTENTS

Illustrations   vii

Preface   ix

List of Acronyms   xi

CHAPTER 1
Trouble in the Accounting Profession   1

CHAPTER 2
A Short History of Accounting   13

CHAPTER 3
The Development of Accounting Thought   31

CHAPTER 4
Generally Accepted Accounting Principles   47

CHAPTER 5
The Auditing Problem   63

CHAPTER 6
International Accounting and Auditing   77

CHAPTER 7
A Conceptual Framework for Financial Reporting   93

CHAPTER 8
Regulation of Financial Reporting—The Disclosure Issue   111

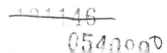

CHAPTER 9
    Financial Reporting and Changing Prices   125

CHAPTER 10
    Current Cost Accounting   147

CHAPTER 11
    The Financial Statements   161

CHAPTER 12
    Improving the Financial Statements   179

CHAPTER 13
    The Future of Auditing   191

CHAPTER 14
    The Future of Financial Reporting   203

    Selected Bibliography   215

    Index   219

ILLUSTRATIONS

FIGURES

3.1	The Accounting Model of the Firm	38
3.2	The Investment Cycle	40
7.1	Conceptual Framework for Financial Accounting and Reporting	97
8.1	SEC Form 10-K Disclosures	115
10.1	Backlog Depreciation	155

TABLES

9.1	Constant Dollar—Current Cost	140
11.1	Value-Added Form of Income Statement	170
11.2	Types of Information	177
12.1	Combination Income Statement, Statement of Cash Flows, and Balance Sheet	184

PREFACE

"I hold every man to be a debtor to his profession," said Sir Francis Bacon. This book attempts to repay a debt that has been accumulating since 1940. It represents an affirmation of the validity of the accounting profession, a critique of current practice, and a prescription for reform.

One who recommends change should be prepared to produce credentials. Since 1957 I have been publishing books, articles, and research reports, providing a good audit trail. In the 1950s I tried, to persuade the profession in the United Kingdom to take a leadership role in Europe. In the early 1960s I pioneered both empirical research and research in international accounting. During this period I drew the attention of my colleagues in the United Kingdom to several practice problems that have only recently received widespread attention. An early attempt at a conceptual framework (1962) was accompanied by writings that drew attention to the possibilities of replacement value accounting. In 1969 I proposed two forms of experimental financial statement, one of which subsequently surfaced as reserve recognition accounting, the other as the statement of cash flows. More recently, my publications have dealt with international accounting and auditing, a 1988 research report having proved prophetic of the BCCI scandal.

On more technical questions, there are many articles and the discussions in my book *Accounting Theory*, which, for example, identified the issues involved in marking liabilities to market. I have been a regular respondent to exposure drafts of the Financial Accounting Standards Board and the International Accounting Standards Committee; my submissions form part of the public record.

This book starts with a historical survey, then subjects the present state of affairs to a critical examination, leading eventually to proposals for action. Some of these proposals may strike readers as radical, particularly those contained in Chapters 13 and 14.

Many thanks to Marie Levine and Dalia Emery who typed much of the manuscript for this book, and to the many colleagues who have contributed to my education over the years, although they may not have perceived it at the time.

LIST OF ACRONYMS

AAA	American Accounting Association
AACSB	. American Association of Collegiate Schools of Business
AAPA	American Association of Public Accountants
AcSEC	AICPA's Accounting Standards Executive Committee
AIA	American Institute of Accountants
AICPA	American Institute of Certified Public Accountants
APB	Accounting Principles Board
APBO	Opinion of the APB
ARB	Accounting Research Bulletin of the CAP of the AICPA
ARS	Accounting Research Study of the APB
ASAC	Accounting Standards Authority of Canada
ASB	Auditing Standards Board (of the AICPA)
ASC	Accounting Standards Committee
ASR	Accounting Series Release (of the SEC)
ASSC	Accounting Standards Steering Committee
BCCI	Bank of Credit and Commerce International
CAP	Committee on Accounting Procedure of the AICPA
CAUP	Committee on Auditing Procedures
CCA	Current Cost Accounting
CCAB	Consultative Committee of Accountancy Bodies
CICA	Canadian Institute of Chartered Accountants

CPA	Certified Public Accountant
CPIU	Consumer Price Index for All Urban Consumers
EC	European Community
EITF	Emerging Issues Task Force
FAS	Statement of Financial Accounting Standards of the FASB
FASB	Financial Accounting Standards Board
FCPA	Foreign Corrupt Practices Act
FRR	Financial Reporting Release (of the SEC)
GAAP	Generally Accepted Accounting Principles
GAAS	Generally Accepted Auditing Standards
GASB	U.S. Government Accounting Standards Board
IAG	IFAC International Auditing Guideline (now standard)
IAS	IASC Statement of Accounting Standards
IASC	International Accounting Standards Committee
IFAC	International Federation of Accountants
IIT	International Investment Trust
IOS	Investors Overseas Services, Ltd.
IOSCO	International Organization of Securities Commissions
LIFO	Last In-First Out (valuation method)
MNC	Multinational Corporation
MWCA	Monetary Working Capital Adjustment
NASBA	National Association of State Boards of Accountancy
NYSE	New York Stock Exchange
OECD	Organization for Economic Cooperation and Development
ROI	Return on Investment
ROWC	Return on Working Capital
RVA	Replacement Value Accounting
SAP	Statement on Auditing Procedure
SCF	Statement of Cash Flows
SCFP	Statement of Changes in Financial Position
SEC	Securities and Exchange Commission
SFAC	Statement of Financial Accounting Concepts of the FASB
SSAP	Statement of Standard Accounting Practice (U.K.)
SSAR	Statement on Standards for Accounting and Review Services

The Future
of the Accounting
Profession

CHAPTER 1

TROUBLE IN THE ACCOUNTING PROFESSION

INTRODUCTION

The accounting profession in the United States is a profession that has lost its way. This does not mean that accountants elsewhere are without problems. Nevertheless, accountants in the English-speaking countries are in the most dire straits, and those in the United States have it the worst. Their product, the financial report, is a costly mess; their generally accepted accounting principles in chaos; their signatures on audit reports suspect; and their education and training declared unacceptable. How did it get this way, and what can be done about it?

ACCOUNTANTS AND FINANCIAL REPORTING

In every type of human endeavor records are kept as an aid to decision-making, to help comprehend outcomes, avoid repeating mistakes, and improve performance. In business, such records take the form of accounting, based on double-entry bookkeeping. Business managers who are accountable to investors, creditors, tax authorities, employees, and others, discharge this duty by issuing financial reports prepared from accounting records (financial statements).

To make sure that business managers resist the temptation to issue false or misleading financial statements, sophisticated users require that a competent and credible independent party audit such statements and provide an audit report stating that they "present fairly, in accordance with generally accepted accounting principles." What constitutes fair presentation in the United States is found in large measure in standards published by the Financial Accounting Standards Board (FASB) and its predecessor organizations. Other countries use similar standards. Public accountants who are responsible for these attestations are known collectively as the accounting profession. In the United States, public accountants are certified by the states (CPAs) and are represented nationally by the American Institute of Certified Public Accountants (AICPA).

The accounting profession has reached a critical stage of its history. During 1990 one of the largest firms of public accountants in the world filed for bankruptcy and closed down, an event that would have been unimaginable ten years earlier. The monetary amount of legal claims that the Big Six[1] faced in 1992 exceeded $7 billion. Yet many saw the situation coming and had published advance warnings.

A letter from the chairman of the board of the American Institute of Certified Public Accountants accompanied dues notices for the year 1986–87. It began: "I am writing you with a great sense of urgency. The accounting profession is confronted with an unprecedented array of issues that threaten the way we practice our profession and the way business is conducted in this country."

The proximate cause of this pronouncement was an investigation of the accounting profession by a committee of the United States Congress (the Dingell Commission), and attempts by some legislators to amend the federal securities laws in order to increase accountants' liability. The chairman sounded a similar note in his inaugural speech to the institute at its ninety-ninth annual meeting in October 1986. Both the letter and the speech were aimed at provoking members to oppose these legislative initiatives; they did not constitute recognition of the underlying causes of the malaise.

I first attempted to draw attention to these in two articles published in *The Accountant* (London) twenty-five years ago.[2] In the United States, Abraham Briloff excoriated the profession for its obvious failures in a series of articles in *Barrons* and in two brilliant books.[3] Similar criticisms can be found in a work by attorney Irving Kellogg.[4]

EARLIER CRITICISMS OF ACCOUNTANTS

The Dingell Commission was simply a new means of criticizing accountants and accounting. Prior to the 1930s the critics were mainly economists, who found it difficult to use financial statements for their analyses. These critics observed the following:

   —Financial reports to stockholders did not show realized and liquidated profits available for distribution or additional investment, or cumulative investment, profit, and dividends to date.

   —Financial statements for credit-monitoring did not reveal current market values of assets or settlement amounts of legal claims against them.

   —Tax assessment required that financial statements be reworked in accordance with tax laws to calculate taxable income.

   —Important information was omitted from financial reports, such as value-added. Value-added is the difference between a firm's sales and its purchases, and is therefore the source of wages, rents, interest, dividends, and capital investment. For this reason it is important, for example, in labor negotiations, because unions seek to maximize labor's share. It is also an excellent tax base, widely used as such in Europe.

In addition, several dubious accounting practices were identified, some of which accountants have changed during the past sixty years. Criticism of accountants by accountants started in the 1920s, and reached a strident level in 1939 with the publication of Kenneth MacNeal's *Truth in Accounting*. MacNeal, a CPA with many years' experience, denounced widespread abuses such as permitting profits and losses to bypass the income statement, which facilitated income manipulation by the creation of reserves in good years and their reversal in bad ones. His main target, however, was the accountant's unwillingness to *value*, recalling Oscar Wilde's definition of a cynic: one who "knows the price of everything, and the value of nothing." Because the figures in financial statements consisted of historical costs, the statements had no relation to "the truth."[5]

The truth, said MacNeal, a student of economists Irving Fisher and John Canning, lay in "the meaning of value in its economic aspect," which he believed was well known and complete enough to serve most practical purposes. "A balance sheet and profit and loss statement purport to state values. In order to fulfil their purpose they must state values according to economic concepts." This was itself a misleading proposition, because economics is not a science of values but of relative prices. Modern economic theory can be said to have started when the medieval schoolmen recognized that the domain of truths that can be proved by reason is limited, and that many doctrines must be accepted on faith alone. The economists who followed Thomas Aquinas and Duns Scotus turned away from questions of value and concerned themselves with price formation (for example, what constitutes the *pretium justum*, or just price). In the words of German economist Fritz von Bülow, price is a reality, but cost is a concept. Present value theory, introduced by Eugen Böhm-Bawerk and elaborated by Irving Fisher, simply attempted to account for the effect of time on the formation of prices.

MacNeal predicted that the accounting profession would decline in reputation and remuneration if it did not occupy itself with values. During the following fifty years, however, the profession flourished as never before, without coming noticeably nearer to "the truth." Its current decline is related to more basic problems. Nevertheless, criticisms based upon economic theory have continued unabated, although they are more likely now to refer to political correctness than to so unequivocal a concept as truth. The values that many desire to see appear in financial statements are not necessarily true, but are desirable because they conform to identifiable decision models. For example, financial analysts are regarded as sophisticated users of financial reports, and they have called for cash flow information that they believe can be used to forecast future cash flows.

T.A. Lee and others have inferred from this a need for financial statements to be based on cash-accounting and omit accruals.[6]

As Richard P. Brief has pointed out, the antiaccountant movement is even older than these paragraphs suggest, and revolt has been brewing for at least 100 years.[7] Accounting in the United States may belong to the category of human difficulties that are impossible to solve. This book will attempt to examine many of the problems, in order to determine whether this proposition is correct. These problems can often be traced to less fundamental disagreements. Because the action sequence is a social problem–accounting problem–auditing problem, resolution of accounting issues is a necessary prerequisite to developing a sound auditing profession, and questions of education hang on both.

DO ACCOUNTANTS HAVE GUILTY CONSCIENCES?

More and more frequently accountants are pronouncing their own mea culpas. Robert K. Elliott, a partner in Peat Marwick's New York executive offices, in an article entitled "Dinosaurs, Passenger Pigeons, and Financial Accountants"[8] claims that "the historical cost-reporting model" was a reaction to the Industrial Revolution and its assumptions may not reflect present economic realities.

First, an accounting model constructed for measuring the production and distribution of goods may not be suitable for an information-based economy producing services. Second, it assumes that money has a constant purchasing power. Third, it fails to account for executory contracts as a category. Fourth, it presupposes a need for annual or quarterly financial reporting. These defects, argues Elliott, have resulted in the growth in demand for supplemental information in financial reports, outside the financial statements. We will examine these criticisms, and attempt to decide if the fault lies with accounting or with accountants, as the conclusion of Elliott's article suggests.

A similar confession is made by Robert Mednick of Arthur Andersen & Co., in a recent article calling for a new approach to auditing.[9] He argues that the current accounting model is irrelevant, and that the practice of auditing has been inhibited by litigation. Mednick looks forward to "more predictive and value-based information" even though this could subject accountants to new forms of predatory litigation. He asserts that the public wants more from auditors than simply an opinion on management's assertions, and also assurance of the auditor's independence. (The latter was the subject of a 1987 Arthur Andersen publication, *Answers to Important Questions about Scope of Practice and Auditor Independence in the U.S.*) But there is no barrier to corporations issuing value-based financial statements (several real estate companies do this routinely) or to auditors reporting on them, and the obvious commercialization of the public accounting profession, which has resulted in several large-scale mergers, is incompatible with the desired improvement in the credibility of financial statements. Indeed, the so-called audit expectation gap results from such mundane matters as failure to report the disappearance of cash, the nonrecoverability of loans, the worthlessness of inventory or fixed assets, and the omission of liabilities.

WHAT IS "ACCOUNTING"?

Accounting is what accountants do, and it has always proved difficult to define the word, or even to describe the activity. The word itself is in dispute, as "accountancy" is often used in its place and none can satisfactorily explain wherein lies the difference.

A widely quoted and accepted definition was contained in the 1941 AICPA publication *Accounting Terminology Bulletin No. 1*: "Accounting is the art of recording, classifying, and summarizing in a significant manner and in terms of money, transactions and events which are, in part at least, of a financial character, and interpreting the results thereof." Obvious weaknesses of this definition are the vagueness of "in a significant manner" and "in part at least." Current practice specifies the object of accounting as "transactions, other events, and circumstances" and financial reports include certain disclosures that are not made "in terms of money." The word "financial" cannot refer to monetary representation, which precedes it, so that it is unclear what restriction, if any, is implied.

More recent attempts at a definition have specified information as a basic component. The Netherlands Institute of Accountants tried "the systematic recording, processing and supplying of information," and a committee of the American Accounting Association (AAA), in a report referred to as ASOBAT, cited "the process of identifying, measuring, and communicating economic information to permit informed judgments and decisions by users of the information."[10]

One problem presented by these definitions is that they include the work of journalists, archivists, and librarians. The information approach was adopted by the Accounting Principles Board (APB) in its 1970 *Statement No. 4*: "Accounting is a service activity. Its function is to provide quantitative information, primarily financial in nature, about economic entities that is intended to be useful in making economic decisions, in making reasoned choices among alternative courses of action."

It will be observed that the obscurity of the AICPA decision is carried forward intact, and the definition has in fact led to the problem of distinguishing between financial statements and financial reports. For, this reason, perhaps, the Financial Accounting Standards Board's (FASB) conceptual framework studies have concentrated on financial reporting: "Financial reporting is intended to provide information that is useful in making business and economic decisions—for making reasoned choices among alternative uses of scarce resources."[11]

Fortunately, we do not have to choose a definition. Fields of knowledge are distinguished by the methodologies they use. Chemists, physicists, and anatomists all study the human body, as accountants and economists study man in society, but use different tools. Accounting/accountancy can be defined as the solution of social problems using accounts. Any definition that restricts the subject to the decision models of economists or the information needs of investors and creditors is too narrow to be of service.

THE POLITICIZATION OF ACCOUNTING

Accounting is now too important to be left to accountants. In recent years there have been more frequent interventions by politicians aimed at improving the practice of accounting. In the United States they may be said to have started with the securities legislation of 1933 and 1934, which first recognized the public's interest in financial reporting. Today these interventions increasingly take the bargaining form that is the recognizable style of a modern democracy. This has been characterized as the politicization of accounting.

We may distinguish between the regulatory process in general, and specific actions to implement a political agenda. Chief among the regulatory systems affecting accountants is the Securities and Exchange Commission (SEC), established by the Securities and Exchange Act of 1934. This agency was given the power to set accounting standards, but preferred to allow first the accounting profession, in the form of the AICPA, and since 1972 an independent agency, the FASB, to promulgate the majority of the rules. The SEC has actively participated in the process, however, both as a grey eminence behind the scenes and by direct action in the form of accounting and auditing releases, staff accounting bulletins, and other guidelines.

An example of the former was the SEC's role in the production of an FASB statement on early extinguishment of debt. In 1974 the SEC became aware that many corporations were realizing substantial gains by purchasing and retiring their own debt securities, then standing at deep discounts because of rising interest rates. These gains were not being separately reported because APB *Opinion No. 30* [1973] precluded their treatment as extraordinary items. The SEC required the FASB to respond immediately to the situation; the FASB announced its intention to issue a standard and produced an exposure draft within days. The customary public hearing was waived, and a new statement (FAS 4) was published in March 1975, in the minimum time period allowed by the FASB's due process rules. The SEC's threatened action resulted in the FASB reversing an important decision taken by the APB only two years earlier, a decision in which the then chairman of the FASB had actively participated. Equally well documented was the role of the SEC in forcing the FASB to adopt a standard on reporting the effects of price-level changes in 1979 (FAS 33) and achieving withdrawal of the requirement in 1986 (FAS 89). The SEC's hand is also visible in the FASB's attempt to produce a "mark to market" standard for financial investments.

But the political process works more directly than through agencies established for the purpose of regulation. Specific U.S. legislative acts have included accounting antiregulation, for example, a provision that no organization can prescribe a particular method of accounting for the investment tax credit (Revenue Act of 1971). Senate Bill 1435, "Capital Cost Recovery Act of 1979," attempted to change the method of depreciation accounting. Political forces occasioned the withdrawal of the rules laid down by the FASB in FAS 19 on accounting for preproduction costs by the petroleum industry. We have mentioned the current drive to legislate auditors' liability.

These new initiatives build upon a movement that started nearly twenty years ago. In 1974 and 1975, committees of the U.S. House of Representatives (the Moss Committee) and of the U.S. Senate (the Metcalf Committee) conducted a lengthy investigation of the accounting profession, and their reports were very critical of the efficacy of SEC oversight and of the extent to which the FASB had been able to reduce the amount of substandard financial reporting. As a result, an oversight committee was appointed, and the SEC obliged to make an annual progress report on the improvement of the accounting profession.

Such criticisms also led to the enactment of the Foreign Corrupt Practices Act of 1977 (FCPA). Mainly intended to make illegal certain payments to politicians and foreign officials, the FCPA also amended the Securities and Exchange Act of 1934 by adding two new subsections, 13(b) 2A and (b). They require every filing issuer of securities to keep accurate books, records, and accounts, and to devise and maintain an adequate system of internal accounting controls. In this connection, it is interesting to quote from the "Report on Questionable and Illegal Corporate Payments and Practices" submitted by the SEC to the Senate Committee on Banking, Housing, and Urban Affairs, dated May 12, 1976:

> The almost universal characteristic of the cases examined to date by the Commission has been the apparent frustration of our system of corporate accountability which has been designed to assure that there is a proper accounting of the use of corporate funds and that documents filed with the Commission and circulated to shareholders do not omit or misrepresent material facts. Millions of dollars of funds have been inaccurately recorded in corporate books and records to facilitate the making of questionable payments. Such falsification of records has been known to corporate employees and often to top management, but often has been concealed from outside auditors and counsel and outside directors.

THE "ECONOMIC CONSEQUENCES" ISSUE

At least since the 1970s there has been a general recognition of the fact that accounting decisions have economic consequences. It is surprising that the implications of this proposition were not addressed earlier, because if accounting does not have economic consequences, it has no purpose. A financial report is to be expected to influence a decision, if only to buy, hold, or sell shares or other securities. More important, it may affect the cost of capital, market competition, management compensation, profit-sharing by employees and others, wages, and even survival.

FAS 8 on foreign currency translation brought the issue of economic consequences into the open. It was alleged that the standard increased the variability of the earnings of international business firms, resulting in the lowering of their security prices, and also reduced profits by forcing them to incur real costs to hedge their foreign currency balances solely to protect themselves against exposure to accounting losses rather than financial losses. These criticisms obliged the FASB to revisit the subject in FAS 52, which was well received because it was perceived to be relatively free of economic consequences.

The importance of the economic consequences of accounting is also revealed by reference to postretirement benefits for employees. For many years management in both the public and private sectors traded future benefits (pensions, health care) for present benefits (wages) under the belief that the latter expense must be accounted for immediately, while recognition of the former could be postponed to the future. The future always arrives, however, and the problem of payment has finally been faced, so that accountants are now obliged by FAS 87 and 106 to provide for postretirement benefits during the period in which they are earned, rather than paid. According to Newsweek (June 17, 1991, p. 49), "A change in the accounting rules is bringing startled executives face to face with the long-term price of the many promises they've made." As a corollary, had accountants understood that they should report the fact that a cost was involved from the time the decision was made, there is some question whether these benefits would have been offered, or at least, about the level of cost that would have been incurred. (FAS 5 is the authority for concluding that a loss must be accrued if a liability has been incurred and the amount can be reasonably estimated.)

The issue reemerged in acute form in 1991, when the SEC pressured the FASB to issue a standard requiring banks and other financial institutions to "mark to market," that is, to carry investments at market value rather than cost. It was suspected that the institutions had been "cherry-picking," improving earnings by selling appreciated stocks and bonds while holding on to those that had depreciated in value but were reported at cost. An intense lobbying effort ensued, not only by the banks but also by other entities that might have an interest in carrying depreciated securities at cost. The banks, however, raised an important economic issue. Since bonds with long maturities have high volatility, changes in interest rates being factored into their prices for more years than for short maturity bonds, it was argued that a mark to market rule would eliminate the U.S. government's ability to raise finance by issuing securities with twenty five or thirty years' maturities. The fear of such an economic consequence may have been behind one board member's change of position in early 1992, which had the effect of postponing the issue of a proposed statement of financial accounting standards.

THE BROADER SOCIAL ISSUE

The prevailing view is that "economic consequences" are identified by reference to firms, stockholders, financial analysts, and other investor- and creditor-oriented user groups (of financial reports). For example, since it began a research program in the 1980s, the Financial Accounting Standards Board (FASB) has investigated the impact of certain of its standards on corporations. This behavior was prompted by assertions that FASB accounting standards had affected corporations by:

—foreign currency translation accounting (Statement No. 8), forcing companies to engage in expensive hedging operations

—lease accounting (Statement No. 13), making it less advantageous to lease equipment

—oil and gas accounting (Statement No. 19), triggering a rash of corporate acquisitions as oil companies realized that they could convert oil and gas reserves amortizable over fifteen years into goodwill amortizable over forty

The mark to market issue is an example of the effect of an accounting standard on a broader social issue.

Today's society is deeply concerned with questions of accountability, and of far greater importance than effects on particular entities are the economic consequences of decisions concerning the role and scope of accounting for society in general, national and international. Is accountability a duty that inevitably accompanies property rights? Should accountability extend to all social entities, individual, corporate, and government? For what are these entities accountable? Is the discharge of the duty of accountability so important that it should be mandated by government?

Accountants' exposure to liability suits is driving them out of the audit market. It is becoming difficult to find auditors who will accept assignments for low fee engagements, which is one of the reasons why the ranks of medium-sized firms are thinning. This could also affect the ability of developing companies to raise capital, because accountants are wary of providing an opinion to enable them to go public. Is auditing a type of social function, like that of policing, which will result in the auditor becoming a public servant?

These questions may extend to property rights. It is already clear that I may not build on my land without obtaining government permission, but how much may I spend, and who will monitor this? They go to the root of the electoral process. Candidates' fund-raising efforts are restricted and they must render account of their expenditures. In what form, and should it be subject to audit? Consider the vital role played in economic decisions by national income accounting, and in international decisions by balance of payments accounting. Who is responsible for fair presentation here?

THE TREADWAY COMMISSION

Many social institutions have suffered a loss of status and credibility in the last quarter of the twentieth century. In some cases this has been due to a failure to adapt, but in others there has been an apparent decline in standards of performance, to a level below society's expectations. This appears to have been the case in public accounting, and the failure of the profession to satisfy social needs has been called the "expectation gap." It manifests itself not only in liability claims, but also in lower earnings and employment. In 1990 the Big Six announced the forced separation of hundreds of partners and thousands of other employees.

Responding to pressures for reform, the accounting profession sponsored the 1987 report of a national commission on fraudulent financial reporting (the Treadway Commission). The profession responded to the commission's criticisms by promulgating new auditing standards in 1988, and forming a monitoring committee to ensure the implementation of the Treadway recommendations.[12] These actions were intended to reduce the expectations gap by forcing auditors to confront the ethical issues involved in auditing, as well as by making explicit the auditor's responsibility to search for and uncover fraud. It may be noted that both the Treadway report and the AICPA's reaction accepted as a fact that fraudulent financial reporting was widespread and pervasive.

Quite apart from the issue of fraud, however, the expectations gap is fueled by such accounting problems as:

- —the existence within generally accepted accounting principles (GAAP) of multiple and often contradictory methods of accounting for the same facts
- —switching from more or less "conservative" accounting methods to the opposite
- —"front-ending" income that should be allocated to the period in which it is earned
- —deferring unrecoverable costs in inventory and fixed asset accounts, followed by "big bath" writeoffs
- —overoptimistic valuation of investments
- —off-balance sheet financing and other devices to avoid disclosing liabilities
- —failure to follow GAAP under the excuse of immateriality
- —accounting for the form, rather than the substance, of transactions designed with the accounting treatment in mind

CONCLUSION

Accounting is an international activity, and trouble in the accounting profession is by no means confined to the United States. Similar chains of events have taken place in Australia, Canada, the United Kingdom, and other countries where the accounting profession is largely self-regulating. Even countries where accounting is heavily regulated by law have experienced and become concerned about audit failures. Because financial reporting is now a global concern, we must look at the process of setting accounting and auditing standards in an international context.

We live in an age of actors who cannot speak, of singers who cannot sing, of artists who cannot draw or paint. This is in part a consequence of the fact that their market consists of uneducated and undiscriminating buyers, and they have prospered in spite of their lack of competence. We may not be able to hold out the same prospect to accountants, however, whose publics tend to be rather sophisticated. It is therefore important to answer the question: What causes a profession to lose contact with its reason for existence to the point where its very economy is threatened? This book will shed some light on this question, and present reasoned proposals for our salvation.

NOTES

1. The Big Six: Arthur Andersen & Co., Coopers & Lybrand, Deloitte and Touche, Ernst and Young, KPMG Peat Marwick, Price Waterhouse.

2. "Problems in the Profession," *The Accountant*, April 16, 1966, pp. 462–63; and "The Great American Accounting Principles Controversy," *The Accountant*, March 23, 1968, pp. 377–81.

3. *Unaccountable Accounting* (New York: Harper & Row, 1972); and *More Debits Than Credits: The Burnt Investor's Guide to Financial Statements* (New York: Harper & Row, 1976).

4. Irving Kellogg, *How to Find Negligence and Misrepresentations in Financial Statements* (New York: McGraw-Hill, 1983).

5. Kenneth MacNeal, *Truth in Accounting* (Philadelphia: University of Pennsylvania, 1939).

6. T. A. Lee, *Towards a Theory and Practice of Cash Flows* (New York: Garland, 1986).

7. Richard P. Brief, "The Accountant's Responsibility in Historical Perspective," *The Accounting Review*, April 1975, pp. 285–97.

8. In *World* 1986, 20, No. 5, pp. 32–35.

9. "Reinventing the Audit," *Journal of Accountancy*, August 1991, pp. 71–78.

10. *A Statement of Basic Accounting Theory* (Sarasota: American Accounting Association, 1966).

11. "Objectives of Financial Reporting by Business Enterprises," *Statement of Financial Accounting Concepts No. 1* (Stamford, Conn.: FASB, 1978).

12. *Report of the National Commission on Fraudulent Financial Reporting* (Washington, D.C.: AICPA, 1987).

CHAPTER 2

A SHORT HISTORY OF ACCOUNTING

INTRODUCTION

Accounting is the second or third oldest profession, depending on how one classifies the military. For the past 100 years archaeologists have traveled the world in search of ancient sites, hoping to discover the secrets of human origins. They usually find accounting records.

A major question is whether we can call these records "accounts," lacking as they do the distinguishing forms recognizable as double-entry bookkeeping. Many commentators divide the history of accounting into two periods, with Luca Pacioli's celebrated book *Summa de Arithmetica, Geometria, Proportioni et Proportionalita* (1494) as the point of partition. Adopting less of a purist position, we shall examine the history of accounting in relation to four time periods:

1. The age of antiquity (prehistory to about A.D. 400)
2. The development of double-entry (A.D.900 to A.D. 1494)
3. The growth of capitalism and the Industrial Revolution (A.D. 1500 to A.D. 1800)
4. The managerial revolution (A.D. 1800 to the present)

ACCOUNTING IN THE AGE OF ANTIQUITY

There are respectable hypotheses that both writing and arithmetic evolved from a need for accounts. The words "count" and "account" obviously share the same root, but it seems that commerce called for written records before they were used for other purposes.

Writing developed from pictographs, which were drawings that represented objects in daily use. Bone artifacts bearing such markings have been attributed to the Paleolithic Age, 30,000 to 12,000 years ago. Subsequently clay tablets were used for writing, and some dating back 6,000 years display similar images. The cuneiform writing of the Neo-Sumerian and Old Babylonian periods evolved from pictographs. Large numbers of clay tokens of various shapes have been found in ancient settlements in the Middle East; these tokens are believed to have represented objects in trade, and scholars have inferred that pictographs replaced these tangible objects. Thus, whereas clay tokens would once have been given by one party to another as evidence of a change in ownership of the goods represented, such an exchange could later be effected by a written record of the transaction.

A key to this transition was the *bulla*, or clay envelope. Clay tokens were placed inside an envelope of clay, which was baked hard; to verify a shipment it was necessary to break the envelope. Subsequently pictorial representations of the tokens were incised on the surface of the envelope, so that it could be used to convey property by manual transmission. Eventually it was realized that the tokens could be dispensed with, the pictographs telling the whole story. The earliest account records were inscribed on clay tablets, the convex surface of which bears evidence of their origins.

A fascinating insight into this period is provided by Geoffrey Bibby in his book *Looking for Dilmun* (1969). Although excavations at Ur of the Chaldees were carried out at the beginning of this century, the clay tablets discovered there were incomprehensible because of their unknown language. It was eventually deciphered with the aid of the Rosetta Stone, and is called *Linear B*. Bibby transcribed the accounting records of a trader, Ea Nasir, who was importing dates from Dilmun; when Bibby looked for this place in the old maps, he found no record. Organizing expeditions, Bibby and his students went looking for Dilmun, and eventually found it in what is now Bahrain in the Persian Gulf. Of significance to us is Bibby's assertion that the records showed Ea Nasir was losing money (but he may have been looking at the merchant's tax accounts.)

The Babylonian Code of Hammurabi, the first written system of laws created about 4,000 years ago, contains several references to accounts. Bailees were required to keep accounts for objects consigned to them, and agents had to provide their principals with written memoranda. The scribe, who could read, write, and do arithmetic, was a kind of professional accountant in those days.

It is tempting to assume that we know more than we do about the life of those times through deciphering these tablets. In fact, only 100 of the perhaps 250,000 fragments known to have survived have been transcribed. They record land sales and other contracts (one contract is to brew a certain quantity of beer). Payments were made in silver and other valuable commodities, and it is clear that accounts were kept, although not in the same form as today. Interest was calculated and charged on loans, inventories taken, and transfers made from one party to another.

After Mesopotamia the center of civilization moved first to Egypt, and then to Greece. Like the Babylonians and Assyrians, the Egyptians kept extensive records that have survived in the form of hieroglyphics (for example, the Rhind Papyrus in the British Museum); translation and interpretation present a problem. Papyrus is paper made from reeds, and on it were recorded shipments to and from their cities and funerary temples.

The coinage of money with uniform value that could be used as a medium of exchange and thus serve the purposes of a unit of account occurred about 800 B.C., when the Greeks ruled much of the then known world. Greece effected the secularization of banking, a function previously carried out by the priests who received tithes in kind and loaned out the seed corn for more extensive cultivation. Money permitted those outside the priesthood to perform this function. Not only did the Greeks bequeath us stone-engraved records of public finance; we also possess the Zenon papyri, which provide a tantalizing glimpse of economic activity in the Greco-Egyptian Empire. Zenon was the steward of the Egyptian farms belonging to Appolonius, finance minister to the ruler Ptolemy Philadelphus II. Not only did Zenon require his managers to keep accounts; he practiced a form of audit by arriving unannounced to count the cash. The Greek citizens appointed auditors to check on their public officials who, then as now, were not entirely trustworthy.

In China, accounting was developing at about the same time. The Chao Dynasty (1122–256 B.C.) demonstrated sophisticated account-keeping. The Chinese used paper and coined money. Because economic activity was centralized in the hands of the rulers, China developed systems of government accounting and auditing. The comptroller-general was a very powerful official, of higher rank than the grand treasurer, who reported to the emperor. Budgets were prepared, funds designated, and taxes assessed and collected. Reports were prepared for ten-day periods called *hsun.*

THE ACCOUNTS OF ANCIENT ROME

We are less well served by the surviving records of Rome, on which the mantle of civilization next fell. The Roman Empire, which lasted from about 700 B.C. to A.D. 400, attained a high point of social order that still distinguishes societies descended from peoples who enjoyed it from those beyond the pale. One would expect that substantial accounting activity was involved, but no records have survived because the Romans used wax tablets, a very perishable material. As a consequence, all that we have from which to infer the account-keeping activities of the Romans are a few Ciceronian orations, a couple of lines of Virgil's poetry, and the legal codes of Gaius and Justinian.

On the basis of this meager evidence we can observe many of the features of modern accounting in Roman practices. The Latin language possesses different words for concepts and their manifestations; an account in general was *ratio*, a specific account *nomen* (hence our "nominal ledger"). They used a *codex accepti et expensi*, probably a cash receipts and payments book, daybooks called *ad-*

versaria, and a special journal for interest called a *calendarium*. But did the Romans use double-entry bookkeeping?

In 1817 a German historian named Bartholdt Niebuhr found a palimpsest in the Vatican Library that attracted his attention. Medieval manuscripts were written on material that was rare and expensive, and scribes often scraped writing off old parchments in order to reuse them; the result is called a palimpsest. Niebuhr deciphered a few of the erased phrases, and found fragments of a hitherto unknown Ciceronian oration, *Pro Fonteio*. Cicero, the great defense attorney of his age, had been engaged to plead the case of one Marcus Fonteius, an official of the Roman emperor who was accused of defrauding the Roman treasury.

At the time, about 100 B.C., inflation was rife in Rome, and caused real hardship because purchases required metallic coins, which were in short supply. To improve matters, a currency reform law was passed, which divided all prices by a factor of 4, and four old sesterces were exchanged for one new one. Fonteius was accused of having received payments, of taxes and other debts due to Rome, in new currency, and accounting for them as though they had been paid in old currency, keeping three-quarters of the money for himself.

In the pleadings, Niebuhr found Cicero saying, ''You praise Hirtuleius [another official] for having kept records of the three-fourths and the one-fourth; he [Fonteius] did the same.'' Now Niebuhr who, like other educated men of the period understood double-entry bookkeeping, asked himself why they should have kept records for the three-fourths, the amount of the writeoff. If they were keeping an unstructured set of individual accounts, it would be sufficient simply to replace the old value with the new one. Only if it was necessary to balance the books, he reasoned, would the bookkeeper account for the amount of sesterces written off.

On the basis of this observation, Niebuhr postulated that the Romans used double-entry bookkeeping ''which was therefore not an invention of the Lombards'' as was generally supposed.[1] The proposition was the subject of considerable debate in Europe during the nineteenth century, incapable of resolution because of the paucity of evidence. The view that this system first appears in Italy in the thirteenth or fourteenth century has prevailed.

We shall never know. The fall of the Roman Empire occurred when the Goths and Visigoths swept down from northern Europe, burning, raping, and pillaging. Most books and other documents were destroyed, leading to the long night of the Dark Ages. It was not until Charlemagne (A.D. 742–814) restored law and order by means of the feudal system, that the peoples of Europe were confident enough in the future to resort to saving, and the resulting economic surpluses provided the capital that gave birth to the rise of capitalism. This capital permitted voyages to take place like that of Marco Polo, by means of which Europe became aware of the culture of the Orient, and of course financed the Crusades, which discovered the culture of the Arab lands. This knowledge produced the Renaissance, of which Pacioli is such a luminary. There has been some speculation whether account knowledge was also brought back to Europe from North Africa,

India, or China, thus stimulating the development of the Italian method of double-entry.

THE MIDDLE AGES

Wealth accumulated and by the eleventh century it was enticing adventurers such as William the Conqueror. One of his first acts after defeating King Harold at Hastings in A.D. 1066 was to call for the creation of the Domesday Book, a record of all properties in Britain that served as a basis for assessing taxes. The process of accounting for government receipts during this period is evidenced by the Pipe Roll, the great roll of the Exchequer, which, beginning in A.D. 1130, documents the levying and payment of taxes, fines, rents, and other dues, and related disbursements. The proffer system that accompanied this account involved an early form of audit, in this case an oral examination of taxpayers (from the Latin *audere*, meaning "to hear").

Then, as now, government accounting was primitive and uninformative. The developments that led to accounting as we know it took place outside government, in the medieval manors, banks, and merchant firms. There were two kinds of manors, those of the church and those of the lay lords. The church accumulated great wealth through bequests and other gifts from persons who were concerned about building up a treasury of merits in the world to come, and acquired lands that were administered as agribusinesses, on the model of the lay manors. Records of the medieval church manors reveal that they were meticulously organized and kept account of production, consumption, and distribution. Sales of products in excess of personal consumption needs were reported to the abbot as profits from the operations of the manor. Although church manorial records were largely statistical in nature, they did involve bookkeeping, and the personnel needs of the church led to the creation of the first chair of accounting at Oxford University, in the fifteenth century.

The lord of the manor, on the other hand, had more of a financial interest in his estates. The administration of these manors was in the hands of stewards and other managers, who were perhaps less virtuously inclined than their religious counterparts. Many lords spent years away from their estates, fighting the Crusades in the Middle East. By the fifteenth century there developed what has come to be known as the "charge and discharge" statement, by means of which the steward accounted to his lord. Essentially his object was to satisfy the latter that his property had been faithfully administered; there was no profit measurement involved, and indeed, no distinction between capital and revenue. Such statements were also subject to audit. It is not surprising that one modern theory of financial reporting is based on the "stewardship function" and its associated duty of accountability.

But it was in the banks and the offices of the merchants who did business with them where modern accounting developed. The bilateral account form reappears. Known to the Babylonians, it had been replaced by superimposed sections because of the narrowness of papyrus sheets. Transfers between accounts were used in antiquity (we have the record of a journal entry in 3000 B.C.), but the creation of a closed system of accounts, with movements between them by journal entry, was achieved sometime between A.D. 1200 and 1340. The Massari ledger of the city of Genoa for the year 1340 is generally regarded as the earliest known record of a double-entry accounting system, but the Massari (the city's treasurers) asserted that they were following the practices of the banks. The books of the Salon (France) branch of the Florentine Farolfi family of merchants for the year 1299–1300, which on first examination did not balance, were made to balance by Geoffrey Lee when bookkeeping errors were corrected. These are probably earlier evidence than the Genoa books.[2]

Why did double-entry bookkeeping develop in Italy during the early Middle Ages? A. C. Littleton postulates seven preconditions: writing, arithmetic, private property, money, credit, commerce, and capital, but all of them existed 2,000 years before.[3] Further, private property and capital have not proved essential in the communist countries, where double-entry bookkeeping is just as valuable as elsewhere. Werner Sombart, whose contribution to the history of accounting will be discussed later, referred to double-entry bookkeeping as the first wholly abstract system conceived by the human mind, and believed that it inspired later scientists, notably Harvey who represented the circulation of blood in the human body as a closed system. It need not surprise us that this should be so.[4] In Sombart's view, a mechanistic image of the firm, which underlies its representation by means of an accounting system, is associated with other mechanical inventions of the time, such as the clock and the gun.

One mechanical device that may have had a major impact was the transition from Roman to Arabic (actually, Indian) numerals, popularized by Leonardo of Pisa in his *Liber Abacci* of 1202. Most likely, however, necessity was the mother of invention; the Italians extended their trading businesses throughout the then known world by means of agents operating without direct personal supervision. They needed not only a means of enforcing accountability, but also a measure of internal control. The self-checking feature of double-entry provided this. At any rate, long before Luca Pacioli's *Summa* the new Italian method of accounting was in widespread use.

LUCA PACIOLI

Luca Pacioli was born in Tuscany in 1445 and lived until about 1523. Although he achieved contemporary fame as a mathematician and university professor, and became a Franciscan friar to assist his career development, he had considerable business training. At the age of twenty he became tutor to the sons of a Venetian merchant, a position he held for six years. During this period he traveled with this family in ships that carried goods. Friend of artists such as Leonardo da Vinci (who illustrated one of his texts), he was a leading Renaissance character.

His *Summa* (1494) is a treatise on mathematics, but some twenty chapters are devoted to a description of the accounting methods of the merchants of Venice of his time. In all important respects, the double-entry system demonstrated by Pacioli was, in conception and implementation, identical with the system that we use today. For this reason he is known as the father of double-entry book-keeping, but of course it had been long in use, for perhaps two centuries. Surviving records of the Medicis' textile-manufacturing business show that a more sophisticated and complex system was used by them fifty years or more prior to 1494. Pacioli's text was reproduced, translated, and plagiarized, and thus circulated throughout the known world during the next three centuries, and therefore provided training for many generations of accountants in many countries.

Corporations were few in number at the time, but Pacioli did illustrate accounting for multiple capital accounts. His accounting proceeded from the viewpoint of the proprietor of the business, which has been referred to as the proprietary theory. (From the nineteenth century the corporation itself assumes a position of prominence; and corporate accounting is said to be based on the entity theory. The distinction seems to lack a difference, however, as both theories lead to virtually the same results.) Pacioli illustrated profit measurement primarily with reference to voyages and lines of business, rather than proprietors or entities.

THE SOMBART PROPOSITIONS

Werner Sombart was a German economist who lived from 1863 to 1941. Even for an economist his forecasting was poor; he predicted a reduced world population, the end of large-scale wars, and that capitalism would reach its zenith in the twentieth century and then decline. He studied law, history, and philosophy as well as economics, and his research inspired him to prepare a major work on the origins of capitalism, which he published as *Die Moderne Kapitalismus.*[5]

The accounting books and records of the early Middle Ages led Sombart to certain conclusions about the causes of the growth of capitalism during that period. For example, the firm was viewed as an entity separate from the persons who owned and managed it; it was a legal entity, a market entity, and an accounting entity. The legal system provided the firm with a social framework, and the market, a financing mechanism; accounting was a business management, or organizational, framework. This last facilitated, or even made possible, the development of capitalism:

1. By representing the flow of capital through the firm "from the capital account to the transaction accounts through the profit and loss account and back to the capital account."

2. By restricting the entrepreneur's field of vision to those observations that could be represented in the accounts, the origins of economic

rationalism. "Quod non est in libris, non est in mundo" (What's not in the books doesn't exist).

3. By permitting a systematic organization of the complex operations of the firm.

4. By separating the capital of the firm from the wealth of the owner(s), permitting management to concentrate on increasing capital, "the wealth-producing sum."

Inherent in this analysis was the view that double-entry bookkeeping depersonalized the firm, rendering it distinct from all humanistic influences and goals. This proved sympathetic to critical theorists engaged in denouncing capitalism. Although some economists quoted Sombart with approval, several denounced his conclusions as placing far too much importance on accountants who, on the economists' scale, occupy a very lowly position. Contemporary studies fail to find empirical evidence in support of the Sombart propositions, and conclude that the main contribution of double-entry bookkeeping was in assisting the entrepreneur to introduce order into the chaos of events (not a minor managerial achievement). They ignore the point, however, that the factors identified by Sombart were largely psychological, as indeed were the fundamental skills that he believed distinguished the capitalist entrepreneur from the pirate or freebooter: the ability to calculate and save.

THE AGE OF STAGNATION

Because accounting remained relatively unchanged in theory and practice from A.D. 1500 to 1800, this has been called "the age of stagnation." It is assumed that there were few economic changes in the basically agricultural societies of Europe during this period, and therefore little pressure on accountants to innovate. Yet with major and fundamental economic changes occurring during the next two centuries, the theory and practice of accounting remain visibly similar to Pacioli's method. Even communist states utilize similar systems for their enterprises. On the other hand, major changes did take place in accounting during the period 1500–1800, which challenge the title of this section. Among them are the following:

1. Pacioli described three books of account: the waste book (a kind of diary), journal, and ledger. It became apparent that the journal was the book of original entry, and the waste book was replaced by such documentation as sales and purchase invoices. This led eventually to today's voucher (slip) systems.

2. The single journal was replaced by a set of day books (cash book, sales day book, purchases day book, payroll, etc.). The journal became a summarization and posting medium.

3. The concept of the control and subsidiary account was developed. It was recognized that the account could model a whole or any part thereof, which permitted division of labor in the counting house and improved methods of internal control.

4. Pacioli described the closing and balancing process in relation to the completion of a venture or the necessity to open a new account book, the old one being full. Nevertheless, he recommended annual balancing. Annual closing and balancing became the norm during this period.

5. Single-entry accounting developed as an economical method of achieving the same ends as double-entry. (Many people believe that single-entry preceded double-entry, but as Sombart pointed out, the former presupposes the latter, of which it is a modification.) Those, like Jones of Bristol, who advocated the simpler system began the practice of totaling the two columns of the journal, as an arithmetical proof of the entries.

6. The scope of accounting was extended from transactions to other events and circumstances. This was done notably by means of accruals and deferrals, which began to be reflected in accounts. Depreciation, although not unknown prior to the Medicis, became an accounting problem.

7. Other technical innovations were the compound journal entry, the practice of posting monthly totals, and subsidiary ledgers.

8. Pacioli's accounting cycle ended with the trial balance, which, after closing, becomes a balance sheet. The practice of journalizing the closing created the profit and loss account that complemented the trading account (for profits and losses) and thus led to the modern form of income statement.

9. Cost accounting for products and processes was developed. For example, Christopher Plantin, a famous Antwerp printer, kept a set of books for his partnership covering the period 1563–67, consisting of a journal and ledger; ledger accounts included equipment, inventory of paper, manufacturing expense, and finished goods inventory (for unsold books).

10. Theoretical issues began to appear in the literature, such as the personalization theories that explained debits and credits, and the debate on whether accounting was an art or a science.

Corporations contributed greatly to these developments. The early trading ventures were for single voyages, and financed with terminating stock. Magellan equipped five ships to travel around the world in 1519, but only one returned; ship and cargo were sold and proceeds divided among the surviving venturers (a liquidating dividend). Later ventures, although dangerous, proved more profitable, and it became the custom to subscribe stock for successive voyages. From these beginnings grew the modern corporation.

The corporation was (and is) a more convenient form for doing business than the partnership. A corporation is a separate person at law, and therefore does not terminate on the death or incapacity of any human person. This feature is known as "perpetual succession" and avoids many of the problems that can arise when humans contract with each other, or form partnerships. Limited liability is simply an optional extra, but we may note that Italian limited partnerships existed before trading corporations.

By the end of the sixteenth century there were several large trading corporations operating throughout the world, under charters granted by the rulers of England and The Netherlands. These chartered companies included the English and Dutch East India companies, the Hudson Bay Company, the Russia Company, and the Virginia Company. Shares in these companies were traded in coffee houses, the forerunners of the modern stock exchange, providing liquidity to investors. Separated from management, investors had to be provided with accounts to explain and justify the use of their money, and accountants had to grapple with issues of accrual and deferral in order to apportion profits between time periods. For example, unpaid expenses had to be provided for, and unsold merchandise from one voyage would be left in the ship's hold until the next, so that deferral of cost in inventory became an acute accounting problem. The accounts were often audited.

THE GROWTH OF ACCOUNTABILITY KNOWLEDGE, 1775–1990

The Industrial Revolution ostensibly began in 1768 with Arkwright's invention of a cotton-spinning machine. The mechanization of production proceeded rapidly, resulting in the creation of large-scale manufactuing firms and of wealth that far exceeded anything previously experienced. Large firms needed to obtain capital from the savings of many thousands of investors, and the consequent separation of ownership from management has been called the managerial revolution.

The principal factors responsible for the expansion of the accountant's functions were the following.

The Industrial Revolution

One result of the transition from domestic production to factory production was the growth in the size of the firm and its capital requirements. To raise capital of the required magnitude, it was frequently necessary for the firm to incorporate; the number of registered corporations increased from a few hundred to tens of thousands between 1800 and 1900. The need for meaningful accounts to be rendered by the promoters and managers to the stockholders greatly increased the responsibilities of accountants, and company legislation in Great Britain calling for these accounts to be audited, created a need for public accountants. In the United States, where the greater part of industrial capital was provided by foreign financial institutions and domestic banks, audited financial statements resulted from their requirements.

A second aspect of the Industrial Revolution that had an impact on accounting was the lengthening of the production time period. This feature of industrialization called attention to accounting for overheads and the allocation of costs to cost centers as well as products. Industrialization also led to the development of standard costing, and to the separation of cost accounting from financial accounting, which has been characteristic of accounting at least since the nineteenth century.

A third aspect was the successive waves of industrial bankruptcies that took place in Europe and the United States during the latter part of the nineteenth century. The growth of the industrial sector was accompanied by overcapacity. Many marginal firms were unable to survive economic upheaval such as that which followed the American Civil War. The need for qualified persons to manage and liquidate insolvent businesses for the benefit of their creditors placed additional burdens on private and public accountants. The need to establish forms of industrial cooperation, particularly to avoid the more lethal forms of price-cutting, led to the creation of national trade associations. Many of these developed uniform accounting systems that were published for the benefit of members.

The Railroad Companies

The biggest single users of corporate capital during the nineteenth century were the railroads. These companies were illustrative of additional problems presented by the Industrial Revolution because they were highly capital-intensive, and their fixed assets had longer useful lives than customary. Many people in the industry believed that maintenance of the tracks and rolling stock would make railroad fixed assets virtually everlasting, and there was thus no need to charge depreciation in the income statement (then called the profit and loss account). Coupled with the overstatement of profits, many less excusable abuses occurred, such as paying dividends out of capital contributed for investment, and the creation of excess capacity leading to business failures, which caused investors and creditors substantial losses.

These problems directed attention to the critical necessity to distinguish capital from revenue, to the importance of the income statement, and to the need to calculate depreciation on a systematic basis. In many countries railroad finances became a matter of public concern, and legislation regulating their operations was enacted. In most countries the railroads have gradually been taken over by government and are now operated as state enterprises. In the United States certain states prescribed the form of railroad accounts; regulation was later taken over by the Federal Interstate Commerce Commission, which issued a uniform classification of accounts in 1894.

These developments were followed by regulation of other industries of public interest, such as public utilities, broadcasting, interstate gas pipelines, and aviation. In each case, regulation included the requirement to use a uniform accounting system for recording and reporting, and in each case the system was different. Thus, the case of the railroads provides an example not only of the growth of accountability knowledge but also of the emergence of acceptable alternatives in accounting.

The Rise of the Accounting Profession

The profession of public accountant gradually became organized in the English-speaking world during the nineteenth century. The Institute of Chartered Accountants in Scotland was the first such organization (founded 1854), followed by the Institute of Chartered Accountants in England and Wales (1880). The New York State Society of Certified Public Accountants was formed in 1896 and a national organization, the predecessor of the American Institute of Certified Public Accountants, in 1887.

These professional organizations laid down rules of conduct for their members and issued pronouncements on technical questions that added substantially to accountability knowledge from about 1900.

Personal and Corporate Income Taxes

After several abortive attempts, the U.S. Treasury finally succeeded in imposing an income tax in 1913. Although challenged as unconstitutional, this form of taxation was eventually validated by constitutional amendment. Other countries, notably Britain and Germany, had imposed income taxation before the end of the nineteenth century.

The significance of this development lies both in the contribution it made to strengthening the accounting profession by opening to it a new field of accounting, and in the additions to knowledge made by a succession of revenue acts and related commentaries, case law, and textbooks. The necessity to determine income, as a preliminary to the determination of taxable income, provided a major impetus to the extension and improvement of accounting practice, and the essentially legal ideas and concepts of the tax laws influenced the development of accounting theory in subtle ways.

The First and Second World Wars

In the First and Second World Wars the governments of the countries taking part utilized to the fullest extent the industrial sectors built up during the nineteenth and early twentieth centuries. In the United States large portions of the industrial sector were engaged in the production of weaponry, ships, ammunition, motor vehicles, military clothing, and a wide variety of goods and equipment needed for the war effort.

Only a small part of this production was carried out by the government itself; the greater part was allocated to private industry through the medium of the defense contract. There was considerable fear, in many cases justified, that defense contractors would exploit the ignorance of civil servants by overcharging for their products, but the government was a powerful force in this situation and gradually succeeded in laying down regulations for costing defense contracts (Section XV of the Armed Service Procurement Regulation) and establishing audit agencies to ensure that costs were fairly reported.

The relations between government agencies and private firms created by defense contracting and its regulation led to further consideration of cost accounting problems, and the refinement of methods of standard costing and differential or incremental costing is attributable in large part to this situation.

Government Accounting

Politicians do not favor disclosure. When in power they resist it, and the opposition does not fight too hard for fear it will inherit the obligation. It is no accident that in most countries government accounting is a byword for backwardness and obscurity.

The tremendous increase in government revenues that followed the introduction of income taxation, particularly at the level necessary to finance the First World War, vastly increased the problem of government accountability. In the English-speaking countries, government accounting has traditionally been accounting for receipts and payments, which paradoxically is less informative than the accrual system. It may be noted, however, that the Kingdom of Sweden in the seventeenth century, and the Austria of Maria Theresa in the eighteenth, developed sophisticated forms of government accounting comparable to contemporary business systems, and that the cash basis is no more essential to government accounting than to any other kind.

Beginning in the 1890s, attempts were made in the United States to reform the federal budgeting and financial reporting process, and similar movements were discernible elsewhere. The Taft Commission, which reported in 1912, resulted in the establishment of an executive budget only nine years later, and the Budget and Accounting Act of 1921 enacted some of the Taft recommendations. In 1949, the 81st Congress completed the task of legislating the Taft Commission's report by passing Public Law 784. Nevertheless, even now, the actual implementation of reforms proposed by the Taft Commission is a long way from completion.

In addition, state and local government accounting have developed their own techniques and literature as the revenues from sales and property taxes have increased through both legislation and inflation.

The Fruits of Scientific Management

By the end of the nineteenth century many of the problems of industrial organization and management had been identified, and a scientific approach to their solution was proposed by F. W. Taylor, the Gilbreths, and others between 1885 and 1920. Imitating the dictum of Lord Kelvin, this approach has been summed up in the phrase: "What cannot be measured, cannot be managed."

It was clear to the pioneers of scientific management that accounting had a large part to play in the measurement of cost and output and in the evaluation of managerial performance. The business schools established after the turn of the century placed emphasis on the study of accounting as a tool of management control, and a substantial literature has developed on this aspect of accounting. We may note as landmarks the early work of Emile Garcke and J.M. Fells and Hamilton Church on standard costing and the invention of breakeven charting by Henry Hess in 1904. This literature, which grows more extensive daily, belongs to the area designated management accounting, the title of the monthly publication of the Institute of Management Accountants in the United States.

The development of management accounting has been marked by two significant changes in emphasis, which cannot be ignored by any student of accounting. One is the attempt to apply to accounting data the mathematical methods that have proved powerful tools for investigating the world of natural phenomena. This field of statistical method has produced many experiments of varying success. The use of ratios and averages has a long history, but such techniques as discriminate analysis, multivariate analysis, and others, applied to accounting ratios in order to evaluate their usefulness as predictors, is a fairly recent development. Compound arithmetic as a tool of financial mathematics is likewise of some vintage, but present value techniques for accounting valuations are new.

The other change is the attempt to solve accounting problems within an interfunctional, and consequently interdisciplinary framework of management. Before the Industrial Revolution it was common for merchants, bankers, and artisans to keep their own accounts. As specialization became necessary in the growth of manufacturing firms, accounting was one of the first functions the manager transferred to someone else. The accountant became increasingly isolated from the decision-making centers of the firm, leading to the separation of accounting from operating management. Outside pressures created a tendency for accounting aimed at such external users as financiers, creditors, and the tax authority to acquire the major share of the resources available for the accounting function. The twentieth century has seen a reversal of this trend.

In the process, the accountant has both contributed to and taken from the other functions of management. To production planning and control he has given standard costing: from it the statistical techniques used in quality control have been taken over for variance analysis. To marketing he has given cost/volume/profit analysis, and from marketing he has taken one of the principles of valuation of joint products, the relative sales value method.

A HISTORY OF AUDITING: THE BRITISH EXPERIENCE

That it is sometimes necessary to give people a chance to be honest has been known since prehistory. We have observed that audits were performed in the Greco-Egyptian era, in ancient Greece, and in medieval England in connection with the Pipe Roll. Here we shall try to trace the history of the corporate audit.

Before doing so, however, we should take note of the role that accountants played in bankruptcy cases. An English bankruptcy law of 1542 attempted to protect creditors against fraudulent bankrupts, and by the nineteenth century related accounting work had become an important business. Accountants were regularly appointed trustees of bankrupt estates as well as instructed by the court to audit their records for evidence of fraud. As late as the second half of the nineteenth century, such work provided more than half the fees earned by public accounting firms. It was soon overtaken in importance by the corporate audit.

Most of the investors in the chartered companies were businessmen who understood the temptations to which traveling executives are prey. It was common to appoint one or several stockholders as auditors, to check the accounts of the company and report to the members. During the seventeenth century speculation took over from investing, and companies were formed and capital raised for the flimsiest purposes. Those who follow contemporary financial events will recognize the phenomenon.

In 1720 speculation in Britain came to head with the collapse of the South Sea Company, an event that has gone down in history as the South Sea Bubble. Originally formed for a practical purpose, the company became the instrument of greedy and irresponsible directors, who sold stock far in excess of the economy's ability to service it. Eventually it became known that the directors' promises were incapable of fulfillment; many investors lost fortunes. The government intervened, and an accountant named Charles Snell was appointed to examine subsidiary records. This appears to be the first recorded instance of an independent company audit, although in fact it was more of a fraud investigation.

Because of this scandal an act of Parliament, the Bubble Act of 1720, virtually closed the door to those who wished to form corporations. In the early years of the Industrial Revolution businesses had to be conducted as partnerships. Because this restricted their expansion, pressure was brought on the government to repeal the Bubble Act, which was done in 1825. An act of 1844 provided for company formation by registration and from that time on the corporation became the chosen instrument of economic expansion.

An 1845 act required directors to keep account books and balance them periodically, something that has not yet found its way into U.S. corporation laws. The directors had to prepare and also sign an annual balance sheet; the SEC has attempted to impose such a signature obligation on U.S. registrants, without success. The balance sheet, with other information, was to be filed as an annual report with the Registrar of Companies. The balance sheet had to be examined by one or more stockholders, and this is the origin of current company laws in

Britain and (elsewhere) imposing auditors on companies. They were and are to be given unrestricted access to the company's books and records and to report to stockholders that the company's accounts present a "true and correct" (today, true and fair) view of the company's affairs; the accounts and audit report must be sent to stockholders within a specified period prior to the annual meeting before which they are to be laid. The 1844–45 acts provided that skilled accountants could be employed as assistants to the stockholder-auditors, and ultimately these accountants took over the audit function.

All did not go smoothly for the corporate audit. Acts of 1855–56 omitted the accounting and audit requirements, although they did provide a model balance sheet for use by companies that failed to provide one in their statutes, and related audit and accounting provisions that could be adopted voluntarily. These model articles of association also specified that the auditors need not be stockholders. An 1862 act refined these provisions and provided a model form of audit report. Following a major bank failure in 1878, annual audits were required for banks, and similar obligations were placed on building societies (savings and loans), public utilities, and other public service corporations. A series of legal cases during the nineteenth and early twentieth centuries clarified the rights and duties of the auditor. A 1900 act restored the accounting and auditing requirements of the 1845 act, and in 1907 differential disclosure was applied to private (small) companies, which did not have to file their balance sheets, leaving the other accounting and audit provisions applicable to them also. Subsequent legislation has expanded the financial disclosure provisions of the law, and in 1948 audits were restricted to professionally qualified individuals. Company laws enacted in the 1980s have implemented the directives of the European Community, which has imposed consistent accounting, auditing, and financial reporting requirements on all corporations in the twelve member countries.

AUDITING IN THE UNITED STATES

The history of auditing in the United States is quite different. During the nineteenth century, as a developing country, its capital needs were met from European sources. A critical event was the creation of the Scottish investment trust, a financial intermediary that invested in a number of trading and manufacturing firms in the United States. These trusts sent accountants over to audit their investments in the United States, since although there were public accountants in this country, there was no tradition of bankruptcy or corporate audit. Some of these individuals stayed and formed branches of the British firms that had sent them; this is the origin of Price Waterhouse, Peat Marwick, and other public accounting firms, many of them since merged and known by other names. Gradually native accounting firms were established: Haskins and Sells (now part of Deloitte and Touche), Lybrand, Ross Bros., and Montgomery (now part of Coopers and Lybrand), and much later, Arthur Andersen & Co.

The important distinction between U.S. and European auditing is that the former is contractual, whereas the latter is statutory. For whatever reason, the states, in whom the power resides, have never legislated for corporations to keep accounts or render audited financial statements to stockholders. That is why the federal government intervened with the Securities Act of 1933 and the Securities and Exchange Act of 1934, which, however, apply only to corporations that are obliged under those acts to file with the SEC, that is, corporations whose securities are traded on markets. No matter how large a U.S. corporation may become, or how much profit it earns, if it does not meet the threshold requirements (500 shareholders, $5 million in equity) it does not need to file, and therefore need not appoint an independent auditor. Many public service type organizations that are required by law to file financial statements are not required to have an independent auditor. As to sending financial reports to stockholders, even SEC registrants must do so only if the directors solicit proxies.

The fact that auditing is based on contract in the United States, rather than law, has had a significant impact on the development of the accounting profession. Whereas the British auditor is given statutory rights, the U.S. auditor must bargain for access to books and records. Like the British auditor, the U.S. auditor is technically appointed by the stockholders, but actually by the directors; nevertheless, stockholders in Britain have important rights that are not enjoyed in this country, such as the power to apply to the courts to appoint an auditor, or to order an investigation. U.S. auditing had to be justified as cost-effective, and the detailed checking that characterized auditing in other countries was expensive. Hence the peculiarly U.S. concept of the selective audit.

Apart from foreign investors, the main market for auditing services in the late nineteenth century was the banks. Lacking a base of domestic capital, U.S. industry was financed largely through bank borrowing. Banks were interested in getting their money back, and began to use account information as a basis for granting credit. They required balance sheets certified by public accountants, and this was a major part of auditing activity during the first half of this century. But it was easy to persuade bankers that a complete audit was unnecessary and uneconomic. Hence the balance sheet audit.

A balance sheet audit essentially was a verification of liquidity and solvency. There was no interest in uncovering fraud or reporting on stewardship; the questions were whether the corporation's current assets exceeded its current liabilities (ability to pay interest as it fell due) and whether total assets that could be turned into cash exceeded total liabilities (ability to repay debt on maturity). For these purposes it was concluded that careful examination of selected accounts could provide the auditor with a degree of assurance that was satisfactory for the matter in hand. Eventually, auditors adopted statistical sampling techniques and even extended their activities to compilation and review services that involve virtually no auditing at all.

On the other hand, it may not be assumed that U.S. auditors were more incompetent than their European counterparts. In the first place, many of their clients were foreign parent companies, who exacted a higher standard than the domestic banks. Enlightened and responsible directors in the majority of U.S. corporations voluntarily contracted for detailed audits to assist them in discharging their duty of protecting the company's assets. Internal auditing was developed to achieve the same objectives as external auditing, but at lower cost. The rapid growth of business and accounting education in U.S. universities produced a flowering of knowledge about accounting and auditing that had no counterpart in countries where training was mainly by apprenticeship. And following the 1933–34 federal legislation, the SEC became heavily involved in supervising auditing, ensuring auditor independence, and penalizing substandard performance.

CONCLUSION

This brief survey of accounting and auditing history demonstrates the important role that the accountant has played in society throughout the ages. Starting with a simple and logical device, the account, accountants have constructed complex systems based on double-entry that have permitted large-scale enterprises to be managed effectively, and by means of financial reports have opened the door to large-scale financing through financial intermediaries.

The process is by no means complete. Computer systems have drawn attention to the fact that double-entry is simply a special form of multiple-entry; the same thinking that produced the journal underlies the database; the worksheet has given birth to the spreadsheet. Financial statements as a device for communicating information about a firm have become financial reports that extend to narrative form the data that used to be restricted to accounts. Many accountants feel that the complexity of contemporary financial reporting has placed upon them responsibilities that exceed their competence.

Yet in the last analysis, nothing has changed. The model of the firm that Pacioli recognized is still taught to students in the form of the basic equation. The need for audit remains paramount in a world where fraud and deception are rife. Repeated attempts to reformulate basic accounting principles have led nowhere, and audit failures invariably can be traced to poor performance rather than inherent defects of the auditing process itself.

NOTES

1. B. G. Niebuhr, *Römische Geschichte*, 2nd. ed., Berlin, 1830. II, No. 1319, p. 673. This note was omitted from the English translation (London, 1844).

2. G. A. Lee, "The Coming of Age of Double Entry: The Giovanni Farolfi Ledger of 1299–1300," *The Accounting Historians Journal* Fall, 1977. 4, No. 2, pp. 79–96.

3. A. C. Littleton, *Accounting Evolution to 1900* (New York: American Institute, 1933), p. 12.

4. "Look where a man's treasure is, there will his heart be likewise" (Matthew 6:21).

5. A shorter work was published in English as *The Quintessence of Modern Capitalism*, trans. M. Epstein (New York: L. P. Dutton, 1915).

CHAPTER 3

THE DEVELOPMENT OF ACCOUNTING THOUGHT

A basic issue is whether we can include in discussions of accounting the unsystematic records that existed before double-entry bookkeeping came into general use. Even though the logic of the account, and the device of the journal entry that moves data between accounts, were known thousands of years before the Middle Ages, when double-entry bookkeeping first appears, our interest lies with the later period, and the financial reports to which systematic bookkeeping gave birth.

EARLY ATTEMPTS AT EXPLANATIONS

We see from the earliest books on accounting some indications that the authors attempted to explain why as well as describe how. Pacioli, of course, presented the basic accounting equation: assets = liabilities + proprietorship (equity). The objective of accounting was to give the trader without delay information as to his assets and liabilities, and therefore, his proprietorship interest. This formulation corresponded with the nature of an essentially static process described by Pacioli, and the contemporary method of calculating an increase in wealth by comparison of balance sheets at successive dates. He advocated the use of current market prices.

The limitations of current market prices become apparent in manufacturing businesses, where commodities are removed from the market for the purpose of transformation. Heinrich Schreiber was the chief accountant to the Fugger mining and manufacturing conglomerate, and wrote a book on accounting (under the name Grammateus) that was published in Erfurt (Germany) in 1523. Inventory accounting proved very difficult to explain, and it appears that he experimented with several valuation methods, including last in-first out (LIFO), which proved unsatisfactory. Simon Stevin, tutor and adviser to the Prince of Orange, published a treatise in 1605–8 in which he argued for the use of double-entry bookkeeping for the royal estates and the army.

For the most part, however, the authors of accounting texts published prior to the nineteenth century were strong on method and weak on theory. One exception was Abraham List, who in his 1660 book *Amphithalmi, or the Accomptant's Closet,* raised the question whether accounting was an art or a science. He chose art, and argued that arts are taught differently from sciences, a viewpoint that bears examination three centuries later. The principal development during this period was the progressive abstraction of accounting entries; starting with fairly detailed narrative accounts, accountants gradually evolved the basic elements: name (title), form (bilateral), date, shorthand description, and amount. Businesses used many different currencies, and values fluctuated widely. We find a variety of methods of asset valuation illustrated by these authors. Holding gains and losses were recognized in some systems. Most contemporary scholars hold that the main purpose of the accounting system was to bring order into the merchant's affairs rather than to ascertain profit; however, Stevin illustrated a form of profit and loss account, to accompany the balance sheet, suggesting that the objective of accounting included the measurement of period income.

Eighteenth-century fraud and misrepresentation were very much in the minds of those responsible for nineteenth-century company legislation. For this reason, company laws provided that officers should keep proper records, including books of account, and render account to shareholders in the form of an annual balance sheet. They also provided that the shareholders should appoint auditors to audit the balance sheet before it was presented at the annual (general) meeting, and gave the auditors certain powers and the duty to report that the balance sheet was "true and correct." Disputes concerning the truth and correctness of accounting practices were regularly adjudicated by courts of law, resulting in the beginnings of a legal theory of accounting.

The second influence the Industrial Revolution had on accounting arose from the lengthening of the time period of production. In an artisanal society, the consumer provides the producer with materials and the producer delivers a product directly to a known market. In a mass production society, the producer acquires materials and other factors in advance of production, and transforms them into products that are often held for an unknown market. Credit was required to finance this process, calling for short-term information about profitability and liquidity that annual balance sheets did not provide. The need to prepare frequent financial statements, including the profit and loss account, drew attention to acute difficulties of measurement, of accruals and deferrals in particular, that called for new accounting rules. The accountant had to explain the reasons for methods of inventory valuation, depreciation accounting, revenue recognition, and provision for future expenditures arising out of past acts. Accounting for transactions was expanded to cover other events (for example, production of finished goods) and even circumstances (news that a debtor had fled the jurisdiction).

Finally, large-scale enterprises called for internal accounting to assist managerial planning and control, in addition to external accounting for shareholders and creditors. This monthly, weekly, and even daily provision of information required far more resources, and began to influence the form and contents of financial statements. It also led to a conflict between financial and management accounting personnel, which, because of the critical importance of financing decisions, has led the financial accounting tail to wag the management accounting dog.

CONTINENTAL EUROPEAN ACCOUNTING THEORY

Accounting theory developed in nineteenth-century England as a consequence of the Industrial Revolution. Paradoxically, other European accountants were producing ideas without the same stimulus. A striking illustration is the great contribution of nineteenth-century Italian writers at a time when Italy had a basically preindustrial society.

We can see three different movements in the writings of European accountants. Emphasis was first placed on the account itself, leading to the so-called personification theories. But an account is not a person, and this redirected attention to the transactions, and eventually other events and circumstances, which are the stuff of which accounts are made. Rules designed to ensure that objective economic facts were recorded and reported took precedence over the mechanical functioning of the accounts themselves. Next, the perspective from which economic facts were observed came into question, leading to the substitution of the firm, instead of the proprietor, as the central concept. Finally, the very concept of "economic facts" came in question, and scholars began to examine the theory of accounting itself, as distinct from accounting theories that purport to answer questions about financial statements and reports.

With regard to the first of these, early writers found it difficult to explain exactly what their students were expected to do. Lacking a theory, they resorted to precept and admonition, bolstered by appeals to the deity. Personification helped students memorize rules and procedures, leading to the rule "debit him that receives, credit him that gives." Some accounts were those of persons with whom the firm did business, but personification took three additional forms:

—the attribution of human qualities to inanimate objects represented by accounts—"Mr. Cash"

—the fiction that each account was an extension of the proprietor's personality—"John Smith his goods"

—the view that each account was a clerk who received and gave on behalf of the proprietor

From these beginnings came the classification of accounts into three categories:

—personal accounts (accounts for persons with whom the firm transacted)

—real accounts (things owned)

—nominal accounts (accounts for abstractions, such as sales, expenses, profit)

Whereas personal accounts followed rules of reciprocity, the other accounts were not so constrained. Expanding the scope of accounting to cover other events, and even circumstances, increased the importance of nominal accounts, which presented problems: How does one personify cash discounts received or given? This type of problem led to a search for a classification scheme, or taxonomy as it is called in other sciences.

Another major influence on accounting theory at this time was the law. Whether the objective of accounting was to provide evidence for the settlement of civil litigation, as in Germany and Spain, or for discharging the duty of accountability placed upon bankrupts and corporate officers, as in Britain, it functioned within a legal framework. The rise of the corporation provided jurists in European countries with a philosophical problem of some magnitude: Does the corporation exist separately from its shareholders and officers? That this was not an easy question to decide can be seen from the fact that as late as World War II in a celebrated British criminal case in which a company was the accused, the defense argued that a corporation cannot have *mens rea*, a guilty mind (R.v. The Houndsditch Warehouse Company, Ltd.). This problem produced a nineteenth-century accounting theory, the entity theory, to replace the prior proprietary theory, with consequent effects on the principles of valuation. The distinction was also made by later American accounting writers, who ignored the fact that a comparable legal framework did not exist in this country.[1] The entity theory was one reason why personification theories were abandoned.

The transition from a proprietary to an entity theory of accounting had the important consequence that, even for unincorporated businesses, accountants began to distinguish the business affairs of the firm from those of other firms owned by the same proprietor, and from his or her personal assets, liabilities, income, and expenses. Thus was born the entity assumption, one of the basic concepts on which modern accounting is founded, and its corollary, the going concern assumption.

Entity theory is also responsible for the historical cost principle that dominates accounting in many countries. Other valuation methods are feasible where the objectives of the proprietor are paramount, but not from the standpoint of the firm. Historical cost provides an objective measurement that is difficult for shareholders and creditors to challenge, although the effects of price-level changes have led to such a challenge in recent years. The assumption of a constant value monetary unit is attributable to the same cause. The ability to substitute one shareholder for another, through sale and purchase of shares, underlies the revenue principle, which requires accruals and deferrals in order to treat outgoing and incoming shareholders fairly. It is also a factor in periodicity, the use of commensurate accounting periods. These are often referred to as the basic assumptions underlying financial statements.

THE CLASSIFICATION PROBLEM

The classification of accounts was originally viewed from the standpoint of the proprietor. Thus, Abraham de Graef in a 1693 book published in Amsterdam divided accounts into three groups:

—Accounts of the merchant as a person: capital, profits and losses, insurance, reserves, housekeeping, interest

—Accounts of other persons: debtors, creditors, participants in trade ventures

—Accounts for merchandise: goods in store, goods in ships, cash (available for purchases)

Edmond Degrange, in a 1795 book published in Paris, used five classes: cash, goods, bills (notes) receivable, bills payable, and profits and losses. In the nineteenth century, the Belgian H. Godefroid applied a classification to an integrated financial and cost accounting ledger, using titles, chapters, and sections. One of the titles was used for cost accounts. Such schemes were increasingly used in business, and following the popularization of the universal decimal system in the 1890s, led to the use of decimally coded charts of accounts.

The accounting implications of the entity theory were most clearly perceived in France, by writers such as Rene Delaporte and J. F. Dumarchey. Delaporte saw through the limitations of classification of accounts, arguing that there were really two classes, assets and liabilities. (The modern entity theory form of the basic equation is assets = equities.) He included owner's equity under liabilities. He favored the use of the symbols + and − in place of the words "debit" and "credit." Dumarchey attempted to create a science of accounting, related to economics and sociology. Dumarchey is responsible for first distinguishing between static and dynamic accounts, a distinction that was examined in depth by the German writer Eugen Schmalenbach.

SCHMALENBACH'S GENERAL CHART OF ACCOUNTS

Schmalenbach was the leading European accounting theorist of the first half of the twentieth century, recognized as such not only in his own country, but throughout Central and Eastern Europe. He founded the discipline of business economics, which he taught at the University of Cologne, and the first business research journal, *Zeitschrift für Handelswissenschaftliche Forschung*, in 1906. He argued that the legalistic nature of prevailing accounting practices, which revolved around the balance sheet, led to static accounting. He called for a new approach, based on a business model of the firm, which he called dynamic accounting.[2]

Schmalenbach believed that the balance sheet was incapable of presenting financial position. It did not reflect the value of the business as a going concern, that value being more or less than net assets because under the cost principle, some self-generated assets such as goodwill, and also contingent liabilities were not included, and those that appeared in the balance sheet were not valued at market or liquidation prices. He argued that accountants should leave the unattainable objectives of the static balance sheet aside, and make the period statement, the profit and loss account, a dynamic measurement of results. If the balance sheet became merely a list of leftover balances, a step between two income statements, so be it.

Schmalenbach's classification scheme, derived from his model of the firm, was as follows:

Class 0	Fixed assets and long-term capital
Class 1	Current assets and liabilities (working capital)
Class 2	Neutral (nonoperating) income and expenses
Class 3	Materials inventories
Class 4	Operating expenses
Class 5	Cost accounts
Class 6	Cost accounts
Class 7	Work in process and finished goods inventories
Class 8	Revenues
Class 9	Financial statements (closing and balancing accounts)

Note that the chart was coded decimally, and that more classes were allocated to income statement and operating accounts than to balance sheet accounts. Note also that, unlike many contemporary Anglo-Saxon charts of accounts, the classes conform to the basic principle of classification, namely, that the members of any class should have more common features with each other than with the members of any other class.

Schmalenbach's schema was disseminated through his writings, but gained unusual prominence from a circumstance totally unconnected with his life and work. The economic policy of the National Socialists who governed Germany after 1933 relied on total control of all factors of production and production entities. They mandated use of the general chart of accounts to facilitate the collection of economic statistics and control over firms; a government inspector would find the same account used for the same observations in every business firm. As Germany occupied other European countries from 1940 on, the occupiers introduced the same chart of accounts in firms as they acquired control over them. France, in particular, became familiar with the general chart of accounts in this way, and French accountants and economists learned its usefulness and simplicity. Some economists who entered government in post-World War II France saw that a general chart of accounts would lead to improved national income accounting, notably Pierre Lauzel, who was instrumental in creating a National Accounting Council, of which he was the first secretary-general. The National Accounting Council promulgated a general chart of accounts *(Plan Comptable Général)* in 1947, since revised twice.

Originally made obligatory for state agencies, defense contractors, and very large commercial corporations, the chart rapidly commended itself for training accountants and improving their mobility, as well as for expediting the audit. I witnessed an illustration of this last when working as an auditor in France in the early 1950s. At the time, the French National Bank exercised strict control over foreign currency transactions because there was a substantial black market, particularly in U.S. dollars. To check whether the French subsidiaries of U.S. corporations were exchanging dollars on the black market, instead of remitting them through the French National Bank, the bank sent auditors to examine their accounts. I was present when one such auditor arrived and asked to see account number 10. This was the account for contributed capital in the general chart of accounts, and was indeed the account that the company was using for remittances from the U.S. parent. The bank auditor was in and out in under an hour.

Similar general charts of account are now in widespread use in a number of other European countries. Rather than illustrate the French *Plan Comptable Général*, therefore, we will use the even more generalized International Chart of Accounts to demonstrate the theory and practice of the genre.

THE INTERNATIONAL CHART OF ACCOUNTS

At an international accounting conference in Paris in 1951, *Les Jourees Internationales de la Comptabilite*, it was proposed that a well-designed chart of accounts should be applicable to all firms, in any country. Such a chart would represent the universal characteristics of business activity, free from national laws, accounting conventions, or professional standards. The conference committee eventually adopted for this purpose a classification scheme that had been published by a French accountant, Joseph Anthonioz, in 1947, that was itself based upon a paper entitled "The Cycle of the Economy" presented by Maurice Lucas at the World Congress of Accountants held in Barcelona, Spain, in 1929. This chart, adapted to represent an accounting model of the firm, is shown in Figure 3.1.

The classification starts with an economic definition of the firm. The firm is a production entity that receives savings from other entities (households, other firms), invests them in fixed assets and working capital, and incurs costs by transforming these assets into products and services. The products and services

Figure 3.1
The Accounting Model of the Firm

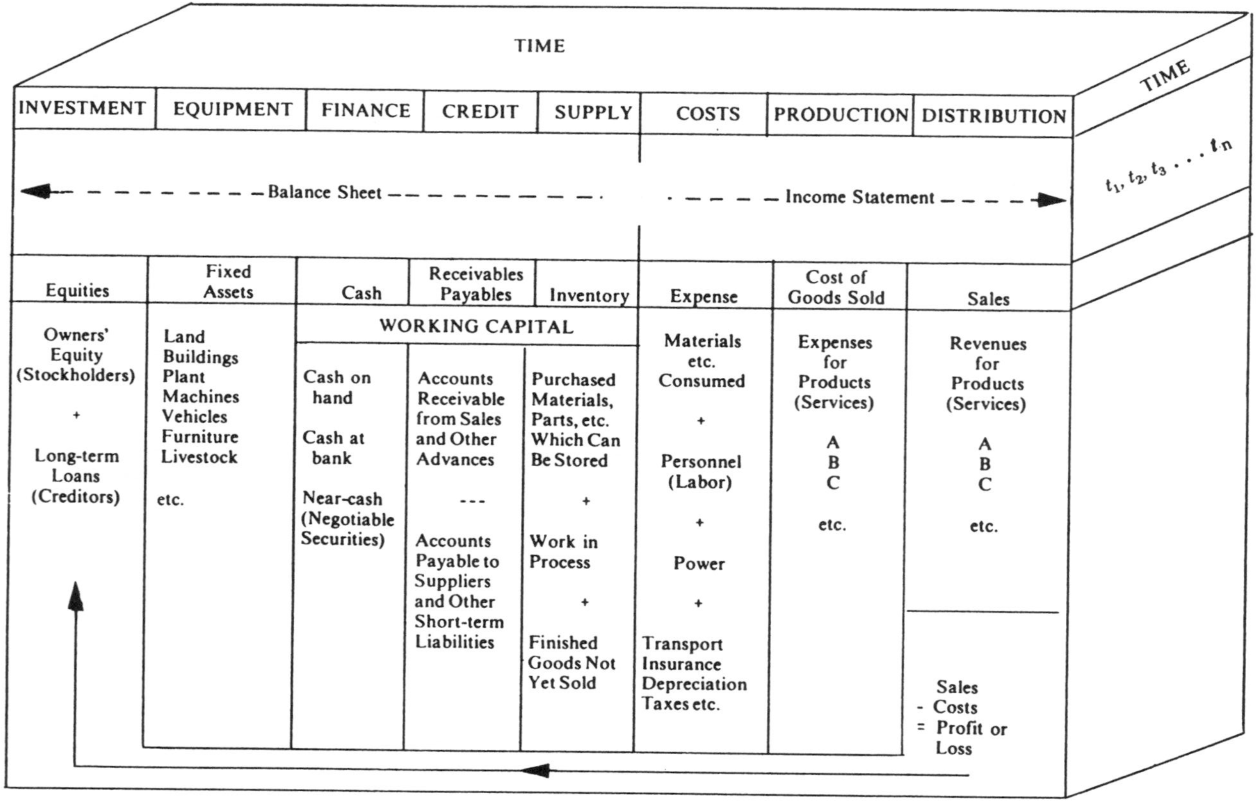

TIME

INVESTMENT	EQUIPMENT	FINANCE	CREDIT	SUPPLY	COSTS	PRODUCTION	DISTRIBUTION	TIME
– – Balance Sheet – –				– –	– – – –	Income Statement – – –		$t_1, t_2, t_3 \ldots t_n$

Equities	Fixed Assets	Cash	Receivables Payables	Inventory	Expense	Cost of Goods Sold	Sales
		WORKING CAPITAL					
Owners' Equity (Stockholders) + Long-term Loans (Creditors)	Land Buildings Plant Machines Vehicles Furniture Livestock etc.	Cash on hand Cash at bank Near-cash (Negotiable Securities)	Accounts Receivable from Sales and Other Advances — — — Accounts Payable to Suppliers and Other Short-term Liabilities	Purchased Materials, Parts, etc. Which Can Be Stored + Work in Process + Finished Goods Not Yet Sold	Materials etc. Consumed + Personnel (Labor) + Power + Transport Insurance Depreciation Taxes etc.	Expenses for Products (Services) A B C etc.	Revenues for Products (Services) A B C etc.

Sales
- Costs
= Profit or Loss

are distributed to other entities, and in the process the firm adds value to all factors of production transformed, that is, makes a profit. According to this definition, a loss is antisocial, because it involves a reduction in the value of society's savings. The various parts of the definition form the headings of the eight columns in Figure 3.1, so that the basic classification is a logical analysis of a firm's operating characteristics. Following Descartes' rule in his *Theory of Method*, the analyst has divided the problem to be solved into the parts necessary for its solution.

In Figure 3.1 the first five columns constitute the balance sheet elements. Note that the analysis assumes the basic equation of finance, rather than the basic equation of double-entry bookkeeping. That is, finance = investment, where investment is defined as fixed capital (assets) + working capital. It is a financial reporting model rather than a purely bookkeeping model, and has been used in Britain during the past thirty years, where balance sheets display, not total assets, but net assets (total assets − current liabilities), and equate them with capital employed (stockholders' equity + long-term debt). The model ties in with the macroeconomic equation, saving = investment, leading to the observation that micro- and macroeconomic models can be integrated by social accounting methods.

It is argued that suppliers of short-term credit (accounts, expenses, wages, taxes, etc., payable and accrued) are not providing capital to the firm. These credits are known in corporate finance as "spontaneous finance" because they arise out of the nature of business operations, rather than a conscious decision to provide capital. As a corollary, because these creditors do not expect interest or dividends, they should not enter into the asset base on which the firm calculates return on investment, and thus should not affect the determination of selling price.

The last three columns constitute the income statement elements. Missing from this presentation are the elements of the statement of changes in stockholders' equity, suggesting that it is not a basic financial statement. One type of transaction that does not appear is payment of dividends, which have traditionally been accounted for as distributions to owners, that is, as the opposite of contributions from owners.

The third dimension of the chart is that of time, and it depicts changes during a period of time. These are known generally as *changes in financial position*. The net effect of operations is found through the income statement as net income (profit) or loss, but changes in specific assets and liabilities are not shown in the balance sheet or income statement although they may be calculated from successive balance sheets. The statement of changes in financial position was created to solve this problem, but has been abandoned in favor of a statement of cash flows (changes in the cash account).

THE CHART OF ACCOUNTS AS PLANNING MODEL

The model serves also as a planning model of the firm, thus permitting financial planning and control to proceed within a consistent framework. The planning

Figure 3.2
The Investment Cycle

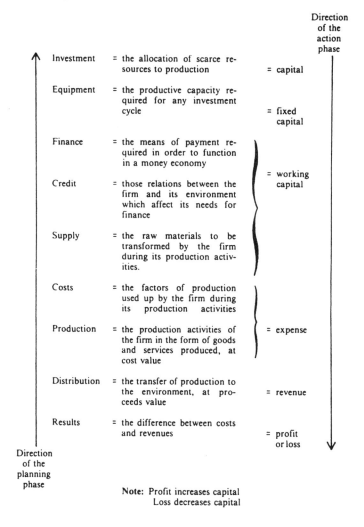

Note: Profit increases capital
      Loss decreases capital

function (in a market economy) starts with the market, that is, distribution. Figure 3.2 shows how the planning phase ties in with the action (implementation) phase.

The columns of Figure 3.1, representing the stages of the investment process, are analyzed into their most commonly encountered components (the items listed are illustrative, not definitive). Savings are tapped in two forms—proprietorship and debt—depending on the attitudes to risk and material needs of the saver. The fundamental difference between them has been obscured in recent years by the issue of financial instruments that contain elements of both. (The consequent accounting problems will be discussed in a later chapter.) However, the total capital requirements of the firm are found with reference to planned sales.

Although the chance of profit and risk of loss are implicit in any investment, profit or loss (net income or loss, in U.S. terminology) cannot be separately calculated. It is the result of the process that substitutes revenues for costs, and may be zero. It follows that the accounting model illustrated is applicable to not-for-profit production entities, including governments, and the U.S. Government Accounting Standards Board (GASB) is engaged in adapting a similar model developed by the FASB to state and local government needs.

A general chart of accounts includes, besides the structure demonstrated in Figure 3.1, definitions of technical terms and bookkeeping rules. The French general chart of accounts has been so well prepared in these respects that it constitutes a virtually complete theory of accounting, within which most (if not all) accounting problems can be solved. Failure to accept such a general theory in the English-speaking countries means that every accounting problem must be solved independently, leading to a great waste of time and duplication of effort. For example, the question of valuation and amortization of an investment in a brand name was easily resolved in a one-page accounting standard issued by the French National Accounting Council, but one can foresee at this time (1992) that the FASB will be obliged to issue one or more complex monographs on the subject when it eventually gets round to dealing with it.

LIMITATIONS OF THE TRADITIONAL MODEL

We have traced the development of the double-entry model from bookkeeping to accounting to financial reporting, showing how accountants have integrated accounts into a system of financial statements. This model of the firm is immediately recognizable, with minor modifications, by accountants throughout the world. Yet the constraints inherent in such a closed system have become increasingly visible during the past thirty years. One such constraint is illustrated by the distinction between *financial statements* and *financial reporting*, which represents the interface between a closed and an open system.

The basic issue is the concept of information, and in this context the accountant confronts an apparently insoluble problem. We define information as ''purpose-oriented data,'' that is, data selected according to the need for inputs to a particular decision model. Those critics who view accounting as a branch of economics have in mind decision models derived from price theory, but these call for data collected at the margin (marginal cost and revenue) that are normally unobservable. Any information system presupposes a selection from available data, yet the accountant is concerned with the accumulation of data, which are massaged into a ''one size fits all'' set of financial statements. How can the accountant become responsible for additional data, which do not lie within the traditional classification? What is the nature of the notes to financial statements, which purport to be part of the financial statements themselves?

There is also the threshhold problem. Transactions, other events, and circumstances do not come labeled "account for me." In the words of the French theorist J. Meyer, there are no accounting events as such. A good example of this problem is presented by the purchase order. Nearly 100 percent of purchase orders issued by firms, and accepted by their suppliers, become purchases and sales, yet most accounting systems admit them only when an invoice and delivery are at hand. There can be no question that from an economic rather than a legal standpoint the purchaser has incurred an obligation. What is perhaps not so clear is that in many cases the supplier, by accepting the order, has also incurred an obligation, for example, to manufacture a product. In the former case, if the market price of the goods declines, GAAP requires the purchaser to accrue a loss prior to delivery, but it is silent on the need for the seller to accrue a loss if the cost of manufacture is expected to exceed the value of the order.

Second, the model abstracts from the question of valuation. Here we define valuation as the representation of an object as an amount of money, a quantity multiplied by a price. True, the need to maintain costs in evidence that underlies the profit measurement function of comparing costs with product revenues, implicitly assumes a multiple valuation focus: accounts receivable at selling prices, inventories at cost prices. But whereas price is a reality, cost is a concept. Currently accounting theorists use the word "attribute" to denote the kinds of cost concept that might be used: historical cost (acquisition price), replacement cost (current input market price), and even opportunity cost (current output market, or exit price). In addition, relaxing the monetary unit assumption by recognizing changes in the purchasing power of money implies an additional cost concept, cost in constant dollars.

Further, unlike economic statisticians, accountants date all observations, so that the discussion of cost concepts cannot ignore the time dimension implicit in the model depicted in Figure 3.2. Equipment purchased depreciates—how is its cost to be allocated over its useful life? Materials purchased in advance of production are removed from the market—to what extent should changes in cost during the period between purchase and sale be reflected in the accounts, and how? Capital fluctuates in value according to changes in capital markets, quite apart from any increases or decreases attributable to the operations of the firm. Are these changes accounting circumstances?

THE CONCEPTUAL FRAMEWORK

Questions such as these provided the inspiration to construct a conceptual framework, an explicit theory of accounting to which problems could be referred for their solution. The process that led to the FASB's conceptual framework project will be described in Chapter 7. Since its promulgation began in 1978, other English-speaking countries have adopted comparable frameworks, starting with Canada,[3] and the International Accounting Standards Committee (IASC) has recently begun a similar project.

So far, the FASB's conceptual framework consists of the following Statements of Financial Accounting Concepts (SFAC):

SFAC 1, "Objectives of Financial Reporting by Business Enterprises," November 1978.

SFAC 2, "Qualitative Characteristics of Accounting Information," May 1980.

SFAC 3, replaced by SFAC 6.

SFAC 4, "Objectives of Financial Statements by Nonbusiness Organizations," December 1980.

SFAC 5, "Recognition and Measurement in Financial Statements of Business Enterprises," December 1984.

SFAC 6, "Elements of Financial Statements," December 1985.

The FASB referred to the conceptual framework as a constitution, "a coherent system of interrelated objectives and fundamentals that can lead to consistent standards and that prescribes the nature, function, and limits of financial accounting and financial statements." It was expected to

—guide the FASB in its deliberations

—provide a frame of reference for resolving accounting questions for which there was no GAAP

—determine bounds for judgment by financial statement preparers

—increase financial statement users' understanding of, and confidence in, financial statements

—enhance the comparability of financial statements

There is no evidence that any of these objectives has been achieved, and some evidence that users' confidence in financial statements has in fact decreased since the project started. Further, few of the accounting standards promulgated by the FASB since 1978 have relied explicitly on the conceptual framework, a notable exception being Statement No. 95, which replaced the statement of changes in financial position with a statement of cash flows. Unlike a statement of financial accounting standards, an FASB concepts statement does not constitute GAAP, leading to the result that GAAP rests on fundamentals that are not part of GAAP. This is in fact consistent with the premise that a theory of accounting must be found outside accounting itself, in the same way that a definition of a word may not contain the word being defined.

THE NEED FOR UNIFORMITY

One of the underlying assumptions of the standard-setting process in the United States, made explicit in the conceptual framework, is the need for uniformity in financial reporting, particularly the financial statements. This assumption also supports the work of the IASC. It has acquired global significance because of the globalization of finance and the ability of corporations to select among countries in raising capital for their needs. Financial analysts and stock market regulators have called for the elimination of differences among accounting practices that handicap interfirm comparisons and enforcement activities. It is believed that uniformity would also improve the reliability of financial reporting as information for decision-making by investors and creditors.

A widely held view is that financial reports are manipulated by corporate officials, leading to fraudulent financial reporting. It is not clear, however, that uniformity would limit opportunities for fraud, even if it succeeded in increasing the information content of financial reports internationally. The case for regulation rests on other factors:

1. The "free-rider" argument maintains that information about corporations is a public good, in the sense that its benefits cannot be restricted to those who pay for it. Economists believe that public goods will be undersupplied unless paid for by the public, or else the producers forced to produce them.

2. Efficient capital markets call for the same financial information to be available to all traders. Dissimilar information and misinformation lead to market failure, in that capital flows to some firms, and away from others, in a suboptimal pattern.

3. Agency theories of the firm suggest that corporate officials will choose accounting practices that benefit them, either by making the firm look better than it is (increase net income, decrease debt/equity ratio) or possibly, to avoid or foil regulators (the opposite).

None of these propositions bears close examination. U.S. public corporations published financial reports long before the stock exchanges called for them, and have improved their form and content in advance of the promulgation of GAAP; private corporations still are not required to do so. Information efficiency is only one factor in creating market efficiency, and capital markets would still be inefficient even if all security issuers provided comparable information. A corporation is not simply a set of contracts, as contemporary legal theorists maintain, so that response of a corporate official to a given situation cannot be predicted on the basis of a perceived cost/benefit relationship. Most corporate officials are experienced enough to realize that the consequences of manipulating financial reports are unpredictable, even from quarter to quarter.

The case for uniformity must also face contrary arguments, however.

1. There is the view that consistency is more important than an ideological "correctness." Changes in accounting standards render financial reports

for periods before and after the change noncomparable, and undermine their credibility. The words "on a consistent basis" have now been dropped from the U.S. audit report.

2. Accountants have historically adopted a situational approach to accounting questions, distinguishing between ostensibly similar sets of facts where differences can be identified. Uniformity restricts, even suppresses, the ability of accountants to respond to such situations. It is interesting that the one major change that the FASB has made to its own standards, the replacement of the foreign currency translation rules of FAS 8 by those of FAS 52, arose out of a recognition that situation-specific factors must be considered, notably the functional currency.

3. Users of financial reports are sophisticated enough to understand and adapt to accounting differences. It is clear that the principal users of financial reports are investors and creditors, represented by investment managers and financial and credit analysts and those individual investors who have similar skills and interests. Unsophisticated investors are unlikely to read financial reports, even if made wholly comparable.

These arguments lose some of their force in the global marketplace. Even though Italian financial reports may be adequate for sophisticated Italian users, they present difficulties to their counterparts in other countries. Thus, there is a great need for international accounting standards that lead to uniform financial reporting for reasons of comparability; domestic standards such as GAAP will eventually have to conform to that need.

CONCLUSION

The gradual development of accounting and financial reporting over the past 500 years has created a system of great complexity and infinite variety. Accompanying attempts to explain, or perhaps rationalize, accounting practices have culminated in an accounting model of the firm, demonstrated in some countries by a general chart of accounts, and in others by a conceptual framework. There is no substantial difference between either of them, although the general chart of accounts has proved easier to work with than the essentially narrative form of the conceptual framework.

Explanation strains, however, have increased in recent years with the increasing complexity of the political, social, and economic environment and the need for accountants and auditors to adapt. A noted philosopher of science, Thomas Kuhn, has called the set of concepts agreed upon by scientists within their field a paradigm, and shown how they attempt to work within it until the strain of doing so becomes unbearable, when a new paradigm emerges. Some accountants argue that accounting is approaching such a change, and the problem of distinguishing between financial statements and financial reports may provide critical evidence on this point.

NOTES

1. The proprietary viewpoint has proved hard to kill in the United States. Lacking a legal framework, accounting writers have looked to economics, particularly that branch known as corporate finance, as a source of ideas. Because economic theory abstracts from the institutional framework of society, finance theory proceeds from the assumption that shareholders own the assets of the firm, rather than the firm as an entity. This underlies the avowedly proprietary viewpoint adopted by many writers. W. A. Paton was a notable exception.

2. E. Schmalenbach, *Dynamic Accounting*, trans. G. W. Murphy and K.S. Most (London: Gee, 1959). The first edition of this book was published in Germany in 1916.

3. The Accounting Standards Authority of Canada, *Conceptual Framework for Financial Reporting*, Vancouver, B.C.; April 1987.

CHAPTER 4

GENERALLY ACCEPTED ACCOUNTING PRINCIPLES

Financial reporting in the United States is dominated by GAAP (generally accepted accounting principles). In this chapter we will examine what GAAP means, and how it has developed a vast and inchoate mass of written material, similar to the U.S. system of written laws.

PROMULGATED AND NONPROMULGATED GAAP

Many accountants proceed from the assumption that they are capable of solving accounting problems satisfactorily by applying their knowledge and experience, consulting GAAP only to make sure that the proposed solution does not conflict with any of the written GAAP that has been promulgated by an agency established specifically for this task. To the extent that this knowledge and experience is not represented by such writings, it is nonpromulgated GAAP.

Some parts of nonpromulgated GAAP are based on practice; others are found from several sources, discussed later in this chapter. Most influential are:

1. Written regulations other than promulgated GAAP, such as the U.S. Internal Revenue Code and regulations issued under it. Inventory accounting under the LIFO (last in-first out) method is an example. There is also a great quantity of written material published by accounting organizations, including those responsible for promulgation, which has not been officially designated as GAAP.

2. Answers to questions on which promulgated GAAP is silent, or ambiguous, or even contradictory, such as comprise accounting for stockholders' equity. The AICPA's annual review of financial reports,

published under the title *Accounting Trends and Techniques*, provides one source, and accounting textbooks another.

THE HISTORY OF GAAP

The concept of GAAP is not old, and we can examine it in relation to three fairly recent time periods: 1917–33, 1934–57, and 1958 to date.

Prior to World War I there was little public interest in U.S. corporate accountability, private interest, as we have pointed out, having resulted from foreign investment. As the American economy grew and savings accumulated in banks and other financial institutions, these became an important domestic source of business capital.

By the 1930s individual and institutional investors other than banks had come to dominate the financial world. Whereas banks were interested primarily in liquidity and solvency, investors wanted information about profitability. These two influences were behind the securities legislation of 1933–34 and the accounting regulations that resulted.

The period following World War II saw a great expansion in the volume of institutional funds seeking investment, not only from banks and other savings institutions but also through a variety of financial intermediaries, including pension funds, insurance companies, and specialized finance houses such as those involved with leasing. Individual investment also grew, and with it the size and importance of mutual funds, investment trusts, and brokerage houses operating in stock and bond markets. These developments placed new and increased responsibilities on financial analysts, whose needs were regularly expressed in journal articles and by direct lobbying of the SEC and the FASB, as well as by face-to-face meetings with corporate finance officials. The FASB has been particularly responsive to their wishes.

The Period Preceding 1933

As early as 1894 the American Association of Public Accountants (AAPA) had attempted to lay down rules governing the order of balance sheet items.[1] In 1900 the New York Stock Exchange passed a rule requiring all corporations applying for listing to agree to publish annual financial statements. In 1910 the AAPA formed a committee to establish uniform definitions of accounting technical terms, and of course, the introduction of a corporate income tax in 1916 increased pressure to regulate accounting practice.

Additional pressure built up during World War I, when government agencies had to contract with industrial corporations for war materiel, and sought a degree of accountability to counteract profiteering. An anonymous letter was presented by Edwin Hurley, chairman of the Federal Trade Commission, at the first meeting of the American Institute of Accountants in 1916, expressing the dissatisfaction of the Federal Reserve Board and others with the financial statements certified by public accountants. He threatened to impose a uniform accounting system for each industry, and proposed a registry of accountants whose certificates would be recognized by federal agencies. The American Institute of Accountants (AIA) as it was now called responded to this by issuing a memorandum on the subject, which was endorsed by the Federal Reserve Board and published in the 1917 issue of the *Federal Reserve Bulletin* and subsequently under the title *Uniform Accounting*. It was republished in 1918 as *Approved Methods for the Preparation of Balance Sheet Statements*, and revised in 1929, with an emphasis on auditing, as *Verification of Financial Statements*. Finally, the AIA revised it in 1936 under the title *Examination of Financial Statements by Independent Public Accountants*, after which, as we shall see, the institute's direction changed.

These early attempts at standards for financial statements and their audit are responsible for many of the features that characterize present-day accounting in the United States. Preoccupation with the balance sheet is marked, and although the 1936 revision provided a new emphasis on the income statement, the balance sheet view has reemerged in the work of the FASB, notably in standards for accounting for leases, pensions, and income taxes. The influence of the banks is apparent from the decision to list assets in declining order of liquidity, and liabilities in the order in which they will be met. This order is virtually unique to the United States, as most other countries use the reverse presentation. The going concern convention and the related historical cost basis of valuation also date from this period.

It is interesting to note another respect in which U.S. practice diverged from other countries. The attempt to direct attention to the income statement was designed to assist accountants in demonstrating what the late G. O. May, a leading practitioner of the time, called "earning power." For this purpose, accountants have used a two- or three-part income statement, the first showing trading (operating) profit, the second showing the effects of nonoperating and extraordinary items, and the third, prior years' items and other income adjustments, to arrive at net income or profit. The uniform accounting publications mentioned led to the adoption of a unitary form of income statement embracing all revenues, gains, expenses, and losses, not only of the period but also *in* the period, such as prior period items. The resulting strain has led the FASB to promulgate standards that effectively permit income statement items to bypass the income statement and go directly to stockholders' equity. This self-inflicted wound has led the FASB to attempt to distinguish "earnings" from "comprehensive income."

The Depression and Its Consequences

The 1920s were a period of financial euphoria in the United States, as stock markets, awash in the liquidity generated by World War I, appeared to know only one way to go. Many critics, including several noted economists of the time, sounded warning notes, and drew attention to deficiencies in financial reporting that could lead investors to unfortunate consequences. There were no company laws to protect them, and in particular, the provision of audited financial statements was purely voluntary, even though a 1926 rule of the New York Stock Exchange required listed companies to supply stockholders with financial statements prior to their annual meeting, as was mandated by law in other countries.

Many of the critics drew attention to rather common problems, in particular, the use of different accounting methods for ostensibly similar situations. Among the problem areas were depreciation accounting, consolidations, absence of essential data such as sales volume and explanatory notes, and practices designed either to under- or overstate profits. The AIA established a special committee on cooperation with stock exchanges, headed by G. O. May, to consider the possibility of a competent authority to set binding rules. This was rejected in favor of another approach: "to leave every corporation free to choose its own methods of accounting within . . . broad limits . . . but require disclosure of the methods employed and consistency in their application from year to year."

Under this system, each listed company would file a statement of its methods of accounting and reporting with the Stock Exchange, together with any changes, and a revised auditor's certificate (as it was then called) would state whether the company had followed these methods, whether they were in accordance with generally accepted accounting standards, and whether they had been applied consistently.

Because there were no written "generally accepted accounting standards" the May Committee specified the following five principles, which were believed to be basic:

1. That income accounts should not include unrealized profit, realization being the consequence of an act of sale.
2. That capital surplus should not be used for revenue items of charge.
3. That earned surplus of a subsidiary created prior to acquisition was not part of the consolidated earned surplus of the parent.
4. That dividends paid by a corporation to itself in respect of holdings of its own stock should not be credited to income.
5. That amounts receivable from officers, employees, and affiliated companies should be shown separately.

It is noteworthy that 1, 2, and 3 of these "principles" no longer constitute part of GAAP. Accounting for long-term construction contracts involves recognizing unrealized profit; losses on long-term investments in marketable equity securities are charged to stockholders' equity; and pooling accounting combines preacquisition retained earnings of a subsidiary with those of the parent. Nevertheless, at the time the list was welcomed, and quoted with approval in a statement issued the following year by the president of the NYSE when he announced that after July 1, 1933, all applicants for listing must agree to have their financial statements audited and submit them on application.

The May Committee's correspondence with the NYSE Committee on Stock List includes a letter from the committee to the governing committee of the NYSE recommending that auditors' reports state

—whether in their opinion the form of the balance sheet and of the income or profit and loss account is such as to fairly present the financial position and the results of operation.

—whether the accounts are in their opinion fairly determined on the basis of consistent application of the system of accounting regularly employed by the company.

—whether such system in their opinion conforms to accepted accounting practices, and particularly whether it is in any respect inconsistent with any of the (May Committee's) principles.

Thereupon the May Committee produced *Revised Suggestions of a Form of Accountants' Report* that stated following the scope paragraph: "In our opinion, based upon such examination, the accompanying balance sheet and related statement of income and surplus fairly present, in accordance with accepted principles of accounting consistently maintained by the Company during the year under review, its position at December 31, 1933 and the results of its operations for the year." A short-form audit report subsequently adopted by the AIA used similar wording, but very significantly dropped the comma after "fairly present." The word "generally" was added to "accepted accounting principles" in 1936, at the insistence of the SEC. Although the audit report was radically revised in 1988, and reference to consistency dropped, the phrase "in conformity with generally accepted accounting principles" has survived intact.

The Search for Principles

By 1935 the SEC had accepted the proposition that accounting principles would be formulated by the accounting profession, and the profession had begun to experience a certain insecurity when reporting "in accordance with" a non-existent set of accounting principles. Perhaps in desperation, it offered a prize for the best paper on the subject, which was won by Gilbert Byrne. The paper, entitled "To What Extent Can the Practice of Accounting Be Reduced to Rules and Standards?", was presented at the fiftieth anniversary celebration of the AIA in 1937, and published in the *Journal of Accountancy* in November of that year.

Byrne's paper had a seminal influence on theory and practice. He quoted the Webster's Dictionary definition of a principle: "a fundamental truth; a comprehensive law or doctrine, from which others are derived, or on which others are founded; an elementary proposition or fundamental assumption; a maxim; an axiom; a postulate.'' This suggestion that there might be a theoretical basis for accounting principles has led to the FASB's influential conceptual framework project. Another of Byrne's propositions, that accounting principles ''like the axioms of geometry . . . are few in number,'' now looks like wishful thinking. It was probably based on an unrealistic analogy with economics, where great superstructures have been erected on the laws of supply and demand.

Among the more practical propositions of Byrne are four restrictive assumptions from which U.S. accountants are striving to liberate themselves nearly sixty years later. They are:

—that ''accounting is essentially the allocation of historical costs and revenues to the current and succeeding fiscal periods''

—that ''while it is not in many cases of great importance which of several alternative accounting rules is applied in a given situation, it is essential that, once having adopted a certain procedure, it be consistently adhered to''

—that ''income shall include only realized profits''

—that ''profit is deemed to be realized when a sale in the ordinary course of business is effected''

Besides Byrne's contribution the search for GAAP was also aided by a committee established by the Haskins and Sells Foundation in 1935. This committee consisted of two accounting professors (Henry Sanders of Harvard and Henry Rand Hatfield of California) plus a legal scholar (Underhill Moore of Yale). Their report, *A Statement of Accounting Principles* (AIA, 1938), included a list of items encountered in financial statements together with justifications of current practice. From these observations a ''Summary of Accounting Principles'' was derived, and made Part VI of the report. This represented the first attempt to identify a comprehensive list of accounting principles, based on the need to distinguish capital and revenue. Thus, the lower of cost or market rule was accepted in respect of current assets, and losses were explicitly excluded from deferral.

Accounting Regulation in the United States

Starting with the establishment of the Interstate Commerce Commission in 1887, the U.S. federal government has created a number of agencies designed to regulate various aspects of the country's economy. Following the financial crises and stock exchange crashes of the period 1929–32, and as a response to the consequent investor losses, the federal government passed the Securities Act of 1933 and the Securities Exchange Act of 1934; the latter provided for the establishment of a Securities and Exchange Commission (SEC). One of functions of the SEC is to ensure that issuers of corporate securities provide the market with information in the form of financial statements.

Section 13 (b) of the 1934 act gives the SEC the power to dictate the form and content of financial statements, the method of valuation of assets and liabilities, and the determination of revenues and expenses. In other words, the SEC may lay down what constitutes GAAP. This power was used to require that financial reports be certified by an independent public accountant who must follow the SEC's rules and procedures. In the beginning, the SEC looked to the accounting profession to lay down accounting principles, a policy formally stated by the first chief accountant of the SEC, Carman Blough. The SEC contributed to the improvement of financial reporting through its *Accounting Series Releases*, and No. 4 (1938) stated that the commission would accept for filing only financial statements prepared using accounting principles having substantial authoritative support, or in accordance with the rules and regulations of the SEC itself. ASR 4 lays down that financial statements using accounting principles lacking authoritative support will be presumed to be misleading or inaccurate.

Impatient with the profession's inability to establish accounting principles, however, in 1940 the SEC issued Regulation S-X, which in effect standardized the content of financial statements. (A special bulletin adopted by the Council of the AICPA in October 1964 confirmed that "Generally accepted accounting principles are those which have substantial authoritative support.")

Working behind the scenes, as it were, the SEC has continued to exercise a major influence on GAAP, sometimes more directly, as in the case of mandatorily redeemable preferred stock, and sometimes more indirectly, as in the disclosure of financial instruments and their related risks. Attempts to differentiate the roles of the profession and the SEC have resulted in a distinction between measurement standards, the responsibility of the former, and disclosure standards, the province of the latter, a distinction that has become increasingly blurred. Perhaps the most conspicuous example of the influence of the SEC on measurement has been its opposition to any attempt to report asset appreciation, other than a short-lived flirtation with supplementary reports on the effects of price-level changes between 1976 and 1984.

The CAP and the APB

The AIA created a Committee on Accounting Procedure (CAP) in 1936, which until 1938 consisted of the chairmen of seven committees, after which it was expanded to twenty-one members appointed for one-year terms. The CAP responded to the various issues that arose in *Accounting Research Bulletins*, of which forty-two appeared in its first fifteen years. Most of these were consolidated into ARB 43, and a further eight were published between 1953 and 1958. ARB 43 included eight reports of the Committee on Terminology, which were published separately in 1953 as *Accounting Terminology Bulletin No. 1*, "Review and Resume."

The CAP was criticized because, in spite of the name of its publications, little accounting research was in fact done, and because it failed to come to grips with a number of problems that became acute following World War II. These arose out of the tremendous increase in financial activity, which resulted in the creation of new types of financial instruments, and even new types of financial institutions that escaped the SEC's regulatory net. In addition, the effects of inflation and "creative accounting" eroded some of the confidence in historical cost financial statements.

In the year 1958, following the AIA's name change to AICPA, it established the Accounting Principles Board to develop and promulgate accounting principles. The board appointed a director of accounting research and a permanent research staff, and announced that it would pursue its objectives on four levels: basic postulates; principles; application rules; and pure research. It was again stated that "postulates are few in number" and it was assumed that the principles would follow logically from these postulates, and rules from principles. The AICPA Special Committee that was responsible for the design of the APB recognized the need for a conceptual framework, to ensure consistency and enhance public confidence in GAAP.

During its twenty-four-year life, the APB had from eighteen to twenty-one members, mainly public accountants but including some from academe, business, and government. It published thirty-one opinions that constitute GAAP insofar as they have not been superseded, and four statements and fifteen research studies, which do not. The research arm started badly, publishing ARS No. 1, "The Basic Postulates of Accounting" (1961) and No. 3, "A Tentative Set of Broad Accounting Principles for Business Enterprises" (1962), which contained propositions that, if accepted, would have radically modified the historical cost basis of financial statements. Because the profession was not ready for such reforms, the studies appeared with a disclaimer, and were in effect replaced by ARS No. 7, an "Inventory of Generally Accepted Accounting Principles for Business Enterprises" (1965), which simply enumerated established practices.

During the APB's lifetime (1958–72) the critical issues that face the profession perennially were supplemented by the problem of inflation. It was the attempt to move toward some form of accounting for price-level changes that tainted ARS Nos. 1 and 3; the APB also published ARS No. 6, "Reporting the Financial Effects of Price-level Changes" (1963) and Statement No. 3, "Financial Statements Restated for General Price-level Changes" (1969), but none of these efforts elicited a positive response. While the APB produced a number of notable improvements in the form and content of financial statements, which were expanded to include a statement of changes in financial position, and in methods of accounting for business combinations, income taxes, intangibles, pensions, and other kinds of transactions, it nevertheless fell short of what financial analysts and the SEC expected of it.

The APB made a major effort to produce a conceptual framework, in Statement No. 4, "Basic Concepts and Accounting Principles Underlying Financial Statements of Business Enterprises'' (1970), which failed to obtain acceptance. Because there was little obvious relationship between what research was published and the Opinions, the credibility problem remained. It was alleged that members from the largest public accounting firms were subject to client pressures, and many Opinions displayed evidence of compromises that resulted in suboptimal pronouncements.

The APB also came under fire from the SEC when it took opposing positions, as in the case of accounting for the investment tax credit. Even the Internal Revenue Service became involved in the debate, forcing the APB to abandon its initial proposal. By 1970 it became apparent that the APB's time had run out, because of these problems and others:

—The promulgation of GAAP had become a matter of public interest, involving the SEC, the IRS, and even Congress, whereas the APB was perceived as a self-serving organ of the accounting profession.

—It had failed to resolve controversial issues such as foreign currency translation and accounting for petroleum finding costs.

—Largely as a result of litigation arising out of fraudulent and deceptive financial reporting, it was concluded that the promulgation of accounting principles should be transferred to an independent body.

Of these various factors, probably the strongest was the view that the APB was simply not getting the job done. Corporate annual reports bore evidence of ''managed'' earnings, the consequence of selecting from alternatives permitted by GAAP. For example, a report to Congress by the SEC dated August 3, 1972 (following the Penn-Central bankruptcy), stated that ''The whole practice of income management which emerges here is made up of some practices which, standing alone, could perhaps be justified as supported by generally accepted accounting principles, and other practices which could be so supported with great difficulty, if at all. But certainly the aggregate of these practices produced highly misleading results.''

In 1972 the AICPA formed two study groups, one on the objectives of financial statements, the other on the establishment of accounting principles. The first produced a report (the Trueblood report) that, in modified form, became the FASB's *Statement of Financial Accounting Concepts No. 1*. The second produced a report (the Wheat Committee report) that proposed a new structure for establishing accounting rules, based on a Financial Accounting Standards Board, which was established on July 1, 1973.

THE FINANCIAL ACCOUNTING STANDARDS BOARD

In creating the FASB, the accounting profession was concerned to demonstrate that the task of promulgating GAAP had been transferred to an independent body that was not part of the profession. Hence the concept of the "sponsoring organizations": the AICPA, the American Accounting Association, the National Association of Accountants (now the Institute of Management Accountants), the Financial Analysts Federation, the Financial Executives Institute, and the Securities Industry Association. These six bodies provide the members of the Financial Accounting Foundation, which elects a board of trustees, now comprising representatives of the sponsors plus a maximum of two at-large. The board of trustees appoints the seven-member FASB for five-year terms, of which the chairman is "first among equals," and also finances the FASB's operations, which have been rather costly.

This is in part due to the generous salaries paid to the members, who are required to serve full-time and to divest themselves of investments that might be construed as rendering them less than independent. By 1979 the majority of FASB members came from backgrounds other than public accounting. The FASB also has a permanent staff, including a director of research and technical activities, usually numbering about forty. The FASB is advised by two voluntary bodies, a Financial Accounting Standards Advisory Council that is consulted on planning and programming and helps to constitute the task forces that work on particular projects, and an Emerging Issues Task Force (EITF), formed to issue statements on pressing problems that cannot await the full process.

The promulgation process starts with identification of a problem area, and the appointment of a task force. Difficult issues lead to publication of a discussion memorandum inviting public comment. Due process requires a public hearing, then one or two exposure drafts of the proposed statement. After sixty days for further discussion a vote is taken. A standard now requires a five-to-two majority. By March 1992, the FASB had issued 109 statements of financial accounting standards, 38 interpretations, and nearly 100 technical bulletins.

The APB was criticized for issuing opinions that were not based on a consistent theory, and attempted to produce such a theory by publishing APB Statements, notably No. 4 (1970). The FASB has taken over this task, called "the conceptual framework project," in the form of six Statements of Financial Accounting Concepts, but it appears that these costly products have not contributed much to the standard-setting process. A basic question is what underlies the transformation of principle generation into standard-setting, but the conceptual statements are silent on this point. We continue to confront the anomaly of auditors referring to generally accepted accounting principles and not standards.

The FASB has been accused of "standards overload" and of insufficient productivity. With regard to the former, most of its publications are unnecessarily prolix and complex, which has given rise to a virtual industry producing straightforward versions for the benefit of practitioner and student. Many standards are a burden upon smaller companies seeking a clean audit opinion. On the question of output, in a Bear Stearns newsletter dated March 2, 1990, Lee J. Seidler analyzed the FASB's output of twenty-two standards for the period January 1985 through December 1989, of which only six could be considered reasonably significant. (He calculated a unit cost per standard of $1.8 million.) This relatively low level of activity was inexplicable in light of the fact that many of the most important financial reporting issues, including inventory and depreciation accounting, have not been standardized. Nor has the FASB responded to current developments in the global world of financial reporting, such as accounting for brand names and reporting both historical cost and current cost profit.

Further, the FASB's output has been undistinguished. Several statements have had to be replaced, revoked, or withdrawn (foreign currency translation; oil and gas accounting; income tax allocation; depreciating churches). Many have passed with bare majorities, including such important pronouncements as No. 87 on accounting for pensions and No. 95 on the statement of cash flows; interestingly, Statement No. 106 on postretirement benefits other than pensions, which lays down virtually the same methods as Statement No. 87, was adopted unanimously. Some FASB statements require future obligations to be discounted, others do not. The FASB's inability to use its own definitions was demonstrated by the two standards on accounting for income taxes. The first of these denied that "deferred tax assets" conformed to the definition of an asset; the second stated that they did.

In spite of attacks from business organizations and individual critics, however, the FASB appears to be sure to survive, if only because no one wants the government to take over the standard-setting function, and no other agency is willing to do the job.

THE "HOUSE OF GAAP"

As a consequence of all these sources, what constitutes GAAP is a problem for the practicing accountant. In an article published in the *Journal of Accountancy* (June 1984, p. 123) Steven Rubin depicted GAAP as a hierarchical structure he called "The House of GAAP." In January 1992 the Auditing Standards Board (ASB) of the AICPA issued Statement on Auditing Standards No. 69 entitled "The Meaning of 'Present Fairly in Conformity With Generally Accepted Accounting Principles' in the Independent Auditor's Report." The proximate cause for this initiative was the necessity to provide an official hierarchy of different levels of authority that would be applicable to the pronouncements of the Governmental Accounting Standards Board (GASB) as well as those of the FASB.[2] The Financial Accounting Foundation had earlier (November 1989) established a GAAP hierarchy for both bodies.

The previously existing hierarchy had four categories:

a. FASB statements and interpretations, APB opinions, AICPA accounting research bulletins, and GASB statements and interpretations (for state and local governments)

b. AICPA industry audit and accounting guides and statements of position and FASB and GASB technical bulletins

c. AICPA accounting interpretations together with practices prevalent in a particular industry

d. Other accounting literature, including professional pronouncements, minutes of the FASB's EITF (emerging issues task force) and FASB concepts statements, international accounting standards, regulatory pronouncements, and articles and textbooks

It had only three levels of authority, however, since b and c were equal. The ASB pronouncement:

—sets up two parallel hierarchies, one for state and local government and one for other entities

—gives each of the categories successively weaker authority

—creates a new category c, consisting of consensus positions of the FASB's EITF and the AICPA's accounting standards executive committee (AcSEC)

—makes category d (formerly c) "AICPA accounting interpretations, Qs and As published by the FASB staff, uncleared AICPA accounting and auditing guides, uncleared AICPA statements of position, and industry practices widely recognized and prevalent"

—expands category e (formerly d)

Interestingly, pronouncements of the SEC are not included in this hierarchy, presumably because, being part of administrative law, they override all promulgated GAAP. The EITF's pronouncements had been endorsed by the chief accountant of the SEC, however, and had to be followed by SEC registrants. The new hierarchy moves these pronouncements from the bottom to the middle of the hierarchy, and makes them applicable to all nongovernmental entities. Perhaps because GAAP is narrowly defined in SEC *Accounting Series Release No. 150*, the question whether it means the same thing to SEC registrants and nonregistrants cannot be answered at this time. We may note here the confusion reigning on this presumably very basic question.

PROFESSIONAL JUDGMENT AND GAAP

Promulgated GAAP is believed to eliminate, or at least reduce, the need to choose between alternatives. Under Rule 203 of the AICPA's Code of Professional Ethics, no AICPA member shall "express an opinion or state affirmatively that . . . financial statements are presented in conformity with generally accepted accounting principles . . . if such statements . . . contain any departure from an accounting principle promulgated by bodies designated by Council to establish such principles that has a material effect on the statements" unless (s)he "can demonstrate that due to unusual circumstances the financial statements . . . would otherwise have been misleading." "Unusual circumstances" presupposes the use of professional judgment. This rule applies only to CPAs who are also members of the AICPA.

Although the FASB is normally silent on the question, both the Canadian and U.K. standard-setting bodies have addressed the issue. In Canada, the "Introduction to Accounting Recommendations" in the Canadian Institute of Chartered Accountants (CICA) *Handbook* states that "no rule of general application can be phrased to suit all circumstances . . . nor is there any substitute for the exercise of professional judgment in the determination of what constitutes fair presentation or good practice in a particular case." Paragraph 5 of the "Explanatory Foreword" to the U.K. *Statements of Standard Accounting Practice* goes further by stating that the statements "are not intended to be a comprehensive code of rigid rules." The Preface to the International Accounting Standards contains similar wording. (FASB statements include the wording "need not be applied to immaterial items," which calls for judgment of a different kind.)

Nevertheless, many, if not most, promulgated U.S. GAAP requires judgment for its application. For example, FAS 52 involves selecting the functional currency, and although guidance is offered, it is by no means definitive. FAS 87 applies to any arrangement that is similar in substance to a pension plan, and even to a series of practices involving payment of postretirement benefits. Alister Mason and Michael Gibbins analyzed a selection of APB opinions and FASB statements, and found the following kinds of judgment issues:[3]

1. Wording of several refers to judgment.
2. Several require judgment to be exercised in choosing between alternatives.
3. Several require judgment as to whether a particular element (e.g., disclosure) is applicable.
4. Several require judgment of the meaning of a phrase.
5. The application of the opinion/statement requires the exercise of judgment.

A concordance study of APB opinions revealed the frequent occurrence of two situations calling for judgment: use of the same word having apparently different meanings, and use of different words meaning apparently the same thing. It is worthy of note that although the Canadian and U.K. standard-setters appear to place more importance on professional judgment as against rigid application of the relevant GAAP, they are no more forthcoming in providing guidance for the use of judgment than is the FASB. Mason and Gibbins recommended that not only should the importance of judgment be affirmed, it should also be defined and its scope reduced. An alternative view would suggest that the inevitability of judgment should be recognized by promulgating GAAP in broad general terms, such as those used for accruing losses in FAS 5. It must be admitted from experience with FAS 5, however, that accountants appear to need specific instructions to force fair presentation out of them.

THE IMPORTANCE OF GAAP

Unsatisfactory audits on unreliable financial statements have from time to time aroused the concern of federal agencies other than the SEC. Whereas state governments were powerless to enact legislation or enforce regulation, the federal government had more success. Even so, such enforcement lacks teeth, and Federal Reserve Board regulations requiring banks and savings and loan associations to file financial reports do not even contain a provision for audit. Some state insurance commissioners have been able to impose financial reporting requirements on insurance companies, although again, not necessarily audits.

We have mentioned the influence on accounting of the SEC, the Federal Trade Commission, and the Federal Reserve Board; the Internal Revenue Service, of course, has laid down record-keeping and reporting regulations for corporations generally and not merely large public companies. The Interstate Commerce Commission, the Federal Communications Commission, and the Federal Power Commission have also imposed accounting regulations on privately owned public utility companies, and financial reports are also regulated in such public-interest fields as transportation, particularly railroads and aviation, and broadcasting. This proliferation of rules, called "preferred accounting principles," does not constitute GAAP until promulgated by the FASB.

The overriding importance of GAAP lies in its place in the legal system of the United States. Consider a routine contract such as a debt instrument, which provides for the maintenance of a minimum working capital, or certain ratios such as debt to equity, earnings to debt service, and the like. Very often it is stated that the underlying measurements are to be made "in accordance with generally accepted accounting principles" and may even be affected by GAAP promulgated after the issuance of the debt.

Even though state corporation laws are largely toothless, they nevertheless contain provisions concerning stock splits and stock dividends, treasury stock, and of course a profits test limiting a company's ability to pay dividends, all of which may be affected by GAAP. Generally speaking, if a company's accounting practices are challenged, the accounting profession will argue that the practices in question could not be misleading if they were in accordance with GAAP. In the case of *U.S. v. Simon* (Continental Vending),[4] however, the U.S. Court of Appeals intepreted the auditor's report as stating that the financial statements were fairly presented *and* in accordance with GAAP, which was the position of the accounting profession before the comma between the phrases disappeared from the auditor's report (and is still its position in Canada and other countries).

CONCLUSION

The traditional view of the accountant was of one who learned a basic technique, and then applied it with judgment to a variety of circumstances. During the 1930s we saw the emergence of a belief that the corporate world was populated with crooks and deceivers, and that even audited financial reports could not be relied upon to be free of fraudulent misrepresentation. It was found necessary to constrain accountants by forcing them to conform to officially promulgated generally accepted principles. This process was reinforced after World War II as investment managers and financial analysts expressed their need for consistent and comparable financial reporting. Events in the 1980s have seemed to justify the view that fraudulent financial statements are a major social problem, but placed in question the effectiveness of GAAP.

We have seen that U.S. GAAP is defective in many respects. Important areas of accounting are not covered. The sheer size and complexity of promulgated GAAP undermine its usefulness. Many, if not most, GAAP promulgations are ambiguous, or require judgment; some are mutually incompatible, some incomprehensible. On the other hand, a "cook book" approach that attempts to cover all possible aspects of the subject invites avoidance tactics unless closely supervised. Many pronouncements result from compromises that leave no public satisfied. The FAS 96 fiasco (accounting for income taxes) has ensured that for seven years at least (1987–93) corporate financial reports will be noncomparable. There is still no prospect of a unified approach to accounting standard-setting, and the need for international accounting standards, discussed in Chapter 6, compounds the problem.

NOTES

1. In 1887 a group of mainly British accountants formed the American Association of Public Accountants; their U.S. counterparts then formed the Federation of Societies of Public Accountants, which merged with the AAPA in 1905. The AAPA changed its name to the American Institute of Accountants of the United States of America in 1916. A rival American Society of CPAs was established in 1921, and merged with the AIA in 1936. The AIA changed its name to the American Institute of Certified Public Accountants (AICPA) in 1957. These events are the subject of John Carey's *The Rise of the Accounting Profession: From Technician to Professional 1896–1936* (New York: AICPA, 1969), and are also discussed in Eugene H. Flegm's *Accounting: How to Meet the Challenges of Relevance and Regulation* (New York: John Wiley & Sons, 1984).

2. The Governmental Accounting Standards Board was created in 1984 to promulgate accounting standards for state and local governments. It is managed by the Financial Accounting Foundation, which was intended to assure consistency with GAAP. So far this has not been notably the case.

3. Alister K. Mason and Michael Gibbins, "Judgment and U.S. Accounting Standards," *Accounting Horizons*, June 1991, pp. 14–24.

4. 425 F 2nd. 796 (2nd Circuit, 1969).

CHAPTER 5

THE AUDITING PROBLEM

INTRODUCTION

That all is not well in the auditor's world is an understatement. At the time of this writing, the accounting profession in the United States has drawn a collective sigh of relief as a judge has denied a claim against one of the Big Six firms, arguing that because the directors of a bankrupt savings and loan association knew about irregularities in its accounting records, nothing the auditors failed to do affected the outcome. Many actions against auditors have not had such happy endings.

Accounting firms are themselves very concerned about their performance; a partner in Arthur Andersen & Co. recently published an article in the *Journal of Accountancy* entitled "Reinventing the Audit."[1] We shall discuss the question of whether the audit should be reinvented or simply done properly.

ORIGINS OF THE CURRENT PROBLEM

In Chapter 2 we described the history of the corporate audit and pointed to some of the inherent limitations of auditing in the United States. These limitations were apparent by the 1930s, and led to the system of setting auditing standards, known as "generally accepted auditing standards" (GAAS). Appendix A to *Codification of Auditing Standards and Procedures, Statement on Auditing Standards,* published by the AICPA in 1973, provided some background.

The process started with "a memorandum on balance sheet audits" prepared in 1917 by the American Institute of Accountants, forerunner of the AICPA, which was endorsed by the Federal Reserve Board and published in the *Federal Reserve Bulletin* for April 1917. Reprints were circulated under the title *Uniform Accounting: A Tentative Proposal Submitted to the Federal Reserve Board.* A

1929 revision, *Verification of Financial Statements*, was published by the AIA, again prompted by the Federal Reserve Board. Significantly, this document asserted the impracticability of laying down uniform auditing procedures, and placed full responsibility for the design and execution of the audit on the auditor. At this date, the auditor's report was still referred to as a certificate. In the important case of *Ultramares Corporation v. Touche Niven & Company* (255 N.Y. 170 (1931)), the auditors were sued for negligence because they submitted an audit certificate without uncovering fraudulent bookkeeping that falsified the related accounts. The case eventually went to the New York Court of Appeals, where Judge Cardozo held that an auditor could be liable for gross negligence that amounted to constructive fraud, and ordered a new trial. Thereupon the parties settled out of court, but following this case, an editorial in the *Journal of Accountancy* proposed that use of the word "certificate" be discontinued because "it is absurd to speak of certifying an opinion." The AIA's 1936 revision of *Verification of Financial Statements* substituted the word "examination" for "verification" in order to avoid "unwarranted implications of certainty." Both of these changes may have had important effects on auditing in the United States; the latter change has now been reversed, and the new form of auditor's opinion states that an audit has been performed.

Between 1932 and 1934 accounting and auditing issues were debated by committees of the AIA and the New York Stock Exchange, and the ensuing correspondence was published under the title *Audits of Corporate Accounts*. This correspondence led to the adoption of the form of audit report used in the United States until it was replaced in 1988. As a consequence of a suggestion by the then chairman of the NYSE, the new report stated that the auditor had made an examination of the client's financial statements and expressed an opinion about conformity with generally accepted principles of accounting, consistently applied.

CONSEQUENCES OF THE MCKESSON–ROBBINS CASE

The next major landmark was the McKesson and Robbins case of 1938. Price Waterhouse and Company had issued audit reports on this corporation's financial statements without uncovering substantial fraud, including reporting nonexistent inventories. Price Waterhouse voluntarily refunded over $500,000 in fees to the client. On January 30, 1939, three weeks after the SEC began hearings into this case, the AIA created a Committee on Auditing Procedures (CAUP). Under pressure from the SEC, the CAUP initiated a series of Statements on Auditing Procedure (SAP), the first of which was published in October 1939 under the title *Extensions of Audit Procedures*. SAP 1 required "where practicable" attendance at physical inventory-taking and direct test counts, and also confirmation of accounts receivable. SAP 1 was adopted by vote of members at the next AIA annual meeting, but did not lead to any further procedural standards, as the CAUP subsequently decided not to issue any more statements "dealing largely with auditing procedures in an abstract manner, without reference to particular circumstances.'' Future auditing standards were to be couched in terms of extreme generality, focusing on objectives and "the hierarchy of ideas, concepts and prescriptions that constitute the intellectual edifice of the profession."[2]

The SEC also took advantage of the profession's initiative to press the AIA to require members to report that the examination was made in accordance with generally accepted auditing standards, and this phrase was duly added to the standard form of report (SEC *Accounting Series Release No. 21*, February 1941). However, the SEC regarded the new wording, "in accordance with generally accepted auditing standards applicable in the circumstances," as a direct representation that certain procedures had been carried out, whereas because no additional procedural standards had been promulgated, the CAUP interpreted the phrase as a statement of the auditor's opinion of the quality of the work performed. The SEC prevailed, and the AIA *Tentative Statement of Auditing Standards—Their Generally Accepted Significance and Scope* was adopted at the 1948 annual meeting of the institute. The new form of audit report dropped the previous categorical statement that a detailed audit was not performed.

An Auditing Standards Executive Committee replaced the CAUP, and eventually became the Auditing Standards Board (ASB) of the AICPA. The ASB's charge is to:

—Promulgate auditing standards and procedures to be observed by AICPA members in accordance with the institute's rules of conduct. (Note that not all licensed CPAs are members of the AICPA.)

—Find new opportunities for auditors to serve the public, and develop standards and procedures that will enable auditors to assume such responsibilities.

—Issue interpretations and guidelines.

The ASB issues Statements on Auditing Standards, which are in practice detailed interpretations and applications of ten basic standards adopted in 1948. Rule 202 of the AICPA's Code of Professional Ethics requires members to adhere to generally accepted auditing standards, and a member must be prepared to justify any departure therefrom. Relatively few disciplinary actions have been taken against members under this rule, but the number is increasing.

IMPACT OF GENERALLY ACCEPTED AUDITING STANDARDS

It was expected that the adoption of a formal code of auditing standards would improve the quality of auditing in the United States, and the assumption that the existence of such a written code is a symbol of high audit quality has been widely accepted. It is important, however, to remember that this code resulted not from the strength of the profession, but from its demonstrated weakness.

Lacking a statutory audit requirement, giving the auditor legal rights as well as duties, and a usable body of case law jurisprudence on accounting and auditing, the accounting profession was continually subjected to client pressures to reduce the cost of the audit. This was supported by user acquiescence, notably by the banks. These pressures resulted in a certain lack of clarity about the nature of an audit, and led to the concept of a "balance sheet audit," the name of which indicates something short of a full audit. The SEC and federal and state courts pursued some of the more egregious audit failures, and these and other published cases drew attention to the fact that many auditors were not doing their job. The profession repeatedly attempted to promulgate new auditing standards that demonstrated a commitment to the public's perception of an audit, without effecting any noticeable improvement. In 1954, fifteen years after the process started, an article in the *Journal of Accountancy* stated that "We certainly cannot hide the fact that there is some substandard performance in the profession."[3]

In recent years, actions against auditors have become increasingly common, and their defenses have crumbled to the point where many large settlements have been made in order to avoid potentially enormous judgments. In spite of this, negligence actions against accountants have succeeded in SEC hearings and in the courts. The Continental Vending case (*U.S.* v. *Simon*, 1968) in which the auditors were sued by the federal government for conspiring to file false statements and for mail fraud, shook the profession to its foundation, and steps were taken to improve its image. These included the creation by the AICPA of two practice sections, one for SEC auditors and the other for private company auditors, and introduction of a system of peer review for members of the former. These measures provided only a temporary respite.

THE ANDERSON COMMITTEE AND THE TREADWAY COMMISSION

In 1983 the AICPA established a committee on standards of professional conduct for CPAs, chaired by George Anderson, to address allegations of audit failures. Initially charged to evaluate present ethical standards and consider the role of the AICPA in setting them, its mandate was subsequently expanded to cover expansion of services and products, competition in the profession, the role of self-regulation, improving the quality of practice, and independence and objectivity. In 1986 the Anderson Committee recommended that the AICPA:

—Restructure its Code of Professional Ethics to improve its relevance and effectiveness. Emphasis should be away from rule compliance and toward "achieving positively stated goals."

—Provide guidance to practitioners in making judgments regarding the scope and nature of services and adherence to professionalism. A key question was that of conflict of interest.

—Establish a new practice-monitoring program to provide quality control and assure compliance with performance standards. All firms performing SEC audits would have to be members of the AICPA SEC practice section.

—Establish AICPA membership requirements for entry (150 hours of college study) and continuing education (to be mandatory).

It is noteworthy that none of the committee's recommendations dealt with the critical issues of independence and competition for business. Besides adopting the 150-hour requirement, the principal response of the AICPA was to restructure its trial board system, by consolidating twelve regional boards into one central board.

Evidence of substandard auditing continued to accumulate, and in 1986 the AICPA sponsored a National Commission on Fraudulent Financial Reporting, known as the Treadway Commission. Its 1987 report accepted the prevalence of fraudulent financial reporting as a fact, and indicated the dimensions of the problem by making sweeping recommendations for directors, managers, internal accountants and auditors, public accountants, the SEC, educators, and others.

The commission recommended that:

—Management should assess risk continuously; all public companies should maintain proper internal controls and adequate accounting records; and the SEC should require that management acknowledge these responsibilities in the annual report to shareholders. (The SEC can impose such requirements under its proxy rules, but only for registrants.)

—All public companies should have effective internal audit functions. The director of internal audit should have unrestricted and direct access to both the audit committee and the chief executive officer.

—All public companies should have audit committees to ensure auditor independence, monitor code of conduct compliance, and oversee the quarterly reporting process.

—The Auditing Standards Board should clarify the auditor's responsibility for fraud detection, and for review and evaluation of internal accounting control. The ASB should include "knowledgeable persons affected by and interested in auditing standards, but who are either not CPAs or are CPAs no longer in practice."

—The SEC should have expanded resources for enforcement, and state boards of accountancy should be encouraged to establish monitoring systems.

—Educators should foster knowledge and understanding of factors that lead to fraudulent financial reporting. (In an article in the September 1986 *Journal of Accountancy* the chairman of the commission, James

Treadway, remarked that fraud detection had been covered in the auditing literature of the 1920s, but contemporary texts did not even mention the subject.)

WHAT IS THE PROBLEM?

In the previously mentioned *Journal of Accountancy* article by Robert Mednick, he and his partners at Arthur Andersen & Co. expressed a critique of contemporary auditing and articulated proposals for reform. They criticized the current accounting model as irrelevant and the inhibiting effect of litigation on practice, and proposed changes in corporate governance, including a wider role for the auditor and a new concept of independence.

The problems facing auditors run much deeper, and stem from a departure from the traditional goals and methods of auditing. The decline of the audit can be traced to the failure of the U.S. system of professional education, an abortive attempt to avoid liability in tort, and the commercialization of the audit function. It is also attributable in part to the absence of any legal powers and protection for auditors. An attempt to regain the public's confidence must put teeth into the audit, by addressing these problems.

CHANGES IN CORPORATE GOVERNANCE

Although the problem of who actually governs the corporation exists in every jurisdiction and indeed, is rooted in difficult philosophical concepts of personal responsibility, it is particularly acute in the United States. This is because corporations are formed under state corporation statutes that fail to provide stockholders with much needed protection against predatory officers. In the present context, they do not require corporations to submit audited financial reports to stockholders (and any other kind are not worth receiving) and consequently do not legislate for the appointment, qualification, rights, powers, and duties of the auditor. How important it is to have such legislation was illustrated in 1991 in regard to the Bank of Credit and Commerce International (BCCI). The British government was able to obtain an audit of BCCI where no U.S. jurisdiction had such a power.

It would appear to be of the greatest importance that accountants join with lawyers to lobby for the enactment of a comprehensive model corporation statute in every state of the Union. The experience of the American Bar Association, however, which has failed singularly to achieve adoption of its model corporation statute, containing some accounting provisions, by even a single state, suggests that the problem must be tackled at the federal level. The time is ripe for such an initiative. The National Association of State Boards of Accountancy (NASBA) has drafted a Uniform Accountancy Act, but this is designed to facilitate reciprocity of practice rights, rather than to improve the quality of the audit.

In 1991 a bill that would require auditors of public companies to report illegal acts (H.R. 3159, the "Financial Fraud Detection and Disclosure Act") (the Wyden Bill) was reintroduced in the U.S. House of Representatives. A similar bill, introduced in 1990, failed to clear committees. The current bill, H.R. 4313, would:

—Authorize the SEC to require special reports by the auditor when it believes material illegal acts are, or may have been, committed.

—Require the SEC to prescribe methods to be used by the auditor to detect illegal activities and report them to the audit committee or board of directors.

—Require the SEC to conduct a study to determine the extent of compliance with the Foreign Corrupt Practices Act and whether mandatory internal control audits would be beneficial.

—Provide a "safe harbor" limiting auditors' liability, to end for fiscal years beginning 1996.

This bill provides a golden opportunity for accountants to support the government's attempt to put teeth into auditing, at least for public companies. As a quid pro quo it might enact a statutory duty to publish audited financial statements, which would give the accountancy profession the powers it needs to maintain its integrity in the face of self-serving and even downright dishonest corporate officers.

As Mednick pointed out, an audit requirement does exist for SEC-filing corporations in the United States, and directors must send stockholders audited financial reports if they solicit proxies. SEC regulations give independent auditors few rights and no powers, however, and many of the biggest financial scandals of our time (ESM; the savings and loans; BCCI) have escaped the SEC's regulatory net. Many believe that insurance companies will be the next problem area, for much the same reason.

Mednick discounted the role of outside directors, and the audit committees of which they are usually members, to support and encourage the auditor in the absence of statutory requirements. Most outside directors are appointed because they are friends or business partners of management directors, or are simply token representatives of the public. They are rarely selected on the basis of their knowledge of corporate governance, or finance, or their ability to protect the stockholders and the corporation's other publics. Indeed, the *Wall Street Journal* has indicated that the existence of outside directors is correlated with subpar profitability, which may be indirect evidence of their lack of independence and ability.

THE PERCEIVED IRRELEVANCE OF THE ACCOUNTING MODEL

Many critics argue that the model of the firm that underlies conventional financial statements is obsolete, and that both the accounting and auditing function should extend beyond their existing scope. There is no doubt that we should be moving toward a form of current value accounting. On the other hand, we have yet to read of an audit failure attributable to this inadequacy. The reason why auditors have lost credibility is because they have failed to report that cash has disappeared, that unrecoverable loans have not been adequately provided for, that receivables have been classified as investments, that inventory and fixed assets shown in the balance sheet are worthless, and that liabilities have been omitted. On occasion, they have failed to observe that sales and other revenues were overstated, and ignored the existence of significant losses. These errors and omissions will not be corrected by changing the accounting model.

On the other hand, there is nothing to stop auditors from expressing an opinion on "more predictive and value-based information" when they can get paid for it. The Rouse Companies pioneered supplementary current value statements in their annual reports, and a number of European companies (Shell, BP) are now reporting current cost earnings in addition to historical cost earnings. The problem is not only that public accounting firms have failed to market new products; to the contrary, public accounting firms have *failed to sell the traditional audit*, preferring to increase their revenues with inferior quality compilations and reviews, and to compete with management consultants, computer systems analysts, and even personnel recruiters. This point was made in an editorial in *CA Magazine* for December 1984: "(A) valid reason for the decline of the audit is that we have not really done a good job of selling it. If a client or his banker doesn't want to 'buy' an audit because neither appreciates the difference between it and a lesser product, who is to blame, the customer or the salesperson?"

As an indicator of this failure we may cite the AICPA's *Omnibus Statement on Standards for Accounting and Review Services—1992*, which deletes the prohibition against a public accountant merely typing or reproducing financial statements as an accommodation to a client!

It should not be lost from view, however, that the objective of including more "future-oriented" information within the scope of the audited financial report runs directly counter to the profession's desire to reduce its liability in tort. Nothing is more sensitive than business credit, and information designed to aid investors and others to predict liquidity, solvency, and profitability provides a litigant with yet another opportunity to sue. This prospect of increased liability could cause the auditor to take refuge behind obtuse "boiler plate" language, in much the same way as directors have done in response to the SEC's requirement for management's discussion and analysis of the financial statements. (A solution to this problem will be proposed in Chapter 14.)

Nor should it be overlooked that GAAS obliges auditors to take some responsibility for financial report information outside the financial statements. Since management uses the financial report as a form of public relations, it has an obvious interest in gilding the lily, or at least omitting the bad news. If auditors had any legal rights, they would presumably be able to take a position on fraudulent or misleading information of this kind, as well as on fraudulent or misleading financial statements.

THE OBJECTIVE OF THE AUDIT

This leads to consideration of the view that "the public has grown to expect more of auditors than merely an opinion on management's assertions." Indeed it has, and in years gone by it received what it expected.

In the first place, the objective of expressing an opinion that financial statements are in accordance with GAAP is too narrow. Obviously, audits are not restricted to financial statements, and in many countries additional duties are spelled out by law. For instance, in France the auditor must submit a special report on transactions between the audited company and its directors. Indeed, the audit is not an end result, but a process, as suggested by the *Living Webster* definition: "An examination into accounts or dealings with money or property by proper officers or persons appointed for that purpose."

The restriction to financial statements prepared in accordance with GAAP is unnecessary. Many accounting problems are not covered by GAAP; many that are can be subject to several incompatible treatments; judgment is almost always called for; and some standards contravene fundamental accounting principles. Attempts to substitute other comprehensive bases of accounting for GAAP result in audit reports that defy comprehension.

The objective of an audit is and always has been to examine accounts and other documents to establish their regularity. (It is significant that in some countries company law provides that the audit "discharges" directors from liability for certain acts vis-à-vis their shareholders.) Evidence that an audit has been performed is provided by the submission of a report, whether on financial statements, circulation statistics, or votes for an entertainment industry award. The examination is primary, the report secondary, and the report must be based on the examination.

The conventional wisdom in the United States is that a report stating that financial statements were prepared in accordance with GAAP and audited in accordance with GAAS will protect the auditor from liability under Section 32 of the 1934 Securities and Exchange Act, but experience, starting with the Continental Vending case, demonstrates this not to be so.[4] The Second Court of Appeals stated that "generally accepted accounting principles instruct the accountant what to do in the usual case where he has no reason to doubt that the affairs of the corporation are being honestly conducted. Once he has reason to believe that this basic assumption is false, an entirely different situation confronts him."

Whether or not the public expects accountants to provide "early warning of possible business failures and setbacks," it certainly wants "assurance the entity is well controlled and has complied with appropriate laws and regulations." The basic assumption on which an audit is based is that the client has kept auditable records; if not, then we are talking about an investigation (at a considerably higher fee) and not an audit. And if a company has contravened laws and regulations, the probable future loss arising out of these acts must be provided for or otherwise disclosed, under FAS 5.

AUDITOR INDEPENDENCE

The official AICPA view is that independence is first and foremost a state of mind. The auditor must not only be independent, but must appear to be independent, and auditors in the United States do not appear to be as independent as they like to think they are. Under French law, for example, only an individual whose name is on an official (court) list may perform the statutory audit. Such an individual must be over twenty-five and of good moral character, pass a competency examination, and complete a three-year experience requirement. (In some U.S. states, Florida for example, an auditor can be licensed without any experience!) In France, independence is the subject of absolute prohibitions. No person on the list may audit a company if that individual:

—Receives any special benefits from the company

—Holds a management position or serves as a director of the company

—Is a relative (through the fourth degree of blood relationship) of anyone who holds such a position

—Is an individual, or the spouse of one, who holds a management position or serves as a director of a company in which the audited company holds a 10 percent interest, or which holds a 10 percent interest in the audited company

—Is an individual or spouse of one who receives any remuneration from any of the companies mentioned above beyond the audit fee.[5]

The United States has no legal or other objective sources from which to gauge the independence of an auditor, although the SEC has ruled on specific cases in a number of its releases. The only other aid available is AICPA Rule of Ethics No. 101, *Independence*, which categorically states conditions that negate independence, yet apparently failed to bar auditors who obtained substantial home purchase loans from the savings and loan associations they audited. Although this situation existed in the Penn Square and ESM cases, no attempt was made to render the rule more specific. An AICPA task force is now examining the question, yet it is difficult to see how a rule on ethics could improve on the bald statement that "an auditor must be free from any moral or material obligation to the auditee" or how independence can be enforced other than by statute.

EDUCATION FOR THE PROFESSION

Many accountants believe that a fundamental problem underlying the decline of the audit function can be found in accounting education. Evidence of this may be adduced from the fact that most academic institutions teaching the subject call themselves schools (or departments) of accounting, whereas the profession is administered by state boards of accountancy. This difference conceals a difficult problem, that of the role of professional studies at the college level.

The fact that college education does not adequately prepare entrants into the profession has been widely acknowledged. It underlies the professional schools movement, which started about twenty years ago, and the 150-hour requirement; the former was intended to bring curricula closer to the profession's needs, the latter to improve the quality of students taking the CPA examinations. In 1988 the then Big Eight accounting firms circulated a memorandum calling for improvements in accounting education, and allocated several million dollars to finance innovation; the American Accounting Association then set up an Accounting Education Change Commission in order to distribute the money to schools promising improved programs.

The outcome of these initiatives is in doubt because of institutional dynamics that are impossible to influence. Shortly stated, the accounting program accreditation process is administered by the American Association of Collegiate Schools of Business (AACSB). The AACSB views business education as a set of techniques, of which economics and mathematics are the most useful, and accounting and business law the least. Accreditation requires most accounting faculty to have doctoral degrees, and for this and other reasons many of them have specialized in corporate finance, statistics, computer systems, behavioral sciences, and other disciplines that, while important, are not accounting, auditing, or taxation. As a consequence, even when an accounting program is organized as a school within a college of business, and even when its accounting faculty believe that they are trying to prepare students for a career as professional accountants, the emphasis of the program is on management techniques rather than professional subjects such as financial accounting and reporting or auditing.

One of the most striking deficiencies in these programs is the relative unimportance accorded to the study of law. No CPA can practice for long without realizing that extensive knowledge of the law is necessary, which has always been the case. This does not refer only to federal tax and business law; the accountant in practice must know state corporation, commercial, tax, and property law; the administrative laws of the regulatory system; tort law that will or will not impose legal liability; criminal law that may lead to prosecution for fraud; bankruptcy and liquidations, and a host of other details. A superficial one or two semesters in ''Business Law'' does not get the job done, especially where, as is so often the case, the instructor would not be deemed qualified to teach law in a law school.

The single most effective decision that the accounting profession could take to restore the audit to its former quality would be to take control of the education of its intake, as the architectural, legal, and medical professions have done of theirs.[6] This is not the place to outline the educational changes that would follow such an initiative, but it is clear that as long as accounting is viewed as a subset of business (or management) education, it will prove impossible to produce trained auditors. On-the-job training is no longer enough.

THE COMMERCIALIZATION OF AUDITING

In a phrase, the auditing profession has succumbed to the temptations of commercialization. Evidence of the retreat from professional standards into a simplistic cost/revenue model has been provided by reference to its preoccupation with legal liability (which has also had a chilling effect on the medical profession), the willingness of public accounting firms to sell their signatures at discounted prices (compilations, reviews, and even worse!), the acceptance of a narrow and superficial audit objective, a cynical view of independence, dilution of its mission through involvement with extraneous business activities, and virtual abandonment of the process of professional education.

One can also point to the effects of competition among accounting firms as an element of this commercialization. It is no secret that such competition often reaches predatory levels; the Anderson Committee was charged to investigate it, and the firms themselves have complained about it. The mergers of 1989 that reduced the Big Eight to Six were clearly aimed at improving the competitive position of the merging firms and increasing the earnings of their partners, despite the proclaimed virtues of size in the provision of professional services.

CONCLUSION

We have described the failure of the auditing profession to improve the quality of its work, leading to an expectation gap between the public's beliefs about the auditor's report and the reality. But what if the external audit has lost credibility because its importance has diminished? Perhaps society, while complaining about them, has decided that it can tolerate a high level of fraud and misrepresentation, in the same way that some businesses can live with theft because protecting themselves appears to cost more. Perhaps internal auditors can do a better job of assuring the quality of financial representations more efficiently, and at lower cost. What if the global financial marketplace effectively permits a business to sidestep regulation and the concomitant legal restraints, leaving to the auditor the depressing task of recording a description of the corpse after it has been picked over by predators? Is the external auditor today more coroner than watchdog?

These are obviously basic questions that public accountants should be asking themselves at the present time, which must be answered before problems of accounting education, corporate governance, legal liability, and auditor independence can be solved. Many accountants have serious doubts about the future of the attest function, not only because of the above-mentioned factors, but also because of the clear possibility that auditing will in the near future be taken over by government. Those who believe that auditing is a vital social function will continue to hope that accountants can ensure their survival through making fundamental changes. This point will be considered in more detail in Chapter 13.

NOTES

1. Robert Mednick, "Reinventing the Audit," *Journal of Accountancy*, August 1991, pp. 71–78.

2. Edward Stamp and Maurice Moonitz, *International Auditing Standards* (Englewood Cliffs, N.J.: Prentice-Hall, 1979).

3. Horace G. Barden, "The Meaning of Auditing Standards," *Journal of Accountancy*, April 1958, pp. 50–56.

4. *U.S. v. Simon* (Continental Vending), 425 F. 2nd 796 (2nd Circuit, 1969).

5. The problematical state of auditor independence in the United States was the subject of a 1987 publication by Arthur Andersen & Co. (*Answers to Important Questions about Scope of Practice and Auditor Independence in the U.S.*).

6. At its July 1991 meeting, the board of directors of the AICPA created an Academic and Career Development Division aimed at "developing highly qualified individuals, attracting them into the profession, and retaining them after they enter."

CHAPTER 6

INTERNATIONAL ACCOUNTING AND AUDITING

The internationalization of the accounting profession has been seen as an accompaniment to the globalization of financial markets, and indeed, the expansion overseas of U.S. accounting firms is often attributed to this. Accounting has always been international, however, because trade has overflowed national boundaries. Interest in international accounting developed as first marketing and then production began to be organized on an international scale in the nineteenth century. Global financial markets present additional reporting and auditing problems.

FIRST SIGNS OF AN INTERNATIONAL PROFESSION

Prior to 1900 a number of international conferences were organized by European accountants. Because of the language barrier, they did not attract Anglo-Saxon participation. The first that did was the international congress of accountants in St. Louis in 1904, an English language function with a few attendees from European countries. Future congresses were held in a number of countries at five-year intervals, except for wartime, and became truly cosmopolitan. Their organization was informal, and their purpose largely social and fraternal; technical papers were presented but the opportunity to establish professional connections was also highly valued. At the congress of 1972 an International Coordinating Committee for the Accounting Profession was formed and given the task of arranging the next meeting. Since 1978 these congresses have been the responsibility of the International Federation of Accountants (IFAC).

After World War II several regional organizations of accountants were established, notably the European Union of Accountants (now the Federation of European Accountants), the Inter-American Accounting Conference, the Asian and Pacific Accountants Conference, and at least two African groups, one anglophone and one francophone. These groups organize conferences and have standing committees that work toward the goal of harmonizing the accounting, auditing, and tax systems of the regions.

In 1973, largely through the efforts of (Lord) Henry Benson, then senior partner of Cooper Brothers (now part of Coopers and Lybrand) and president of the Institute of Chartered Accountants in England and Wales, the International Accounting Standards Committee (IASC) was formed. Its nine original members had all been hosts to one of the international congresses. The IASC has grown to a membership of over 100 professional associations from more than eighty-five different countries. From its offices in London, it has promulgated thirty-one international accounting standards through 1991.

IASC AND IFAC

The IASC was created to formulate accounting standards for financial reporting throughout the world. It suffered an early blow when its U.S. member, the AICPA, announced that it could not ensure conformity with IASC standards, because the process of setting GAAP had been transferred to the FASB. (At the time of writing, only GE in the United States reports that its financial statements are in accordance with international accounting standards.) There was also some U.S. opposition to so important a function being located in London.

As a consequence, IFAC was established in New York, at first in the offices of the AICPA and subsequently moved elsewhere. IFAC had the same membership as the IASC and claimed to represent the worldwide profession in all respects, including accounting standard-setting. The possibility of conflict was resolved by reserving accounting standard-setting to the IASC, but also by removing from the IASC agreement the clause stating that member associations would require their members to report conformity with international accounting standards, and take action against those that did not.

Thus, the IFAC has concerned itself with issuing international auditing standards, statements of ethical standards, and pronouncements on governmental and management accounting. The IASC, on the other hand, has been relatively successful in obtaining acceptance of its standards, primarily by those countries that have adopted them either as published or modified for local conditions. Its successes have come, however, at the expense of its proclaimed goal of harmonization. Some standards admit clearly incompatible alternatives, such as both historical cost and current cost. Some have obviously been designed to reflect U.S. sensibilities, particularly in respect of inventory valuation and consolidated financial statements. The resulting flexibility led to a project to reduce alternatives, represented by the 1988 Exposure Draft 32, but as might be expected, major opposition has delayed action.

THE INTERNATIONAL HARMONIZATION OF ACCOUNTING

The creation and work programs of IFAC and IASC demonstrate that the accountancy profession has adopted the goal of harmonized accounting and financial reporting. The word "harmonized" is undefined, however, and before examining the issues involved it is advisable to distinguish among three distinct, although related, concepts:

1. Uniformity—the elimination of all alternatives in accounting for economic transactions, other events, and circumstances.
2. Standardization—the reduction of alternatives while retaining a high degree of flexibility of accounting response.
3. Harmonization—the reconciliation of different accounting and financial reporting systems by fitting them into common broad classifications, so that form becomes more standard while content retains significant differences.

The arguments for harmonization of accounting rarely distinguish among these separate and separable states. Nevertheless, we are in the presence of a movement from harmonization to uniformity, through a process of accounting standardization.

Several arguments are put forward in support of the harmonization of accounting and financial reporting:

—improving the allocation of resources in a global financial market
—reducing the cost of capital and operating expenses for all enterprises
—facilitating social control over the global corporation

Improving Resource Allocation

According to the conventional wisdom, the allocation of scarce resources by means of equity investment (direct and portfolio) and lending and other forms of commercial credit, is optimal if the market in which such operations are performed is efficient. One of the necessary elements of efficiency is information efficiency, a condition under which all participants can obtain the information they need to make their decisions rationally. If investors and lenders (or their surrogates, such as financial analysts) receive noncomparable information, they cannot choose between alternatives, and investment will not take place. If the information takes different forms, they incur unnecessary agency costs of transformation, which reduces the amount of resources to be allocated. If the information received from different sources is of variable quality, which includes also the quality of extent of disclosure, or is not reliable, there is a possibility that investors and lenders will be deceived and therefore investment will be misdirected.

The resource allocation argument presupposes that financial analysts and investment managers are sophisticated users of financial reports. Indeed, financial analysts have become important influences on accounting standard-setting and harmonization, both directly and through their professional associations. Also, the International Organization of Securities Commissions (IOSCO) which like the U.S. Securities and Exchange Commission (SEC) is sensitive to the opinions of securities analysts, has been a strong supporter of harmonization. Research has established that only a small percentage of financial analysts and investment managers is indeed knowledgeable about finance and accounting.[1] Their support for harmonization may in fact be a plea for simplification. This proposition is supported by the observation that securities analysts have been vocal advocates of the cash flow statement.

The theoretical case for harmonization weakens on recognition of the fact that global financial markets are not perfectly competitive, and therefore not efficient in the economic sense. Thus, the consequences of making them *information-efficient* cannot be predicted, even if it were an attainable goal. Foreign currency exchange rates, interest rates, income taxation, subsidies, and many other instruments of national domestic and foreign policy, affect the global allocation of resources, usually in ways unforeseen by, and not always to the benefit of, the nation adopting or changing them. Under these conditions, it takes an effort of the imagination to argue that harmonization of accounting is capable of improving global resource allocation. The influence of securities analysts, however, ensures that the drive for harmonization will continue, if only because they believe that it will make their work easier, whether this is the case or not.

Reducing Cost of Capital and Operating Expenses

The point that it has proved impossible to harmonize accounting and financial reporting domestically is rarely considered when the case for international harmonization is put. In the United States the conflict between full-cost and successful efforts accounting by petroleum companies provided a cautionary example in the 1970s, but many industries, for example, financial intermediaries, chemical and pharmaceutical companies, airlines, and real estate developers, acknowledge the existence of often diametrically opposed accounting practices; the differences between their financial reports are manifest. On a wider canvas, one need only consider the different inventory valuation and depreciation accounting possibilities available to all firms to appreciate the point. It seems intuitively apparent that these differences impose excess costs when securities are issued, increase outlays on accounting services, and result in higher than necessary audit fees.

In this connection, one should note the opposite situation arising out of the widespread use of the *Plan Comptable Général* in France. Standardization of definitions and descriptions of accounting practices and financial reporting forms permits the detail of financial reports to be kept to a minimum. An accountant terminated by the X Bank on Friday can take up a new position at the Y Stores on Monday and is immediately useful without retraining. And the auditor hits the track running, knowing in advance exactly which number a specific account will bear in the chart of accounts of every company audited.

The majority of countries, however, do not enjoy a system of this nature. Thus, when the *Wall Street Journal* reported (May 23, 1991, p. A10) that the Japanese Saison Group and Scandinavian Airlines System (SAS) own 60 percent and 40 percent, respectively, of Inter-Continental Hotels Corporation, with subsidiaries in forty-six countries, one could imagine the accounting Babel that this combination produced. Saison is a Tokyo-based, family-controlled conglomerate of 120 mostly unlisted companies. SAS is a Stockholm-based airline controlled by Scandinavian governments. Inter-Continental was founded by Pan American World Airways, and presumably endowed with a U.S.-type accounting system managed by U.S.-trained accountants. Its $1 billion of debt is owed in a number of countries. Besides being accountable to parents speaking very different accounting languages, Inter-Continental must also present financial statements to many lenders who speak yet others. The accounting and reporting costs of this situation must bear very heavily indeed.

Lord (then Henry) Benson was seized with this issue when he stumped the world promoting the idea of international accounting standards twenty years ago. The uneconomic aspects of U.S. (also U.K. and other) accounting standard-setting, and the consequent auditing problems, are magnified out of all proportion when seen in an international context. Their effect on cost of capital and on corporate operating expenses is a real reason for international harmonization, as compared with the spurious resource allocation argument.

Control over Corporations

On a national level, governments seek to acquire control over private and public enterprises that challenge them for access to the people's savings. This leads to the utilization of financial reporting systems for the provision of information designed to serve socioeconomic purposes. For example, the French *Plan Comptable Général* was introduced to assist national economic planning by improving the collection of data on the business sector and facilitating control over investment by the Banque de France. Some of the disclosures required by the Securities and Exchange Commission in the United States are for the benefit of its Enforcement Division, which asserts socially perceived public rights. In many civil code countries financial reports are based on the duty of the corporate directors to manage the corporation's assets *en bon père de famille* (like a good parent). Clearly, in communist countries the sole objective of financial reporting by enterprises is to demonstrate the implementation of national plans.

Another aspect of this political dimension is the existence of tax conformity laws in countries such as France, Germany, and Japan. Under such laws, financial reports published to investors and creditors must be identical in all material respects to those submitted to the government taxing authority. By this means, it is believed, socially undesirable behavior (tax avoidance and evasion) can be reduced, if not minimized. Since each government decides differently the question of how to utilize the taxation system for its various purposes (financing government operations, national and international economic development, social justice, environmental protection), it follows that tax conformity effectively restrains each such country from bringing its accounting and financial reporting regulations into line with those of other countries.

This problem exists, although to a lesser extent, in non-tax conformity jurisdictions. For example, a major problem in harmonizing inventory accounting is the tax treatment of LIFO (last in-first out) in the United States. There is no way that U.S. accountants will give up LIFO if their clients would lose tax benefits, no matter how different LIFO accounting is from any of the inventory accounting methods used in other countries.

The principal forum in which the issue of accounting harmonization has been debated from the standpoint of social control is the United Nations. In the 1970s the lesser-developed countries attempted to force their agenda (technology transfer; sanctions against South Africa; redistribution of wealth from North to South, and more) on developed countries by asserting control over multinational corporations (MNCs). This led to the creation of the UN Commission on Transnational Corporations, which undertook certain initiatives designed to establish expanded standardized financial reporting for the benefit of governments in host countries. The countries concerned eventually accepted the fact that it was not in their economic interest to burden MNCs with special reporting requirements, and face was saved by the UN Centre for the Study of Transnational Corporations asserting that the accounting standards of the developed countries provided host governments with virtually all the information they required.

To conclude this section, most commentators on international accounting point out that a country's "accounting system" is a function of its history and culture, and its social, political, legal, and educational systems. Because these differ, they argue, national and ethnocentric motivations stand in the way of harmonization of accounting, because countries will not give up their traditional practices. This is both true and false. It is true in the sense that it may not be possible for a country to change accounting without at the same time changing its political, economic, and even cultural profile. But this has been done, in Meiji Japan, again in post-World War II Japan, in modern China, and in the European Community. There has to be some force that will effect the desired changes.

HARMONIZATION IN THE EUROPEAN COMMUNITY

A number of other organizations have taken actions designed to further accounting harmonization: the World Bank, the International Labor Office, the

Organization for Economic Cooperation and Development (OECD), and various regional groupings of accountants. We will examine the contributions of the European Community (EC) and the IASC.

The EC has undertaken initiatives designed to harmonize the legal systems of the twelve member states. These include measures to harmonize company law and business-related subjects, including accounting and financial reporting. The initiatives have taken the form of directives (of the European Commission, the EC's civil service), legislative instruments proposed to the Council of Ministers. When these are adopted by the council, member states are required to implement the directive's provisions by national legislation within a specified period (which turns out, however, to be a moveable feast.)

Directives on Company Law affecting accountants include:

The First Directive. Mandatory publication of financial statements and other information.

The Second Directive. Minimum capital; restrictions on payment of dividends; virtual prohibition of issuing shares at a discount; valuation of noncash consideration for issue of shares; increase, reduction, and redemption of share capital; a requirement that a shareholders' meeting must be called if accumulated losses exceed 50 percent of subscribed capital.

The two directives aimed at harmonizing accounting are the Fourth and Seventh.

The Fourth Directive applies to all companies except banks and insurance companies, which are being dealt with separately. It covers form of financial statements, valuation methods, contents of annual reports, and publication of financial statements. Financial statements comprise a balance sheet, profit and loss account, and notes, but not a funds or cash flow statement.

The Seventh Directive requires all holding companies to provide consolidated financial statements, and prescribes their form and content in some detail.

At the time of this writing (1992) all member states had legislated to adopt the Fourth Directive, and all except Ireland, Italy, and Portugal, the Seventh.

Because the directives permit a great many options, and because the individual national legislators have taken full advantage of them, financial statements are still far from comparable. The directives are silent on many problems, such as leasing, foreign currency translation, and extraordinary items. In some instances, such as valuation and consolidation, practices in member states diverge widely from EC norms.

Because of this, a conference was convened by officials in the Company Law section of the commission, which took place in Brussels on January 17–18, 1990. The main conclusion, however, was that no further EC accounting harmonization directives are to be expected in the near future. The problem of national accounting standards has proved more intractable than was anticipated.

THE INTERNATIONAL ACCOUNTING STANDARDS COMMITTEE

Although there are many players in the game of accounting harmonization, the principal agent of the accountancy profession is the IASC. Specifically, the objectives of the IASC contained in its constitution are:

a. to formulate and publish in the public interest accounting standards to be observed in the presentation of financial statements and to promote their worldwide acceptance and observance.

b. to work generally for the improvement and harmonization of regulations, accounting standards, and procedures relating to the presentation of financial statements.

Paragraph 9 of IASC's *Objectives and Procedures* (January 1983) states how harmonization is to be achieved:

a. A common approach when two or more countries are working on accounting standards.

b. Some countries will adopt IASs.

c. Other countries will base their standards on IASC principles.

d. Where national standards already exist countries may compare them with IASs and seek to eliminate any material differences.

e. In those countries where the framework of accounting practice is contained in law, IASC member bodies endeavor to persuade the relevant authorities of the benefits of harmonization.

The IASC itself believes that it has had a major influence on reducing accounting alternatives, and can point to the fact that a number of countries have adopted IASs to constitute their own GAAP. The countries concerned, however, are not major participants in the global financial market. Singapore is perhaps the model in this connection. The Council of the Singapore Institute of Certified Public Accountants obtains comments on each IAS from members, the Stock Exchange, the Association of Banks of Singapore, and the Chambers of Commerce. After modifying the IAS in response to these comments, the IAS is promulgated as a Singapore accounting standard. Note that the result may be to adopt an accounting standard that differs from a standard promulgated in another country on the basis of the same IAS.

In the United States, the FASB has recognized some virtue in the objective of harmonization. Early in 1992 it announced a more active and supportive role for itself in the arena of international standard-setting. This would involve:

—Intensifying consideration of IASs in domestic projects.

—Collaborating with the IASC on projects of mutual interest.

—Considering adopting IASs or even foreign standards that are judged superior to U.S. standards.

—Attempting to persuade the IASC and foreign countries to adopt U.S. standards judged superior.

There is also some evidence that the views of the IASC have already influenced U.S. accounting standards, such as those on foreign currency translation and income tax accounting. The SEC has discussed the possibility that it may eventually recognize IASs in considering whether to accept foreign financial statements for filing. Finally, in 1990 the European Community joined the IASC's Consultative Group with the objective of promoting harmonization. This move has reduced the fear that harmonization via IASs would be adversely affected by further EC harmonization via directives.

HARMONIZATION IN PRACTICE

A casual observation of the annual reports of corporations domiciled in different jurisdictions leads to the conclusion that a degree of harmonization is in fact taking place. Not only do the English language versions of the annual reports of companies in non-English language countries resemble those of their English-language counterparts; a similar phenomenon can be seen from their home country language reports. Whether this harmonization is a function of international accounting standard-setting, a flattering imitation of U.S. annual reporting, or simply the result of managers and accountants trying to improve their products, is an unresearched question. Nor is it clear whether the degree of comparability observed is spurious, concealing differences of substance behind a facade of form.

In some cases, this development requires companies to challenge the laws governing financial reporting. For example, German companies have obtained acceptance of the principle of "substantial equivalence" as justification for adopting a valuation method not sanctioned by German company or tax law. In other cases, such as France and Japan, we see a dual system of financial reporting, one orchestrated by the taxing authority, the other by the securities commission. The largest companies, Royal Dutch Shell being an outspoken example, proclaim the right to select the best accounting practices from the several jurisdictions within which they operate, and their auditors subscribe to the view that if the practice is the best, it must of necessity lead to fair presentation.

These developments must be acknowledged by the IASC or any other body working toward harmonization, if only because the companies concerned are large enough to assert themselves in world financial markets. No securities analyst will stop recommending that investors buy Sony's shares on the grounds that the company does not disclose segment profitability. A more powerful reason than the existence of professional standards must be provided such companies if they are to further extend the area of harmony.

THE ROLE OF THE SEC

By 1987, 58 percent of the listings on the Zurich stock exchange were foreign issuers; 50 percent on Amsterdam; 28 percent on Paris (France); 27 percent on Frankfurt (Germany); 22 percent on London. By contrast, only 5 percent of firms listed on either of the far larger New York and American stock exchanges were foreign. It is believed that burdensome accounting, auditing, and financial reporting regulations in the United States have contributed to this difference, and attempts to correlate listing abroad with amount of required disclosure appear to confirm this.

The SEC in the past has applied its function of protecting U.S. investors to foreign issuers by requiring that they provide the same financial information as domestic issuers. In practice, this rule has been relaxed at various times for Canadian, U.K., Dutch, and some other corporations, but most foreign issuers have faced an expensive and inconvenient hurdle when bringing their securities to market in the United States. In response to a mounting chorus of criticism from investment bankers and stockbrokers, reflected in the Congress, the professions, and the press, the SEC has attempted to simplify matters for foreign registrants.

This effort can be said to have started with the integrated disclosure system introduced by the SEC in 1982. The new rules require foreign issuers to file a Form F–20 in place of a Form 10-K. Item 17 of Form F–20 permits non-U.S. registrants to file financial statements prepared in accordance with their domestic GAAP, but requires a discussion of material differences of principle and practice. If this is provided, together with quantitative reconciliations with U.S. GAAP net income and balance sheet items, Item 17 does not require additional disclosures to those made under the foreign country's GAAP. If the foreign GAAP does not require segment reporting, they can omit it, and compensation of directors and top managers may be given in aggregate (concessions much appreciated by the Japanese, who nevertheless have not flooded the U.S. markets with securities). They were also allowed to file up to six months after the date of the financial statements, instead of the 135 days applicable to U.S. filers. The SEC's insistence on an audit in accordance with U.S. GAAS remains.

Since then, the SEC has been reacting to criticism by gradually relaxing its rules for foreign registrants. One change is to a "reciprocal approach" under which bilateral agreements with other countries would prescribe for the acceptance by one of only those financial disclosures required by the other. The first such arrangement was concluded with Canada in 1991; the Canadian regulatory authority is responsible for reviewing a Canadian prospectus to be used in the United States, which would be assigned a "no review" status by the SEC. The reverse process will be used for U.S. securities sold in Canada. Canadian issuers are exempt from the SEC's proxy regulations and other rules, such as reporting insider transactions. For the first time Canadian companies will become foreign registrants, however, filing 20-F forms instead of 10-Ks.

The other approach is to identify a class of sophisticated users and create special rules for offers to them. For example, SEC Rule 144A (April 1990) exempted from registration requirements under the 1933 Securities Act resales of certain securities to "qualified institutional buyers." Such buyers will be institutions responsible for investment of their own funds having assets of at least $100 million. Foreign issuers will enjoy "safe harbor" protection under Rule 144A. As reported in the *Wall Street Journal* (April 13, 1990) a Swedish company (Atlas Copco) and a U.K. company (British Aerospace) quickly took advantage of the rule.

In spite of these measures, however, the SEC has demonstrated a determination to continue to apply its rules to foreign issuers, and has resisted all efforts to have compliance with international accounting standards equated with compliance with GAAP.

A HARMONIZATION PROPOSAL

"The harmonisation of international accounting standards . . . is a worthy objective, but a choice has to be made between the advantages of harmonised standards and its disadvantages. Users should be particularly wary of cases where the same terminology in different countries actually represents very different characteristics."[2]

We started with the proposition that the accounting profession has accepted the case for accounting harmonization, and shown that in spite of some misconceptions and amibiguities, it is a strong one. The members of IASC can achieve real cost savings from pursuing this goal, and the less developed the member organization, the greater these benefits can be expected to be. The other publics concerned, governments and user groups, will not be disadvantaged through harmonization, even if its benefits to them are more difficult to quantify.

We have also emphasized the constraints on harmonization, arising primarily from legal sources rather than national pride, culture, or ethnicity. Lawyers are notoriously hidebound, and it is hard to change their habits and ways of thinking. Even though the elimination of differential legal requirements is acceptable as a goal, it may never be attained, and therefore accountants should direct their efforts toward measures to establish agreed upon international accounting and financial reporting standards existing independently of their national analogs. Such measures should lead to standards acceptable to MNCs and other large companies reporting to global financial markets.

The basic issues are as follows.

Recognition: The threshhold problem. What are the characteristics of accounting transactions, other events, and circumstances? Should we account for corporate capital when it is authorized, or issued, or paid-in? Do liabilities arise out of executory contracts, such as leases, and if so, under what conditions? Is an option an asset? Should brand names and similar intangibles acquired in a merger or acquisition be accounted for separately from goodwill? Is a government subvention revenue of the firm receiving it?

Classification: The display problem. To what model of the economy should financial statements correspond, cash flow or accrual? To what model of the firm should financial statements correspond, assets = equities, or capital = fixed assets + working capital? How should the reporting entity be defined? How should questions about profitability, liquidity, solvency, and efficiency be answered?

Disclosure: The communication problem. Should limits be placed on the extent of disclosure of accounting information? What should be contained in the formal financial statements themselves, and what should be included in notes? How does the accountant resolve disclosure problems in the absence of direct reference to domestic laws or national or international accounting standards? What are the criteria for information overload? Should the nature of disclosure depend on the size of the entity, or does this factor affect only aggregation and disaggregation?

The existing operating method of the IASC, working from specific practices encountered in member countries and attempting through negotiation to reduce variety, is not suited to this objective, which calls for a more scientific approach to the harmonization of accounting throughout the world. Such an approach could well serve to overcome the principal constraint on international accounting standards, their lack of enforceability, by substituting internationally understood logic and conceptual coherence for the national historical accidents of the past.

An example of the logical approach compared to the doctrinaire is the case of intangible assets such as goodwill and brand names. National standard-setting agencies usually prescribe arbitrary amortization periods such as five, twenty, or forty years, the consequence of a negotiating process. The French *Conseil National de Comptabilité*, on the other hand, requires amortization over the period covered in the capital budgeting decision that resulted in the acquisition of the asset. A subjective judgment open to endless argument became an empirical observation capable of verification and acceptance.

INTERNATIONAL AUDITING

The sequence of events leading to auditing standard-setting by other countries has tended to resemble that described in Chapter 5. Events such as the Royal

Mail Steam Packet case in the United Kingdom focused attention on audit failures, and either legislation or professional rules attempted to prevent their recurrence. Case law is a particularly important source of audit standards in the countries of the British Commonwealth, particularly the judicial dictum that "the auditor is a watchdog, not a bloodhound." The belief that high auditing standards are manifested by a written set of GAAS has led to the creation of auditing standards committees in the United Kingdom, Canada, and other countries. Some, such as Mexico and Brazil, have simply translated U.S. GAAS into their own language.

A major effort to promulgate standards applicable to audits in all countries has been made by IFAC, through its International Accounting Practice Committee, which publishes international auditing guidelines (IAGs), since 1991 renamed standards. These IAGs apply whenever an independent audit is performed, if the examination is conducted in order to express an opinion on financial statements. While it is recognized that statutory and professional regulations differ throughout the world, IAGs are intended to bring the quality of auditing worldwide to a uniform level. Very few audit reports refer to IAGs, the Canadian Certified General Accountants' annual report being a notable example. Some countries (Cyprus, Lebanon, Malaysia, Malawi, Zimbabwe) have adopted IAGs, and Australia has integrated them into its own GAAS.

Like the IASs, IAGs are international only in the sense that they are intended to be used in different countries. They do not deal with international accounting and auditing problems (apart from foreign currency translation) such as those that arise when companies go offshore. IAGs do not override local regulations, and in the event of differences or conflicts, members of IFAC member associations are merely committed to implement them "when and to the extent practicable." In Brazil, for example, they conflict with domestic laws. Because U.S. GAAS is generally the point of departure in the preparation of IAGs, they tend to avoid procedural rules and state generalities that may not reflect international consensus, as a prominent practitioner has noted. There is a worry sometimes expressed that standard-setting by the profession is an Anglo-Saxon approach and that international standards themselves result in U.S. standards being foisted upon others because no international standard will ever conflict with a U.S. standard.[3]

Indeed, the response of some members of IFAC to the question of adopting IAGs is that their own auditing standards are either equivalent or superior (France, South Africa, the United Kingdom, the United States). There is little likelihood that the dominant accounting countries will substitute IAGs for their domestic GAAS, for this reason.

THE EC SOLUTION

Another approach has been taken by the European Community, which has issued a mutual recognition directive (89/48/EEC) that came into force on January

4, 1991. This directive provides that a member of a professional association in one EC state will be admitted to full membership in the equivalent body in another state, without having to requalify. The directive applies to auditors, and a key provision is that a host member-state may impose reasonable conditions to ensure competence, either an aptitude test or an adaptation period. A test may only cover essential areas of difference that exist between the two countries, such as tax and company laws.

For example, Germany will grant the title of *Wirtschaftspruefer* (public company auditor) or *vereidigter Buchpruefer* (private company auditor) to statutory auditors from other EC countries who are nationals of an EC country, on successful completion of an aptitude test and swearing a professional oath. The examination consists of two parts and an oral test (the WP examination has seven written papers and an oral) covering commercial and tax law, and legal provisions governing auditing, financial statements, and annual reports. There is an optional subject, which may be specialized tax laws, bankruptcy law, labor and other social legislation, and special types of institution, such as insurance companies and public utilities, which are regulated separately.

By 1992 only the United Kingdom, Ireland, and Germany had passed national legislation implementing the directive, but the EC has announced that it will institute infringement procedures against noncomplying members. In addition, qualified individuals denied entry to professional associations in other EC countries may start proceedings in administrative courts, which are likely, however, to last rather a long time.

Reciprocity is an effective way to ensure that the auditing standards of different countries are comparable, and apart from technical accounting training, knowledge of a country's laws is the most important determinant of professional competence.

CONCLUSION

As accounting standards and laws proliferate, the prospect of harmonized financial reporting practices becomes more problematical. Because many of them are rooted in the legal system, the divergences among the accounting standards of individual countries, of regional groupings such as the EC, and of the IASC, can only become greater over time. Auditing standards are also a function of a country's legal system, and only when the laws of the countries concerned are made consistent with each other can there be any harmonization of auditing standards.

On the other hand, enlightened self-interest, the mother of all ethics, dictates that corporate annual reports, including financial statements and auditor's reports, will become more comparable. It is probable that a consensus will be found that differs from the GAAP and GAAS of the United States or any other individual country, at which point it will be necessary for U.S. accountants to decide whether they will modify their standards in order to conform. The alternative is to fall further behind in the global financial market.

NOTES

1. Lucia S. Chang and Kenneth S. Most, *The Perceived Usefulness of Financial Statements for Investors' Decisions* (Gainesville: University Presses of Florida, 1985).

2. Price Waterhouse, *EC Bulletin*, Issue 91, November–December 1990, p. 15.

3. *World Accounting Report*, May 1986, p. 16.

CHAPTER 7

A CONCEPTUAL FRAMEWORK FOR FINANCIAL REPORTING

Accounting and financial reporting have developed through pragmatic responses to very specific questions: How can we measure and record the complex phenomena of business life? How can we make sure that the firm receives what is due, and pays no more than it owes? What is the minimum information that an investor needs to keep track of an investment? As a result, many accounting practices appear logically suspect to some critics because they cannot be related to an accepted economic theory, or because they represent a conspectus from which important parts are missing. Perhaps for this reason, many accounting scholars have attempted to establish a viewpoint for evaluating accounting practices. Their questions deal with accounting policy issues.

PROPRIETARY THEORY VERSUS ENTITY THEORY

Perhaps the first such policy issue concerned the adoption of a proprietor's viewpoint, which reflected the fact that businesses were sole traders or partnerships. Under this approach, capital (equity) was found by deducting liabilities from assets; it was a residue. As early as 1800, however, James Fulton stated the proposition that capital is also investment plus and minus the effects of operations (including dividends) and can therefore be independently determined. As the corporation became the modal form of business organization, this observation acquired wide currency, so that by the time W. A. Paton published *Accounting Theory* (1922) an alternative to the proprietary viewpoint was beginning to prevail, that of the social entity. This led to an entity approach, in which the proprietary interest did not dictate the perspective of events, but was regarded as another class of obligation.

In spite of the efforts of Paton and others, the underlying assumption of the proprietary theory still dominates American accounting textbooks.[1] It is also convenient to refer to proprietary theory to justify practices that would otherwise be unacceptable. For example, the underlying principle of consolidation is that, given a parent-subsidiary relationship, 100 percent of the assets and liabilities of the subsidiary are combined with the assets and liabilities of the parent. This reflects the essential feature of consolidation: to represent in financial statements all assets over which an entity has control, and all liabilities to which it is obligated. When accountants began to revalue the assets of acquired companies, however, the depreciation and amortization of the plus-values recorded affected profits adversely. Thus arose the practice of limiting plus-value by reference to the parent's shareholding, rationalized as corresponding to the proprietary theory.

Another, more tenuous, reason for the survival of the proprietary theory is the influence of economics on accounting, particularly that branch now studied as corporation finance. Economic theory lacks an institutional framework, although some economists, notably Roger Coase and his disciples, have attempted to study economic problems within a legal framework. It is easy, therefore, for accountants who view accounting from the perspective of economic theory to see the shareholders of a corporation as the owners of the corporation's assets. Nothing could be more false. The only rights possessed by the shareholder are to participate in periodic and liquidating dividends *if declared by the directors*, and to vote at general meetings, *if convened*.

It was recognition of these legal facts that led to the development of the entity theory in the nineteenth century, in which the corporation was viewed as separate from its owners, whose personalities and desires could not affect accounting practices. Paton recognized the significance of the distinction: A proprietary theory directs attention to the balance sheet, whereas an entity theory also places importance on the income statement, the interface between entities. It is obvious from the pronouncements and actions of the FASB that a balance sheet emphasis now informs standard-setting in the United States.

A major problem, however, is that in the last analysis these so-called theories can be used to justify any accounting solution, because $A - L = SE$ and $A = L + SE$ are the same equation stated differently. For example, either theory could be used to justify using historical cost or current market value for asset valuation. "The case against treating an ordinary stock dividend as income is supported under either an entity or proprietary assumption regarding the business enterprise."[2] This appears to be a case of a distinction that had a valid legal origin in Europe, where it originated, being transplanted to an environment that lacked such a legal framework.

INSTITUTIONAL ATTEMPTS AT AN ACCOUNTING THEORY

Besides Paton, a number of other accounting writers have tried to establish a theory of accounting, without success. The American Accounting Association, an organization of accounting academics, was the locus of several committees that attacked the issue directly but ultimately had to confess failure.[3] The most influential publication of this period was Paton and A. C. Littleton's *An Intro-duction to Corporate Accounting Standards*.[4] This monograph identified some of the basic concepts underlying financial statements at that time, and provided a crude framework for the ideas they embodied.

The critical issue, on which all these attempts have foundered, is accounting for the effects of changing prices. On the other hand, that has never been the main issue concerning accounting standard-setters. As the accounting profession grappled with the problems of promulgating generally accepted accounting prin-ciples, it became increasingly clear that incompatible interests would have to be reconciled. The SEC's focus was the information available to investors and lenders; the corporation's was minimizing unfavorable effects on profits; the auditors', their liability. On the other hand, these groups were by no means monolithic. The SEC was subject to pressure from financial analysts and even from politicians, and the auditors from their clients. One may hazard a guess that some accountants were genuinely interested in improving the form and content of financial statements, in accordance with their own ideas.

For example, ARB 43 adopted the current/noncurrent method of foreign cur-rency translation, but by the birth of the APB there was strong corporate support for the monetary/nonmonetary method, in order to eliminate foreign subsidiaries' inventory translation losses from the income statement. How could the transition from one to the other method be rationalized? Similar problems arose with respect to income tax accounting, pension and other postemployment benefits, and new forms of financial instrument, particularly equipment leases. In addition, there was a suspicion that inconsistencies were arising because of a "piece-meal" or "fire-fighting" approach to accounting issues. It became apparent that the APB needed a wider framework for its pronouncements than the one provided by Paton and Littleton.

APB *Statement No. 4* was an attempt to provide such a framework.[5] It ad-dressed fundamental questions: What is accounting? What environmental factors influence it? How can it provide useful information? What are its objectives? What is the nature of "generally accepted accounting principles"? Unfortunately, the research necessary to answer these questions was not done (and still has not been!) so that the bulk of the statement, the so-called educational part, consisted essentially of a classified list of GAAP as of that date.

In addition, the statement contained a "developmental" part aimed at a for-ward-looking view that would assist future pronouncements. For the first time, accounting was defined in terms of information: "Accounting is a service activity. Its function is to provide quantitative information, primarily financial in nature, about economic entities that is intended to be useful in making economic de-cisions."

This debatable proposition implied that accounting was the servant of eco-nomics, rather than a function of management, and that accounting principles could be evaluated with respect to the contribution they made to producing data for input into economic models. The dichotomy between this view and the belief that business is the prime user of accounting information has survived intact in the FASB's subsequent conceptual framework.

GAAP determines how the information is organized, measured, combined, and adjusted to produce basic financial statements. These statements contained two basic types of financial information: on financial position and on changes in financial position, including:

—a balance sheet

—an income statement

—a statement of changes in financial position

—a statement of retained earnings

—a statement of other changes in owners' equity

—descriptions of accounting policies and other notes

The auditor's report was not included as part of the basic financial statements. Some commentators see the U.S. auditor's report as an integral part of the financial statements, evidenced by its function with respect to the going concern assumption. If the audit report were not part of the financial statements, and a question about the entity's continued existence as a going concern arose, it would simply be necessary for the auditor to verify that the question was adequately disclosed, as is the practice in Canada, for example. U.S. GAAS requires this disclosure to be made in the auditor's report itself.[6]

In APB *Statement No. 4* financial position was defined in terms of the proprietary theory as assets − liabilities = owners' equity. Income statement information was pronounced more important than that on financial position. Economic elements were resources and obligations, but these were not identical with assets and liabilities, which were "related" to them, and to revenues, expenses, and net income. Net income, apparently, was something distinct from revenues and expenses. As we shall see, this confusion of ideas has been carried forward intact into the FASB's conceptual framework.

One interesting feature of APB *Statement No. 4* that has not been adequately discussed is the classification of GAAP into:

—pervasive (measurement principles and modifying conventions)

—broad operating (selection, measurement methods, and display)

—detailed (rules and procedures)

Without considering the contents of each of the classes, it is apparent that a hierarchical classification of this kind could have been very useful to the FASB, both in preparing the conceptual framework and in developing specific standards.

THE CONCEPTUAL FRAMEWORK PROJECT

The FASB's conceptual framework project, which was introduced in Chapter 3, adopted much of the material contained in APB *Statement No. 4* which, to avoid repetition, has not been presented here. Because this book is directed to accounting and auditing for business enterprises, we will also omit any discussion of *Statement of Financial Accounting Concepts (SFAC) No. 4*, "Objectives of Financial Reporting by Nonbusiness Organizations."

An overview of the project has been published, showing its eight major components.[7]

Figure 7.1
Conceptual Framework for Financial Accounting and Reporting

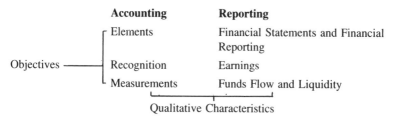

It was intended to provide the FASB with a "constitution," "a coherent system of interrelated objectives and fundamentals that can lead to consistent standards and that prescribes the nature, function, and limits of financial accounting and financial statements." This framework would:

—Guide the FASB's work.

—Permit the resolution of accounting questions pertaining to nonpromulgated GAAP.

—Determine the bounds of judgment allowed preparers of financial statements.

—Increase user understanding of, and confidence in, financial statements.

—Enhance financial statement comparability.

We shall now examine the individual SFACs, except for No. 4.

SFAC 1, OBJECTIVES OF FINANCIAL REPORTING BY BUSINESS ENTERPRISES

APB *Statement No. 4* introduced the proposition that financial accounting and reporting standards must be based on agreed objectives in order to be useful. Previous work had proceeded from a view of the objectives of the process, rather than the product. Regard for the user led to consideration of two kinds of financial statement: general purpose statements for a variety of users, or specified purpose statements for an identifiable user group.

Both APB *Statement No. 4* and SFAC 1 adopted the general purpose financial statements assumption, but it cannot be said that there is universal approval of this viewpoint. In Chapter 6 we referred to the SEC practice of accepting for filing either a foreign company's financial statements, prepared according to its GAAP (with a reconciliation to U.S. GAAP) or U.S. GAAP financial statements. The SEC-mandated reserve recognition accounting statements for oil and gas companies are clearly addressed to a specific class of user. These are clear examples of "different figures for different purposes." Another is the emerging practice of U.S. companies that distribute summary annual reports to stockholders at the same time that a more detailed 10-K report is filed with the SEC.

SFAC 1 was not based on research as such, but its preparation was preceded by extensive consultations with practitioners and others, and the resulting Trueblood report.[8] Like APB *Statement No. 4* it contained certain environmental assumptions:

—In an exchange economy cash is purchasing power.

—Consumption and saving take place on the basis of expectations.

—Production and marketing need saving for investment.

—Savings are invested through financial intermediaries.

—Production is carried out by investor-owned businesses.

—Ownership is divorced from management, and owners are interested in returns (dividends plus appreciation).

—Management is accountable to owner-investors.

—Savings are invested in the form of debt and equity securities that are traded in markets.

—Market transactions set security prices.

—Investors attempt to equate expected risk and return.

—Markets allocate scarce resources to efficient enterprises and away from inefficient ones. Efficiency is defined as adequacy of expected profit.

—There is some government intervention in resource allocation, but its effect on markets cannot be predicted.

—Government supplies economic statistics based largely on financial reports.

—Resource allocation by individuals, enterprises, markets, and government is more effective if based on information about the relative standing and performance of business enterprises.

From these assumptions, it is asserted, flows the primary objective of financial reporting, which is "intended to provide information that is useful in making business and economic decisions—for making reasoned choices among alternative uses of scarce resources."

Because information is costly, SFAC 1 places constraints on the general objective, of which the most important is a focus on the creation of, use of, and rights to wealth, meaning that the information must be expressed in units of money. There is an additional behavioral assumption, that financial reports are aimed at external users who lack the power to obtain the information directly.

SFAC 1 and similar statements purport to deduce from these assumptions conclusions concerning the form and content of financial statements. The information should help users assess the amounts, timing, and uncertainty of cash receipts from dividends and interest, and from the proceeds of sale, redemption, or maturity of securities and loans. Information that helps to assess the amounts, timing, and uncertainty of receipts *by the enterprise* is assumed to serve this purpose, and this has been invoked to justify the statement of cash flows. Information about the resources and obligations of the enterprise, and about transactions, other events, and circumstances that change resources and claims thereto, is more important for predicting cash flows. For this reason, accrual accounting is preferred to simple cash accounting, and SFAC 1 even went so far as to include current market value under the category "historical data" in order to justify the use of market values in historical cost financial statements.

Although it was not immediately apparent why a formal statement of objectives was necessary, consideration of alternatives may help to clarify this question. In Germany, the objectives are not specified by the company law (AktG) but include permitting investors to ascertain whether the minimum distribution of profits (at least 50 percent, to protect minority shareholders) has been made. This could lead to understatement of assets and liabilities, and creating hidden reserves. The British objectives, laid down in *The Corporate Report* of the Accounting Standards Steering Committee (1975), address a wider function embracing the information needs of government, employees, customers, and society generally. The statutory objective, however, is to present a "true and fair view" in accordance with the provisions of the companies acts. Conflict between objectives is also possible there.

SFAC 2, QUALITATIVE CHARACTERISTICS OF ACCOUNTING INFORMATION

This statement was intended to assist accountants in deciding what information would be useful to investors and other users. The two primary qualities were said to be relevance and reliability; if either of these qualities is missing, the information is not useful. Relevant includes timely, and to be relevant information must have predictive or feedback (confirmatory) value, or both; it must make a difference. Reliable includes the ideas of representational faithfulness, verifiability, and neutrality. Comparability is of secondary importance.

It was accepted that a tradeoff must be made between relevance and reliability, and the relative strength of one or the other feature speaks to the value, not the usefulness, of information. For example, the date of a painting may be known with certainty, but its current market price only as a rough estimate. Both pieces of information are useful, but clearly the latter would have a higher value to a prospective buyer than the former. SFAC 2 raised a question that will be examined in subsequent chapters, namely, the choice of ''attribute to be measured for financial reporting purposes.'' By *attribute* the FASB means valuation basis, so that the fundamental issue is ''Will financial statements be more relevant if they are based on historical costs, current costs, or some other attribute?''

Representational faithfulness is the correspondence between a measure or description and the phenomenon it purports to represent. A loan receivable reported as an investment is a misrepresentation. This quality, which in other sciences is often designated as ''validity,'' has an overriding significance because financial statements are a representation—indeed, a model—of the entity for which they are prepared. Verifiability is therefore a quality of representational faithfulness, excluding measurer bias from the measurement; it implies consensus. This brought the SFAC face to face with conservatism.

Although conservatism was not defined, it was described as ''understatement rather than overstatement of net income and net assets.'' Understating inventory this period will mean overstating net income the next, but accountants have historically adopted a skeptical approach to asset and liability valuation, particularly in respect of current assets. The word refers to conservation of working capital, in order to avoid its involuntary liquidation through investment or dividend distribution; hence the lower of cost or market approach to inventory valuation. SFAC 1 accepted conservatism as ''a prudent reaction to uncertainty'' but denied its usefulness as ''deliberate, consistent understatement of net assets and profits,'' thus demolishing its self-erected target. The principle of conservatism is sometimes referred to as the rule of caution, and in International Accounting Standard No. 1 as prudence. The creation of secret or hidden reserves by undervaluing assets and overstating liabilities has never been recognized as a desirable quality of financial reporting, although it is probably an essential element of good management. The race in business goes to the fattest, not the fittest.

Neutrality in SFAC 2 means that the primary concern of a standard should be with relevance and reliability, regardless of effects on particular interests. On the other hand, the FASB was concerned with economic consequences and would monitor them as evidence that a standard might be defective in some way. Neutrality plus freedom from bias produce credibility in financial reporting.

Although SFAC 2 recognized a need for comparability, if only as an aid to investor and other decisions, it rejected consistency as inhibiting progress in accounting. Perhaps for this reason, the consistency assertion has been removed from the U.S. auditor's report. It is difficult, however, to reconcile these propositions, because lack of consistency impedes, and may even render impossible, comparisons over time that are essential elements of investment research.

Finally, SFAC 2 discussed materiality and cost as constraints. Materiality was viewed as a screen through which information must pass; the more important the judgment item, the finer the screen. For example, amounts too small to warrant disclosure or adjustment in other circumstances might be big enough if they affected contracts between the entity and its creditors. Although not stated, this argument also applies to fraud and other illegal acts that may render the firm criminally liable and even threaten its survival. No quantitative materiality guidelines were specified, but reference was made to existing guidelines (Appendix C contained a list); individual judgment was required to assess materiality.

SFAC 2 concluded with a discursive essay on costs and benefits, indicating that the FASB considered these in setting standards.

SFAC 6, ELEMENTS OF FINANCIAL STATEMENTS

This was originally issued as SFAC 3, "Elements of Financial Statements of Business Enterprises," but following the FASB's decision to attempt to influence standard-setting in the public sector it was reissued as SFAC 6. The modifications were slight, and it was burdensome to the public that a new statement was issued rather than a supplement of several pages. Yet this was not the worst feature of the statement; while SFAC 1 and 2 can be seen to do little good, SFAC 6 may be harmful. (Except for matters affecting nonbusiness enterprises, references to SFAC 6 that follow are also references to SFAC 3.)

We start with the first sentences of the "Highlights" page: "Elements of financial statements are the building blocks with which financial statements are constructed, the classes of items that financial statements comprise. The items in financial statements represent in words and numbers certain entity resources, claims to those resources, and the effects of transactions and other events and circumstances that result from changes in those resources and claims." As we shall see, the circular reasoning that embraces classes, items, resources, and claims is never resolved.

The elements are said to be ten in number:

Assets are probable future benefits obtained or controlled by the entity as a result of past transactions or events.

Liabilities are probable future sacrifices of economic benefits arising from present obligations of the entity to transfer assets or provide services to other entities in the future as a result of past transactions or events.

Equity or net assets is the residual interest in the assets of the entity that remains after deducting its liabilities, the ownership interest of a business. (In nonbusiness enterprises this element has three components: permanently restricted, temporarily restricted, and unrestricted.)

Investments by owners are increases in business equity resulting from transfers to it from other entities to obtain or increase ownership in it.

Distributions to owners are decreases in business equity resulting from trans ferring assets, rendering services, or incurring liabilities by the entity to its owners. They decrease ownership.

Comprehensive income is the change in equity of a business enterprise during a period from the entirety of transactions and other events and circumstances from nonowner sources.

Revenues are inflows or other enhancements of assets of the entity or settlements of its liabilities from delivering or producing goods, rendering services, or other activities that constitute the entity's ongoing major or central operations.

Expenses are outflows or other using up of assets or incurrence of liabilities from delivering or producing goods, rendering services, or carrying out other activities that constitute the entity's ongoing major or central operations.

Gains are increases in equity from peripheral or incidental transactions of an entity and from all other transactions and other events and circumstances affecting the entity except those that result from revenues or investments by owners.

Losses are decreases in equity from peripheral or incidental transactions of an entity and from all other transactions and other events and circumstances affecting the entity except those that result from expenses or distributions to owners.

Analysis of SFAC 6

Consider the circumstances surrounding the issue of this statement. SFAC 1 listed as subsidiary objectives of financial reporting by business enterprises: to provide information about an enterprise's economic resources, obligations, and owner's equity, and to provide information about an enterprise's financial performance during a period, measured by earnings and its components.

It was therefore important to define these terms, and this appears to have been the motive behind SFAC 6. The effort failed, however. First, the definitions add two new terms to those identified above: benefits and sacrifices. (Cost is defined in n. 10 as sacrifice, which is undefined.) Only when the meaning of these terms is made clear can we identify equity (assets − liabilities). But equity includes investments by and distributions to owners, here treated as separate elements. Similarly, comprehensive income is the result of deducting expenses plus losses from revenues plus gains, a residual and not a measurable transaction, other event, or circumstance.

The statement also mentions "earnings," left undefined but subsequently explained in SFAC 5 on recognition and measurement. Obligations are described (n. 14) as including legal, equitable, and constructive obligations, but a definition that relies on the word being defined is worthless. It refers to duties, but not all duties are obligations in this sense. Again, not all the observations included in the elements (for example, benefits, resources, obligations) are assets, liabilities, and the like; they must possess other characteristics, notably those that underlie the concepts of recognition and measurement. Additional complications are listed below.

1. From the representation viewpoint, it is more accurate to define an

asset as a *right* to a future benefit; the benefit itself does not appear in a financial statement.

2. Asset and other terms defined appear to be elements of accounts, not of financial statements, which display groupings (classes) of assets.

3. Recognition of the characteristic of a "right" reveals the same ambiguity as noted above for obligations: Not all rights are assets.

4. An asset is a benefit "obtained and controlled" by the entity (para. 19) yet in para. 26 it ceases to be an asset when "collected." This approaches the metaphysical.

5. There are problems in fitting valuation allowances within the definition of asset (or liability, for that matter), especially with respect to those allowances that are treated as components of equity. SFAC 5 included the latter in the concept of equity, as a part of "other (nonowner) source" changes that are included in comprehensive income.

6. The definition of liabilities is wide enough to embrace stockholders' equity, and para. 49 acknowledges that the distinction is often "obscured in practice."

7. With respect to a corporation, the definition of equity is incorrect. Stockholders own the corporation, not its net assets. This is particularly important in the case of groups of companies, where the fact that the corporation owns 100 percent of its assets is vital to both finance and accounting.

8. The idea that revenues are inflows of assets conflicts with the objective of performance measurement, as well as logic. A credit sale creates an account receivable; how can the recognition of the latter determine the former? Both problems are solved by regarding revenues as outflows of goods and services, a definition widely used in the literature prior to SFAC 6.

9. The definition of revenue would not exclude an advance deposit on a sale.

10. The idea that expenses are outflows of assets and incurrences of liabilities is subject to the same criticisms as for revenues. It would not exclude payment of insurance in advance, and might embrace nonmonetary exchanges of assets and/or liabilities. Again, these problems are solved by regarding expenses as inflows of goods and services (payment being the outflow of cash).

11. How do we distinguish gains/losses from revenues/expenses? What constitute "ongoing major or central operations" and "peripheral or incidental transactions"? Is the company cafeteria part of ongoing operations or peripheral thereto? The issue is particularly critical in the age of conglomerates.

12. Which gains/losses are "net results"? (para. 70).

The Importance of SFAC 6

The importance of SFAC 6 lies less in the substantive contribution that it makes to definition and classification than in raising questions that must be answered before agreement on the form and content of financial statements can be reached. In addition to definition, classification, measurement, recognition, and display (which are discussed in SFAC 5) these are:

—The meaning of "financial statements." The elements are those of the balance sheet and income statement, the statement of retained earnings or its alter ego, the statement of changes in stockholders' equity, and the notes (including accounting policies). But the statement of cash flows is also a financial statement, and we have suggested that the auditor's report also belongs in this category. The notes include disclosures required by the FASB, such as segment reports, and in the case of petroleum companies, extensive supplementary statistics. Earnings per share disclosures form a part of the income statement.

—The basic equation of accounting. From SFAC 6 we can infer that an expanded basic equation has been adopted:

assets + expenses + losses = liabilities + revenues + gains + equity

equity = investments by owners − distributions to owners + (−) comprehensive income

—Articulation. The double-entry system is a closed system, in which all parts are specified. Abstraction of some observations, such as those representing changes during a period of time, leaves a residue of observations, called balances. In this system, the difference between the debits and credits in the period accounts (income) is equal and opposite to the difference between the debits and credits in the balance accounts. It is easy to see that dividends (distributions to owners) fit badly into this dichotomy, and also gains and losses on Treasury stock, but the so-called equity adjustments are a more difficult issue.

Until recently accountants were working toward the goal of a "clean surplus." In this approach, there is no resting place for period changes of net assets (assets − liabilities) outside the income statement, an assumption that corresponds with the FASB's concept of comprehensive income. The FASB has ruled that certain additional changes must be carried directly to stockholders' equity, namely, valuation allowances on long-term investments in marketable equity securities, the effects of changes in exchange rates on assets and liabilities denominated in foreign currencies, and the cost of employee stock options. There is also a very odd provision in FAS 87, that a liability for accumulated pension benefits in excess of unrecognized prior service cost should be reported as a reduction of stockholders' equity. A 1992 Exposure Draft of the FASB would require some gains resulting from a prospective FASB standard requiring all financial investments to be marked to market, to go directly to equity.

The FASB's "comprehensive income" might include another set of period observations: those resulting from changing prices when recognition and measurement rules are changed to accommodate such changes (n. 29).

—Capital maintenance is an associated concept, because it distinguishes return *on* investment from return *of* investment. In the classical view, profit (net income) may not be said to have arisen until capital (equity) has been maintained intact. This postulate underlies the clean surplus doctrine, and has therefore been disregarded by the FASB on several occasions. In para. 57, however, the concept is raised in a different context, namely, that of accounting for changing prices. SFAC 6 specifies four different capital maintenance concepts in this context. Both this and the articulation issue will be discussed in Chapter 8.

SFAC 5, RECOGNITION AND MEASUREMENT IN FINANCIAL STATEMENTS OF BUSINESS ENTERPRISES

In the FASB's terminology, "measurement" means the valuation method used for monetary amounts appearing in financial statements, together with a unit of measure, normally the currency of the country. The valuation method is referred to as an "attribute" that may denote "historical cost" (itself an amalgam of different valuation methods), current cost (value), found from either input or output markets, either of these adjusted for changes in the level of prices, specific or general, or present value. These attributes will be discussed in Chapters 8 and 9.

As we have pointed out, many of the critical issues in financial reporting were to be covered by this statement, specifically, those of measurement, recognition, and display. It was widely believed that the time was ripe to depart from the historical cost model and to embrace either a current value approach to accounting, or at least a method of adjusting historical cost financial statements for the effects of changing prices, notably those resulting from inflation. But this was not to be. According to para. 2, "The recognition criteria and guidance in this Statement are generally consistent with current practice and do not imply radical change."

As in the other concepts statements, financial statements were defined narrowly to exclude, for example, the notes. The statement lays down that disclosure "by notes or parenthetically on the face of financial statements, by supplementary information, or by other means of financial reporting is not a substitute for recognition in financial statements for items that meet recognition criteria." While this is correct in the sense that notes to financial statements should not be used as substitutes for accounting entries, it nevertheless begs the question of disclosure generally.

Thus, recognition was restricted to a subset of financial statement items, and described as "the process of formally recording or incorporating an item into the financial statements of an entity as an asset, liability, revenue, expense, or the like." Again there was no mention of the accounts from which financial statements are constructed, and the problem of equity, a residual according to SFAC 5, was not formally acknowledged. The problems that the FASB itself created for stockholders' equity, however, are at the center of the discussion.

Para. 13 stated that "A full set of financial statements for a period should show: Financial position at the end of the period, earnings (net income), comprehensive income, and cash flows for the period, and investments by and distributions to owners during the period." This not only renders suspect all existing financial statements, none of which shows comprehensive income, but also SFAC 6, since revenues, expenses, gains, and losses are not mentioned. One would have expected that, being elements, they would be important. A subsequent discussion of classification and aggregation led nowhere.

Worse followed. In para. 27 it was stated that the statement of financial position should provide information useful to those who want to value a business, but not all assets and liabilities are included in a statement of financial position. If they are elements of financial statements, how can they not be? (Perhaps the words "resources and obligations" should have been used instead.)

The concept of earnings presented "is similar to net income in present practice" but excludes the cumulative effects of certain accounting adjustments (a change in accounting principles, for example). It also excludes prior period adjustments, which, with only two exceptions, are currently included in the period of recognition. SFAC 6's error in defining revenues and expenses became apparent in the discussion of earnings: "Earnings focuses on what the entity has received . . . for its output (revenues) and what it sacrifices to produce and distribute that output (expenses). Earnings also includes . . . gains and losses." The statement devoted considerable space to reconciling earnings and net income, and earnings and comprehensive income.

Recognition requires an item to meet four criteria:

1. Meets (i.e., falls within) the definition of an element.
2. Is measurable with a sufficiently relevant and reliable attribute.
3. The information about it is relevant.
4. The information about it is reliable—representatively faithful, verifiable, and neutral.

Revenues and gains are not recognized until realized or realizable. They are realized when products or other assets are exchanged for cash or claims to cash. They are realizable when "related" assets received or held are readily convertible to known amounts of cash, or claims to cash. Revenues are not recognized until earned, that is, "when an entity has substantially accomplished what it must do to be entitled to the benefits represented by the revenues." So far, so good, if a little vague.

Para. 84 effectively abandoned realization as a criterion for revenue recognition. The two conditions are usually met at the time of sale, and if receipt precedes production and delivery, revenues are earned on production and delivery. The percentage-of-completion method may be used for contracts in process. Some revenues are recognized in accordance with the passage of time. Revenues from certain agricultural and extractive products may be recognized on production. If products are exchanged for nonmonetary assets that are not convertible into cash, revenue or gain may be recognized on the basis that they have been earned and the transaction is complete. It is hard not to interpret this paragraph as a production theory of revenue.

The definition of expense in SFAC 6 was disregarded and a consumption (of economic benefits) criterion adopted for expense and loss recognition. An expense or loss is also recognized if it becomes evident that previously recognized future economic benefits of an asset have been reduced or eliminated or that a liability has been incurred without associated economic benefits (para. 87).

It is not surprising that SFAC 5 has been viewed as a disappointment by those concerned with accounting theory. The great surprise is that the other statements have not, and that the FASB's conceptual framework has been imitated in other countries.

THE GLOBAL ADOPTION OF THE CONCEPTUAL FRAMEWORK

Why, with all its faults, has the FASB's conceptual framework proved attractive to other countries, and to the International Accounting Standards Committee?[9]

As with accounting and auditing standards, the fact that so much time, effort, and money have been expended in the United States has suggested to others that an economical approach is simply to copy, making relatively minor changes where necessary. This was made explicit in the Canadian conceptual framework.[10] "Full credit is given to the FASB, in that the SFACs were the starting point for this Framework" (p. viii). The Canadian document differs from the FASB's framework in several respects, however, in particular by attempting to embrace accounting for changing prices. The principal other differences are:

—A wider objective, including contractual and retrospective uses in addition to the predictive one.

—Relevance is ranked above reliability in the hierarchy of qualities.

—Financial statements are defined to "include" a statement of earnings and comprehensive income, a statement of owner's equity, a statement of financial position, and a statement of changes in financial position: cash flow, and "indirectly" notes and parenthetical disclosure, and supplementary schedules. The all-inclusive concept of "earnings and income" with avoidance of "discretionary omission of gains and losses" is postulated.

—The capital maintenance issue is dealt with, and the statement adopts the financial concept.

—Current price (selling price, replacement cost, or net [*sic*] present value) is preferred to historical cost.

—Measurement in purchasing power units is preferred to use of "nominal dollars" (money dollars), but may not be well enough understood.

On the other hand, the Canadian framework adopts almost verbatim the SFAC 6 definitions of financial statement elements (even though its financial statements are different!), proceeding from an explicit asset/liability view, and the concept of comprehensive income. A cardinal virtue of the Canadian framework is its length (less than fifty pages).

The International Accounting Standards Committee has also published a *Framework for the Preparation and Presentation of Financial Statements* (1989) which, as might be expected, is more flexible and permissive in nature. (It is also more virtuous, at less than forty pages.) This framework adopts an even broader set of objectives, possibly based on a listing of uses of financial statements.[11] The user group includes investors, creditors, employees, lenders, suppliers, customers, government, and the public. Primary responsibility for financial statements rests on management, which is also a user. Qualitative characteristics are stated as in SFAC 2.

Financial statements include notes and supplementary schedules. The elements of financial statements are similar to those of SFAC 6, but more general and therefore less subject to attack. For example, although equity is defined as a residual interest, para. 65 states that it may be subclassified, indicating that it is a concept separate and distinct from assets and liabilities. The statement raised additional problems, however, by the observation that gains, which are part of income, include those resulting from foreign currency translation. U.S. GAAP treats these as equity adjustments; they only affect the income statement on whole or partial liquidation of a foreign investment, and they are then included in the gain or loss on liquidation, under the heading of "discontinued operation," and not under the heading "translation gain (or loss)."

The IASC framework admitted a variety of measurement attributes—historical cost, current cost, realizable value, and present value—merely pointing out that historical cost was most commonly used. It also stated that a financial capital maintenance concept was adopted by most enterprises.

THE CONCEPTUAL FRAMEWORK FAILS ITS PURPOSE

An example of how the conceptual framework fails its purpose was provided by the case of Chambers Development Co., reported in the *Wall Street Journal* on March 19, 1992. The company had for a number of years capitalized direct and indirect costs of developing new projects, such as landfills for waste disposal. In 1991 its auditors apparently took exception to this asset, and as a consequence the company changed its accounting practices and expensed $27 million (after tax).

It appears that the size of the asset was a critical factor in the auditors' change of position, as it may have been argued (surely with great difficulty!) that the effect of the previous treatment was immaterial. The problem however, is that there is no GAAP covering this issue, and accountants traditionally look at analogous situations to solve these problems. Such situations would include development stage companies (FAS 7) and research and development costs (FAS 2), both of which say "expense." They also include inventory valuation (ARB 43) and capitalization of interest cost (FAS 34) as well as nonpromulgated GAAP for own construction of fixed assets, all of which mandate, or at least sanction, the capitalization of indirect costs.

What is interesting is that none of the managers, accountants, investors, and analysts consulted by the Journal's reporters referred to the conceptual framework, in particular, the definitions of "asset," in their discussions of the point at issue. Further, none of the accounting scholars with whom I have discussed this case, all of them incensed by the idea of capitalizing parts of executive salaries, displayed any belief that assistance might be obtained by consulting the SFACs.

We may also cite in this context the FASB's reliance on its definition of asset to first support the view that deferred tax is not an asset (FAS 96) and then to argue that it is (FAS 109).

CONCLUSION

The conceptual framework statements published by the FASB have been welcomed by other countries and adopted with few changes. This raises an important question: Are differences in financial reporting between countries really superficial? If this is so, it renders suspect the need for international accounting standards. On the other hand, if, as demonstrated in this chapter, the conceptual framework is seriously flawed, the fact that it has traveled so easily speaks volumes about the intellectual level of the accountancy profession, and knowledge of basic principles of accounting and financial reporting.

The FASB's framework is defective because of its political nature as well as its methodology. The FASB wanted to create a constitution, a set of propositions that would serve as the intellectual underpinnings of the standard-setting process in the absence of a legal, or even a social, framework. In tackling this issue, however, it fell between the two stools of the normative and the positive, the "should be" and the "is." This problem affects all attempts to replicate the framework internationally.

The methodological defects demonstrate the failure of the accounting profession to resolve the issue: Is accounting an art or a science? If accounting is a science, then epistemological methods appropriate for explaining phenomena and predicting outcomes should be used to formulate hypotheses and test them to arrive at acceptable propositions. If it is an art, then positive description should take precedence over normative proposition; nobody told Beethoven how to write a symphony. The descriptive approach does not prohibit innovation, as Beethoven showed.

NOTES

1. Michael Chatfield, *A History of Accounting Thought* (New York: Robert E. Krieger, 1977), p. 223.

2. Donald E. Kieso and Jerry J. Weygandt, *Intermediate Accounting*, 6th ed. (New York: John Wiley & Sons, 1989), p. 724.

3. Committee of the American Accounting Association, *Statement on Accounting Theory and Theory Acceptance* (Sarasota: American Accounting Association, 1977).

4. American Accounting Association, 1940.

5. New York: Accounting Principles Board, 1970.

6. D. B. Thornton, "The Financial Reporting of Contingencies and Uncertainties," *Research Monograph No. 5* (Vancouver, B.C.: Canadian CGA Research Foundation, 1983).

7. *Scope and Implications of the Conceptual Framework Project* (Stamford, Conn.: FASB, 1976).

8. Report of the Study Group on the Objectives of Financial Statements, *Objectives of Financial Statements* (New York: AICPA, 1973).

9. One should not underestimate the influence of a single individual on the various English-language conceptual frameworks. See D. Solomons, *Guidelines for Financial Reporting Standards* (London: Research Board of the Institute of Chartered Accountants in England and Wales, 1989).

10. The Accounting Standards Authority of Canada, *Conceptual Framework for Financial Reporting* (Vancouver, B.C., 1987).

11. CF. Kenneth S. Most, *Accounting Theory* 2d ed. (Toronto: Holt, Rinehart and Winston of Canada, 1986), p. 160.

CHAPTER 8

REGULATION OF FINANCIAL REPORTING—THE DISCLOSURE ISSUE

The provision of information about corporations by means of financial reports is everywhere the subject of regulation. The regulations constrain corporations and their accountants and auditors by prescribing specific disclosures and by limiting choice of accounting method.

The response by different countries to a perceived need for regulation has been very different, and in this chapter we will review these different approaches in order to attempt to shed light on the subject of disclosure generally.

WHY IS REGULATION NEEDED?

Why should a society regulate the production of financial information? Until the nineteenth century this was regarded as a private matter between partners, or between shareholders and directors. Not until the U.K. companies acts of the mid-nineteenth century were there any laws on the subject, and for 100 years these laws covered relatively few matters. It used to be said that a clerk in the U.K. Registrar of Companies office was instructed to file reports of court cases that revolved around accounting issues. Whenever a new companies act was being drafted, the clerk would try to introduce a clause making the decision a statutory requirement, but beyond that there was no overall regulatory objective.

Further, the practice of issuing annual reports containing financial statements developed precisely during this relatively permissive period. Sophisticated approaches to disclosure, such as consolidated financial statements and funds statements came into widespread use without any state or other organized intervention. This observation, documented by George H. Benston, conflicts with the view of the annual report as an example of the economist's public good, one that will tend to be underproduced because, being freely available, the producer cannot exclude anyone from its benefit.[1]

Rationalists of regulation put forward a number of arguments in support of it:

1. *Accountability*. The corporation, being a creation of society, is accountable to it. This is simply a specific case of the general legal proposition that there can be no right without a corresponding duty.

2. *Efficiency*. Investment is optimal if transactors in securities markets have all the information they need for their decisions.

3. *Comparability*. Investment involves choice, and rational choice requires comparable information about each alternative.

4. *Morality*. People need to be forced to behave honestly. Without regulation they would issue fraudulent or otherwise misleading financial statements.

None of these arguments is very strong. Not all social entities are obliged to publish audited financial statements; government is a notable example. Securities markets are widely held to be efficient in spite of known defects in publicly available information. Investors in many countries have found it possible to make rational decisions on the basis of very different kinds of financial statements; interest and currency swaps have not been hampered by the absence of accounting harmonization. Finally, the growth of regulation has not reduced the incidence of fraudulent financial reporting, which has become a considerable problem as accounting regulation has increased. Some argue that the costs of regulation exceed any possible benefits.[2]

REGULATION IN THE UNITED STATES

Prior to 1934 there was virtually no accounting regulation for corporations in the United States. There were, however, accounting regulations for public service and utility companies, both federal (the Interstate Commerce Commission) and state (the railroad and public service commissions). This regulation had an identifiable cause—the granting of a monopoly, of state property, or of powers to acquire the property of others—and has since been extended to banks, insurance companies, telecommunications companies, and utilities generally.

From 1934, the federal government has had power to regulate the financial reporting of corporate issuers of publicly traded securities, which it effectively delegated to the accounting profession (by a three-to-two vote of the commissioners in 1938). This function was institutionalized in the Accounting Principles Board in 1959, but removed from the accounting profession with the creation of the Financial Accounting Standards Board in 1972. The members of the FASB demonstrate their independence by accepting full-time, salaried appointments, and by severing any previous relationships with firms and corporations. The FASB has sought to rationalize its function by issuing a conceptual framework. Its proceedings are characterized by openness and adherence to due process.

The FASB has no enforcement powers; these reside in the Securities and Exchange Commission. The commission has adopted a policy of "selective enforcement" largely for reasons of cost. The Code of Ethics of the AICPA could lead to disciplining or even expelling a member for failing to comply with accounting standards, but this has been rarely done, and not all CPAs are members of the AICPA. State boards of accountancy also have power to discipline or expel CPAs, but their enforcement record is not as good as that of, for example, the state real estate commissions.

REGULATION IN CANADA

Canada has attempted to merge features of the U.K. and U.S. regulatory environments. The Accounting Standards Committee (ASC) of the Canadian Institute of Chartered Accountants (CICA) promulgates accounting standards. An Accounting Standards Authority of Canada (ASAC) was established to be a representative group of preparers and users of financial information. User organizations include consumers, business, labor, government, and the banking and investment communities. ASAC has published a conceptual framework for financial reporting. Membership in these bodies is part-time and unremunerated.

The ASC includes members of other accounting bodies, but the non-CICA members both of it and of ASAC have complained that the standard-setting process is in fact dominated by CICA. Canada's Business Corporations Act and a number of provincial laws prescribe the preparation and publication of financial statements and specify that they must be in accordance with Canadian GAAP. Hence, CICA standards have legal authority.

Enforcement, however, rests on the accounting profession, which has not been noticeably energetic in this regard. Indeed, some view the relatively closed process of accounting standard-setting in Canada as a "family affair." Canadian accountants maintain the position that choice of accounting method is a matter of professional judgment, which can override accounting standards in any specific context.

THE UNITED KINGDOM AND IRELAND

Although Ireland is a separate state, for practical reasons Irish accountants work closely with colleagues in England and Wales and Scotland. The Institutes (England and Wales, Scotland, and Ireland) have established common accounting standards since 1974 through the Consultative Committee of Accountancy Bodies (CCAB). The three institutes have also formed a joint international committee; merger between the English and Scottish institutes has been attempted once, and probably will eventually succeed.

In earlier chapters we have discussed the legal regulatory framework in the United Kingdom. This has been the subject of frequent major changes in recent years, in part a function of membership in the European Community and in part of imitation of U.S. regulation. The Companies Act of 1990, for example, contains a remedies clause that can be used to force companies to reissue financial statements considered fraudulent or misrepresentative, a power that has long been possessed by the SEC. With a few exceptions, however, the provisions of the company laws do not promulgate specific accounting standards.

Until the 1960s this function was performed by the Institute of Chartered Accountants in England and Wales and the Scottish Institute; the latter demonstrated a characteristic independence of thought. The resulting pronouncements were called "recommendations" and it was felt that the individual accountant's judgment should prevail in any conflict of opinion. In 1969, however, the Accounting Standards Steering Committee (ASSC) was created as a joint venture of the leading accountancy bodies in the United Kingdom, signaling a trend to make the application of standards less flexible. The ASSC later became the Accounting Standards Committee, with a more representative membership. In 1990 the ASC was replaced by an Accounting Standards Board (ASB) and although the membership is still largely part-time and unremunerated, the chairperson and technical director are full-time and must demonstrate independence by severing professional relationships. The standard-setting process, now very closed, will become more open, and less subject to the influence of the accountancy bodies.

The ASSC attempted to produce a conceptual framework in 1975 (*The Corporate Report*), which proved unacceptable to the profession. A second attempt has been made by David Solomons, who has been critical of the FASB's conceptual framework project.[3]

DISCLOSURE

In the United States, the debate concerning what should and should not be disclosed in financial statements revolves around the SEC. "SEC Regulation S-X, together with the various releases issued by the SEC on the subject, governs the form and content of financial statements required under the Securities Act. The said Regulation expressly prescribes balance sheet forms to be used by certain types of companies."[4] In the United Kingdom and Germany the form and content of financial statements are laid down by statute, and in France by the *Conseil National de Comptabilité*.

Regulation S-X serves a similar purpose, but applies only to registrants, that is, public companies and some other issuers of securities. The securities acts of 1933 and 1934 were purportedly modeled on the British company laws, but there are significant differences. The 1934 act requires regular quarterly, annual, and occasional filings (Forms 10-Q, 10-K, 8-Q) of which the 10-K is the most important. These filings are public records that can be inspected or obtained by electronic retrieval (the EDGAR System). Because corporate annual reports include only a part of the 10-K filing, most companies publish a statement in their annual reports to the effect that copies of Form 10-K can be obtained from the company without charge. These 10-Ks are incomplete, lacking important schedules and other data, including the names and percentage holdings of subsidiaries and affiliates. The SEC permits this information to be withheld and a charge to be made because it may extend to hundreds of pages; many investors, however, are unaware of its availability.

The information contained in Regulation S-X falls into three categories:

—disclosures assumed important to all users

—disclosures assumed useful only to sophisticated users

—disclosures responding to specific user needs

Figure 8.1
SEC Form 10-K Disclosures

General Instructions

Part I

   1. Description of the business.

   2. List of properties.

   3. Report of any significant legal proceedings.

   4. Ownership of securities—special features.

Part II (The basic information package)

   5. Market for registrant's stock.

   6. Selected financial data.

   7. Management's discussion and analysis of financial condition and results of operations.

   8. Financial statements and supplemental (e.g., quarterly) data.

Part III

   9. Directors and executive officers.

   10. Management remuneration and transactions.

Part IV

   11. Exhibits, financial statement schedules, and Form 8-K reports.

Signatures

Supplemental information

Central to this model is the *basic information package* (see Figure 8.1), which is presumed to meet the first of these needs. The problem is a complex one, however. Many companies have begun to send stockholders a summary annual report in place of the basic information package, and the SEC raised no objection to the practice when asked by General Motors if this was permissible. (SEC regulations require a financial report to be sent to stockholders only if their proxies are solicited, but they have become customary.) Form 10-Q quarterly information requirements are limited to a balance sheet and income statement for the current quarter, together with explanations for any changes in accounting methods. How can these rules be reconciled with the need for disclosure?

An Outline of the Disclosure Problem

The disclosure problem is viewed here in the context of the financial report. There can be a variety of information that a social entity is obliged to make public other than through the financial report because of a perceived societal interest, such as the environmental impact of its actions. Some matters that may be deemed of interest to investors, such as the ages, other occupations, and addresses of the directors, are not normally viewed as essential ingredients of a financial report. The problem may be examined by asking the following questions:

1. What is the characteristic of the information that is peculiar to the financial report?
2. Who is responsible for the accuracy of the information?
3. When will this information be disclosed?
4. In what form should the information be disclosed?

What to Disclose? Much of the contemporary accounting literature displays impatience with the conventional accounting model. It is argued that the profession's publics demand more information than financial reports disclose, and that it is the accountant's responsibility to report matters outside the accounting system. In previous chapters we have identified ''value'' as an early theme of this movement, and it has come to extend to so-called soft data concerning the future, for which value is clearly the all-inclusive term. More recently, politicians and other critics of the profession have claimed that accountants must disclose illegal and other unethical acts.

Some of the additional information called for could readily be incorporated in financial reports were it not for the apathy of accountants and the narrow focus of management. The issue of value is dealt with in the replacement value accounting system described in Chapter 10. A critical element in projecting the future is the order position, both sales and purchases. Accounting for sales and purchases at the point of order rather than at the point of sale is technically simple. Again, recording contingent liabilities that arise from guarantees and endorsements is the normal practice of banks in some countries, and there is no practical reason (especially in the age of data processing) to treat this information by memorandum, that is, outside the accounting system.

Thus, if we define the boundaries of financial report disclosure by reference to the accounting system we are by no means restricting the subject. Indeed, accounting history since Pacioli reveals a continuous expansion of the domain of accounting, in terms of the observations that are admitted into the system as well as the complexity of the devices whereby they are reported. A debate may well continue concerning non-accounting disclosures, for example, those parts of the Form 10-K that lie outside the basic information package, but they belong to the general topic of corporate governance, and not to the subject of accounting and auditing.

Nevertheless, financial reports contain many so-called voluntary disclosures on employee relations, socially responsible acts, environmental protection, composition of the shareholder body, technological innovations, and even photographs of officers and employees. This is because the annual report serves purposes beyond the needs of financial reporting: financial public relations, communication with present and prospective employees, and combatting political opponents of private enterprise.

Who Is Responsible? Involvement of public accountants with the preparation of financial statements may have contributed to a perception that they were in some way responsible for their contents. Because of the SEC's emphasis on independence, however, auditors have sought to distance themselves, and this has been achieved in two ways. First, chief financial officers of corporations were persuaded to state in the annual report that the financial statements were the responsibility of management. Second, the new form of auditor's report adopted by the AICPA in 1988 contains a specific representation of this fact: "These financial statements are the responsibility of the Company's management" (SAS 58).

The auditor's responsibility is to express an opinion on the financial statements, based on an audit (SAS 1). As far as the other parts of the financial report are concerned, the auditor is required by SAS 8, "Other Information in Documents Containing Audited Financial Statements," to read them for reasonableness and consistency with the financial statements, but is not required to express an opinion unless it is negative. Such a negative expression is unheard of.

The demand for public accountants to take responsibility for financial statements, coupled with resistance to paying the cost of an audit, has led U.S. accountants to issue reports on unaudited statements. This function, called "compilation and review," has been the subject of a separate set of standards (SSARs) issued by the Accounting and Review Services Committee of the AICPA. Such reports are said to provide "limited assurance" that CPAs are satisfied to associate their name with the statements. A recent SSAR permits CPAs to merely reproduce financial statements prepared by someone else. Unaudited financial statements are inherently suspect, and by pretending that they are reliable auditors are in fact selling their services short.

In the early nineteenth century medicine was practiced by barber-surgeons and purveyors of homeopathic remedies. In response to scientific discoveries, some of the former abandoned the shave and haircut and devoted themselves exclusively to medical practice, whereas most of the latter became pharmacists and no longer went into the forest searching for plants. The accounting profession has been challenged with the same decision, but has failed to opt for progress. The regular shave and haircut have proved too attractive a business to give up.

As indicated in Figure 8.1, representatives of management must sign the Form 10-K, but not the financial statements as such. In many countries the company law requires the directors to sign the financial statements, and the SEC has attempted to force this change in corporate governance on U.S. corporations, without success.

Timeliness of Disclosure. A widely accepted proposition of corporate finance is the *efficient market hypothesis.* It is argued that although individual participants in stock (and other financial) markets use financial reports as a source of investment information, such information cannot affect the outcome of their decisions. That is, because market prices are a function of the behavior of the aggregation of participants, they are efficient in the sense that financial information cannot permit individuals to earn abnormal returns.

The efficient market hypothesis takes one of three forms:

Weak form. Market prices fully "impound" all the information that can be obtained from a study of past price movements.

Semistrong form. Market prices impound all information available to the public.

Strong form. Market prices impound all information, including insider information.

It is universally believed that the weak form is valid, leading to the so-called random walk theory, that future prices cannot be predicted. (The phrase likens the movement of share prices to the path taken by a fly that might walk across a sheet of paper.) Huge changes in market prices unaccompanied by new information, such as their fall in October 1987, have produced much soul-searching, but researchers closed ranks behind the random walk hypothesis, arguing that the hypothesis does not rule out large and unexpected price changes, but that they will be infrequent. Research aimed at validating the semi-strong form has produced ambiguous and often contradictory results, some concluding that financial reports do influence market prices, and others that they do not. One would need to be very ingenuous to accept the strong form.[5]

Another critical problem is not addressed by the efficient market literature. If markets are information-efficient they will tend not to attract investors seeking abnormal returns. If they are information-inefficient (for example, as a consequence of inadequate regulation) they may attract investors with the prospect of abnormal returns. The resulting equilibrium may be more efficient in the social welfare sense.

Assuming here that financial reporting does make a difference, and that the information it contains is not immediately and without friction "impounded" in security prices, when should it be made available? Legislative responses to this question tend to allow lengthy time periods (for example, the annual report will be laid before the company in a general meeting within six months of the end of the period that it covers, and will be in shareholders' hands at least fifteen days prior to the date of the meeting at which it will be considered). Stock exchanges and regulatory bodies like the SEC tend to prefer shorter periods, generally ninety days from the end of the fiscal period (forty-five for quarterly reports).

The SEC's 8-K form indicates an alternative view of timeliness. In effect, if a company acquires or disposes of assets, records extraordinary charges or credits or other items of an unusual nature, makes a material provision for a loss, changes its auditors, and so on, this must be reported within ten days of the close of the month in which it occurred. The Wyden Bill would require the SEC to be notified within twenty-four hours in some cases.

The Form of Disclosure

It would seem as though the form of disclosure should be the most variable of the elements of the disclosure package. In fact, disclosure by means of a balance sheet and income statement, although often under different names, is the most universal aspect of financial reporting. They are even found in the countries of the world that are or were communist, although not as important as the nonmonetary statistical reports. Notes to the financial statements became necessary as the items in them became more obscure.

After World War II it became a common practice for statements of funds flows to accompany the other financial statements, and in the United States this table was made a part of the financial statements by APB Opinion No. 19, under the title "statement of changes in financial position." It was regarded as a new form of financial statement, and other countries, and international accounting standards, followed suit. Then, in 1987, the FASB replaced it with a statement of cash flows, which defines "funds" as "cash and cash equivalents." The rest of the world, and international accounting standards, again followed suit. The FASB rejects the concept of "basic financial statements" and argues that financial statements are what it, the FASB, says they are.[6] Even more ambiguous is the status of other disclosures mandated by the FASB: statements of segment sales, profits, and assets (SFAS 14); reserve recognition accounting by oil and gas producers (SFAS 69); the voluntary disclosures (that few companies provide) in respect of the effects of changing prices (SFAS 89). The auditor's report does not refer to them, and although the financial statements may say that the notes are part of them, the issue is unclear, as we pointed out in Chapter 7. For example, research has demonstrated the inconsistent manner in which segment data have been disclosed, yet during the period when "on a consistent basis" formed part of the wording of the audit report, no auditor ever drew attention thereto. Indeed, the auditor's involvement with segment disclosures was discussed in SAS 21, "Segment Information," where it was laid down that auditors need not apply audit procedures to them to the extent required if they were to issue an opinion on the segment information alone.

The SEC has mandated the publication of three years' income statements and statements of changes in financial position (now cash flows) and two years' balance sheets. There is no U.S. GAAP requirement for comparative financial data, but the laws of a number of countries call for those of the preceding year. The SEC requirement is perhaps indicative of a general lack of understanding of the concept of disclosure; financial analysts need one more balance sheet than the number of income statements provided if they are to use ratio analysis effectively.

The other contents of the financial report are less universal. A review by the chief executive or board of directors of the period's operations is customary, and the SEC made a "Management's Discussion and Analysis" mandatory (Accounting Series Release [ASR] No. 279 and Financial Reporting Release [FRR] No. 501 of 1980). These parts of the report usually contain such pellucid observations as "accounts receivable increased between 19XX and 19XY because more customers owed us money." Most European companies provide summaries of the results of operations of important subsidiaries and affiliates; FAS 94, "Consolidation of All Majority-Owned Subsidiaries" required summary financial statements to be provided for previously unconsolidated subsidiaries "either individually or in groups" when FAS 94 was implemented, to compensate for the omission of data previously provided. Narrative reports on major subsidiaries are sometimes given.

Other commonly encountered features of financial reports are a "highlights" page, a discussion of products and markets, names and addresses of directors, officers, auditors, attorneys, share transfer agents, bankers, and the like, and of course, an auditor's report. Photographs and other graphical illustrations are considered a must, as is a five- or ten-year summary of key financial data. This last increasingly includes financial ratios such as profit/sales and profit/equity.

DISCLOSURE AND FINANCIAL REPORTING

Everyone agrees that financial reports must disclose information, and that this disclosure must be "full" and/or "fair," or at least, adequate. But what is information?

We define information as "purpose-oriented data," that is, data selected as input for a specific decision model. Thus, information presupposes a surplus of data, from which either the accountant or the decision-maker makes a selection. In the case of the financial report, management decides which data will be provided to users, and the accountant, which data will be provided to management.

Even in countries where the entire form and content of the financial report are dictated by law, such as Germany, so that *suppressio veri* and *suggestio falsi* can have serious legal consequences for managers and accountants alike, the question abides. We observe even there that some companies include observations over and above those required by law. No meaningful concept of disclosure can be found in the legal or accounting literature.

Disclosure requirements are often ambiguous and sometimes in conflict. In the United States, for example, the valuation of inventories is a function of GAAP, Internal Revenue Service regulations, and the SEC's Regulation S-X, and it is not at all clear, for example, how to report a change to LIFO from any other valuation method.

The traditional view of disclosure in accounting was that it revolved around the financial statements, which became increasingly complex and more detailed to reflect new business finance and investment decisions. This constraint is viewed as burdensome, and financial reports include more and more ''soft'' data, data that cannot be objectively verified through the accounting system. Users would like accountants to be associated with the verification of this soft data, and accountants would like to oblige. So far it has not proved easy.

At the same time, the attempt to improve the quality of financial statements has generated a vast quantity of regulations, compliance with which is clearly uneconomic for all but the largest corporations. Even when the data required by GAAP are provided, in the view of many the result is ''information overload.'' This has led to a demand for *differential disclosure*, which is being achieved in different ways:

—The SEC has reduced requirements for small corporations.

—GAAP contains exemptions for nonpublic companies (earnings per share; segment disclosures) and the former requirement for information on the effects of changing prices (FAS 33) applied only to very large corporations.

—The EC countries have a three-tier system that reduces the amount of disclosure for small and medium-sized companies.

—There has been an effort by the Private Companies Practice Section of the AICPA to establish other comprehensive bases of accounting as acceptable substitutes for GAAP in the case of smaller corporations. These are the cash basis and the tax basis, the former being comprehensive only through a large stretch of the imagination. The objection to the tax basis is less conceptual; accountants might find it difficult to request payment for auditing figures for which they had already been paid as tax preparers.

MATERIALITY

Another way out of the information overload problem is through the concept of materiality. All FASB statements and interpretations state explicitly that they apply only to material items. What is material, however, is not defined in GAAP, and SFAC 2 explicitly refrained from placing a fence around it. The AICPA's *Accounting Research Study No. 7* came close: "A statement, fact or item is material, if giving full consideration to the surrounding circumstances as they exist at the time, it is of such a nature that its disclosure, or the method of treating it, would be likely to influence or to make a difference in the judgment and conduct of a reasonable person." The SEC's definition in Regulation S-X is basically the same.

On the other hand, the idea that an accountant's definition of materiality is of any legal significance is questionable. In *Escott v. Barchris Construction Corporation* (283 F. Supp. 643, SDNY 1968) the plaintiff alleged that the auditor certified materially misleading financial statements. The court cited a definition of a "material fact" as one "which if it had been currently stated or disclosed would have deterred or tended to deter the average prudent investor from purchasing the securities in question." In this case, the court made its own assessment of materiality.[7] The Foreign Corrupt Practices Act of 1977 made use of the word "significance," which is believed to be more comprehensive than "materiality."

It is because of the obscurity of the accounting concept of materiality that conformity with GAAP has become a voluntary undertaking. Many corporations depart from GAAP or omit GAAP-mandated disclosures on the grounds that the result is "not material." SFAC 2 relegated materiality to a position of lesser importance than the primary qualities of relevance and reliability. Yet this cavalier approach to materiality undermines the basic view of financial reports as information for investment and other decisions.

AGENCY THEORY

It seems obvious that, if the objective of financial reporting were to provide information for decisions, future-oriented data would be preferred over historical. Continued emphasis on historical data suggests strongly that the objective lies elsewhere, probably in the evaluation of management's performance. This was, after all, the original purpose of financial reporting, the "stewardship function."

A contemporary byway of accounting theory, known as "agency theory," has attempted to build on this view. The corporation is a set of contractual relationships, among which are those between managers and shareholders, and managers and creditors. Accounting and auditing are seen as devices for monitoring the resulting agency relationships, and the question of disclosure is thus reduced to one of cost and benefit. The assumption that agency theorists test is that management will maximize its own welfare and minimize agency costs;

obviously, these two propositions must be investigated separately. Managers are subject to "moral hazard" and must therefore be given a chance to be honest. Disclosure belongs within this framework.

Unfortunately the practitioners of agency theory research have chosen to utilize the methodology of economics, and particularly the mathematics of cost/benefit analysis, which has proved so unrewarding in economics generally. By this means they have rendered their studies impervious to accountants, and ensured that their debates will be endless. The research that might have contributed to our knowledge on the economic significance of disclosure has not been done. For example, some U.S. banks publish audited financial statements and some do not. Do the former benefit from a lower cost of capital than the latter? How can cost of capital be measured for such an experiment?

CONCLUSION

In the currently fashionable jargon, this chapter has dealt with the supply of financial information for external users. If financial reports were really intended to provide information useful for investment and credit decisions then we would expect to find them loaded with future-oriented data, including budgets and possibly even the forecasts from which these were derived. Indeed, John Burton when chief accountant of the SEC suggested that if this were done, then the only historical data to provide would be variances from budget. (We shall return to this subject in Chapter 14.)

It is obvious that the historical data of which financial reports are composed must serve some other purpose. Edgar Edwards and Philip Bell state that "The principal purpose to be achieved by the collection of accounting data (other than prevention of fraud and theft and the like) is to provide useful information for the evaluation of past business decisions and of the methods used in reaching those decisions." (A subsidiary purpose is to serve the needs of the taxation authority.)[8] Evaluation of managerial performance and compliance with perceived or real governmental needs better explain the form and content of *historical* financial reports than does the information hypothesis.

Further, corporations regularly survey their shareholders in order to find out whether they are satisfied with the annual report, and to elicit their suggestions for improvement. Presumably bondholders, bankers and other creditors, and investment advisers who counsel corporations about the type of disclosures they need, have sufficient clout to influence suppliers to make necessary improvements. This factor may be the determinant in the gradual changes that have taken place in financial reporting in the United States and throughout the world.

Critics (who include some accountants) are becoming increasingly vocal in demanding the provision of more "soft" information in financial reports. Whether this is an ideological response to repeated indoctrination with the objectives stated in SFAC 1, or to some other political influence, or whether it arises out of a real social need, is an interesting question. It should not be forgotten that the SEC is staffed by lawyers, whose standards for disclosure have little to do with accounting information, and everything to do with prosecuting a case in the courts. At any rate, supplier improvements in historical financial reporting are conceivable under any of the disclosure hypotheses. In the next two chapters we will consider perhaps the most important of them, accounting for the effects of changing prices.

NOTES

1. George H. Benston, "Required Disclosure and the Stock Market: An Evaluation of the Securities Act of 1934," *American Economic Review*, March 1973, pp. 132–55.

2. For an economist's analysis, see George J. Stigler, "Public Regulation of the Securities Markets," *Journal of Business*, April 1964, pp. 117–42. For an accountant's, see George H. Benston, "The Market for Public Accounting Services: Demand, Supply, and Regulation," *Journal of Accounting and Public Policy*, Spring 1985, pp. 33–80.

3. David Solomons, *Guidelines for Financial Reporting Standards* (London: Research Board of the Institute of Chartered Accountants of England and Wales, 1989).

4. Securities and Exchange Commission, *Balance sheets for commercial and industrial companies*, 17CFR para. 210.05–02. See also sec. 232.

5. Early work in this field was summarized by Eugene F. Fama in "Efficient Capital Markets: A Review of Theory and Empirical Work," *Journal of Finance*, May 1970, pp. 383–417. Since then the methodology has improved, but not the results.

6. Personal communication to the author from Dennis R. Beresford, chairman of the Financial Accounting Standards Board.

7. See also *TSC Industries, Inc. v. Northway*, 426 U.S. 438 (1976).

8. Edgar O. Edwards and Philip W. Bell, *The Theory and Measurement of Business Income* (Berkeley: University of California Press, 1961), p. 271.

CHAPTER 9

FINANCIAL REPORTING AND CHANGING PRICES

INTRODUCTION

One of the most persistent criticisms of contemporary financial reporting concerns the failure to report the effects of changing prices. In this chapter we will review the one attempt to confront this problem through U.S. GAAP. The accounting profession, when forced into this position, preferred a solution based upon general price-level adjustment, but the SEC preferred one based on current costs. Pronouncements of the AICPA, *Accounting Research Study No. 6* (1963) and APB *Statement No. 3* (1969), rejected current cost accounting methods out of hand, but the SEC's view eventually prevailed.

In FASB *Statement No. 33* on this subject, affected corporations were required to present supplementary data on both the historical cost/constant dollar and the current cost/constant dollar bases. FAS 33 proved unpopular and was effectively withdrawn by FAS 89. FAS 89, which recommended that corporations report supplementary data on the impact of changing prices, eliminated the historical cost/constant dollar requirement.

Because FAS 33 contained considerably more details of both systems, in this chapter we shall examine the subject of accounting for changing prices from its viewpoint. In Chapter 10 conceptual and practical aspects of current cost accounting will be described. Whether grafting onto this system a set of general price-level adjustments adds to the informational content of the data is very doubtful, and it has led U.S. accountants to overlook important aspects of accounting for changing prices.

CURRENT COST ACCOUNTING IN THE UNITED STATES

The accounting profession's preoccupation with historical cost/constant dollar accounting can probably be attributed to its fear of being exposed to additional litigation. Adjusting historical cost data using an index of general purchasing power is a purely mechanical operation, and accountants are not normally prone to arithmetical errors. Current cost, however, involves judgment and critical evaluation, on neither of which the accounting profession prides itself. It is therefore not surprising that the first exposure draft of a statement on the subject (December 1974) dealt entirely with general price-level adjustments.

After expressing concern about the usefulness of such data, and before the FASB finalized a statement, in March 1976 the SEC issued *Accounting Series Release No. 190* (ASR 190). This required over 1,000 of the largest U.S. corporations to include in the footnotes to their financial statements:

—the estimated current replacement cost of inventories and productive capacity

—the approximate current replacement cost of sales and depreciation, depletion, and amortization expense

—a description of the methods used to arrive at these

This initiative caused the FASB to reconsider, and eventually to require both current cost/constant dollar and historical cost/constant dollar data. As a consequence, in 1980 the SEC withdrew ASR 190.

This sequence of events echoed a similar situation in the United Kingdom. During the 1970s, as inflation grew, the U.K. accountancy profession issued recommendations for supplementary financial statements adjusted by a general price-level index. The government became interested in the impact of inflation on income taxation, and appointed the Sandilands Committee to study the problem. The committee came out firmly against general price-level adjustments and in favor of current cost accounting (CCA). Indeed, the committee wanted CCA accounts to be the primary financial statements, and historical cost statements the supplementary data.

This led to the publication of *Statement of Standard Accounting Practice No. 16* (SSAP 16), "Current Cost Accounting," which gave companies the choice of current cost statements as supplements, or as primary financial statements. As in the United States, users displayed little enthusiasm for the current cost data, and the taxing authority did not recognize it as a basis for taxing income. The rate of inflation subsided, and SSAP 16 was suspended on June 6, 1985. Nevertheless, some U.K. companies have continued to report both historical cost and current cost income, on a voluntary basis.

In the United States a number of leading industrial corporations are known to use current cost accounting data for internal operating reports. Some real estate development companies have published supplementary accounting information in current values, using selling market prices of their assets rather than replacement cost.

FASB STATEMENT NO. 33, "FINANCIAL REPORTING AND CHANGING PRICES"

In September 1979 the Financial Accounting Standards Board (FASB) issued the first U.S. accounting standard calling for the preparation and publication of supplementary information on the effects of changing prices. This culminated a professional debate lasting nearly twenty years, on whether financial reports should reveal the effects of inflation on income and assets, and if so, how. FAS 33 failed to resolve the issues debated. In particular, its application was restricted to approximately 1,200 of the largest U.S. corporations; it required information under both of the two main competing systems (constant dollar and current cost); and the problem of what to do with the accounting differences resulting from restatements was not confronted. For these and other reasons, the statement was designated "experimental."

FAS 33 was the outcome of pressures on the Financial Accounting Standards Board from a number of its constituencies. Public accounting firms, notably Arthur Andersen & Co., Price Waterhouse, and Touche Ross, had been publishing increasingly urgent appeals for some form of accounting for changing prices. The Securities and Exchange Commission (SEC), under the chairmanship of Harold Williams, had repeatedly expressed itself in forceful terms on the need for inflation accounting. Academic publications on the subject increased in number and complexity during the 1970s, and some controllers and business executives went on record suggesting the time had come to depart from the historical cost principle. Thus, wide support for the FASB's innovation was expected, and obtained.

The objective of FAS 33 was to provide users of financial reports with information that would assist them in assessing

a. future cash flows

b. enterprise performance

c. the erosion of operating capability

d. the erosion of general purchasing power (para. 3)

In para. 13 the statement acknowledged a lack of a consensus on the "general, practical usefulness of constant dollar information and current cost information" and in para. 15, that the required information provided a basis for studying this issue:

The Board intends to study the extent to which the information is used, the types of people to whom it is useful, and the purpose for which it is used. The requirements of this Statement will be reviewed on an ongoing basis and the Board will amend or withdraw requirements whenever that course is justified by the evidence. This statement will be reviewed comprehensively after a period of not more than five years.

The five-year review period ended in 1984, and because the information required to be published by FAS 33 was not being used, FAS 33 was suspended by FAS 89, "Financial Reporting and Changing Prices." FAS 89 recommended provision of this type of information, but did not require it.

Among the consequences foreseen if price-level adjusted financial statements were published we may note:

—reappraisals of companies by investment and credit analysts, with possible effects on merger and acquisitions trends, stock market prices, and bond and other credit ratings

—greater intransigence by management in the face of union demands, particularly for wage increases not linked to increased productivity

—accelerated price increases for goods and services, and resistance to fixed-price contracts

—restriction of dividends by reference to constant dollar and/or current cost income

—stockholder criticism of management, which is perceived as failing to earn an adequate real rate of return on assets

No research has been reported that attempted to relate the suspension of FAS 33 to any of these factors.

HISTORY OF ACCOUNTING FOR CHANGING PRICES

Changing prices have always been a feature of business operations, and there is evidence from surviving records dating back to the Middle Ages that accountants have long grappled with the problems they present. In modern times, however, inflation has become the principal factor underlying changing prices, which have tended therefore to increase progressively from this cause. Rampant inflation in Germany in the 1920s, and slightly less acute price-level problems in France in the same period, stimulated accountants in those countries to experiment with accounting solutions to the financial reporting problem. These solutions inevitably fell foul of the legal framework regulating corporate financial reporting, which relied on historical cost valuation principles.

Many Latin American countries have experienced high rates of inflation during the past thirty years, and have adapted the legal framework to permit the effects of changing prices to be reflected in financial reports, using a method known as indexation. The U.S. situation is more similar to the European experience, the SEC providing a legal framework that is likewise based on historical costs.

Accounting for price-level changes[1] became a topic of interest to accountants in the United States following World War I.[2] The first article on the subject, by Livingston Middleditch, Jr., appeared in 1918.[3] These early writings reveal that the authors:

1. recognized the instability of the monetary unit as presenting a problem in measuring results, because of the difficulty of ensuring capital maintenance.
2. disagreed on the concept of capital underlying capital maintenance, some choosing a purchasing power concept and others a physical capital concept.
3. agreed that fixed assets and depreciation accounting were the most affected items in the financial statements.
4. assumed that an end-of-period adjustment could correct the financial statements for the effect of changing prices. There is no mention of continuous indexation in the English language literature.

Instability of the Monetary Unit

Everyone knows inflation as a phenomenon, but its effects on financial accounting are not easily recognized. They combine to overstate profits and give shareholders and others the impression that the enterprise is more profitable than it really is. The principal objection to using money dollars in financial statements, however, was expressed by Paton.[4] "The significance of the dollar—the accountant's yardstick—is constantly changing. We know that the 1920 dollar is a very different unit from the 1910 dollar" (p. 2).

Concept of Capital Maintenance

Two different schools of thought on accounting for inflation emerged from the outset: Middleditch favored an index of general purchasing power for making the necessary adjustments, whereas Paton rejected this in favor of a specific index, corresponding to the replacement cost index of the asset concerned. It is clear that Paton was contemplating the maintenance of physical capital, whereas Middleditch was content with the maintenance of money capital.

Fixed Assets and Depreciation Accounting

These and other writers were preoccupied with the valuation of long-lived assets and the related problem of calculating depreciation. They believed that current assets were turning over rapidly, and therefore did not present much of an adjustment problem. This viewpoint was combined with a general criticism of the unsystematic approach to calculating depreciation expense that had prevailed prior to the introduction of the corporate income tax, and which was in the process of disappearing. The prevailing view, however, was that depreciation was a method of recovering an investment, and therefore, if the cost of an equivalent investment had increased, depreciation must be increased proportionally. There was no recognition of the backlog problem, yet, depending upon the preference of the author, the firm was assumed to desire recovery of money capital or to reconstitute a fund for reacquiring physical capital.

The discussion was influenced by the decision of the United States Supreme Court in *Smyth v. Ames*.[5] The Court's view in this case was that depreciation should be based on reproduction cost, and this became a permitted method of determining the rate base of utility companies. The practice ceased following the decision in *Knoxville v. Knoxville Water Company*[6] and other cases.

End-of-Period Adjustments

The absence of any discussion of the use of indexed or replacement cost accounting data in the day-to-day operation of an accounting system is very marked. Middleditch omitted the income statement (and also the funds statement, which was not discussed by any of the authors during this period) from his terms of reference. Paton also limited his presentation of a system of adjustments to fixed assets and accumulated depreciation. These omissions are all the more remarkable in that several of the writers explicitly mentioned the need for management to have price level-adjusted information, and some even referred to the relationship between such adjustments and product costs.

The instability of the monetary unit became a matter of concern again following World War II, and discussion of the need for price level-adjusted financial statements revived. Perhaps as a consequence of the extended study of the subject by Sweeney,[7] however, the discussion now embraced many details omitted from the earlier literature. The measurement of results was seen to involve restatement of inventories and cost of goods sold; it was suggested that current prices should be used for all income statement items, or that all items in the income statement should be price-level indexed. This was, no doubt, in part at least due to the higher rates of corporate income tax experienced during this period, which also led to the adoption of LIFO, a substitute for current cost of goods sold, for income tax assessment. Management decision-making necessitated a knowledge of current costs, and price-level adjustments were designed to provide this information.

It should be pointed out that many articles published during these two periods reaffirmed the importance of historical cost-based financial statements and opposed price level-adjusted accounting. Indeed, even the advocates of price-level accounting in the United States never went beyond the proposal that such financial statements should be supplements to the historical cost financial statements. The criticisms of opponents may be summarized as follows:

1. Stewardship accountability requires the use of the money (nominal) dollar.

2. In a reasonably well-managed firm, inflationary gains and losses tend to cancel out, with little continuing effect on stockholders' equity.

3. Changes in markets and technology render replacement less and less relevant to decision-making. Both inventories and fixed assets tend to be replaced by different items from those sold or used up.

4. The fact that the monetary unit was specified in law permeated contractual and other legal relationships, including the income tax laws. The users of financial statements would be confused by data based upon a concept of constant dollars, and would not be able to use any of the data in their day-to-day transactions.

The response to these criticisms was that stewardship included the measurement of results; that inflation affected different firms differently; that replacement was a difficult concept, but not impossible to quantify; and that users must be educated to take advantage of the information on changing prices when it became available.

THE DUAL APPROACH OF FAS 33

FAS 33 required public enterprises reporting in accordance with U.S. generally accepted accounting principles to disclose the following supplementary information in annual financial reports, if they met a specified size test: gross property, plant, and equipment of more than $125 million, or total assets amounting to more than $1 billion. Approximately 1,200 public enterprises qualified.

For the current year

—constant dollar income from continuing operations

—current cost income from continuing operations

—purchasing power gain or loss on net monetary items, not to be included in income from continuing operations

—year-end current cost amounts of inventory and property, plant, and equipment

—increase or decrease during the year in the current cost amounts of inventory and property, plant, and equipment, net of inflation, not to be included in income from continuing operations

—information permitting a reconciliation of constant dollar and current cost income with historical cost income, and specifically the amounts of or adjustments to cost of goods sold, depreciation, depletion, and amortization expense, and any reductions of historical cost amounts to lower recoverable amounts in the determination of constant dollar income

—the aggregate amount of constant dollar and current cost depreciation expense if allocated among cost of goods sold and other accounts

—how current costs were calculated; any differences in calculating constant dollar or current cost depreciation and historical cost depreciation; any differences in income tax allocation

For the five most recent years

—net sales and other operating revenue

—constant dollar income from continuing operations, also on a per share basis

—constant dollar net assets at year-end

—purchasing power gain or loss on net monetary items

—current cost income from continuing operations, also on a per share basis

—current cost net assets at year-end

—Consumer Price Index used for each year's constant dollar restatements

We have noted the parallel development of two schools of thought on accounting for changing prices—one advocating a constant dollar method, and the other a current cost method. FAS 33 acknowledged this phenomenon by admitting a dual approach in the requirement to publish both constant dollar and current cost information. It did, however, attempt to combine them in the method known as current cost/constant dollar accounting.

We can identify two kinds of price change.

1. For a given good: if the market price at t_o = $2

and at t_n = $\underline{3}$

the price change is   1

and can be expressed as ½, or 50 percent. A specific price index would show the price of this good having increased by 50 percent.

2. For all goods in a consumer basket:

if market prices at t_o sum to $200

and at t_n to $\underline{240}$

the price change is   40

and can be expressed as $^{40}\!/_{200}$, or 20 percent. A general price-level index would show inflation at a rate of 20 percent for this period.

We can therefore study the impact of changing prices on a firm holding this specific good in relation to two effects: the *inflation effect*, or the extent to which the price change is attributable to inflation; and the *market effect*, or the extent to which the price change is attributable to specific market factors. Examining the $1 increase:

Inflation effect = $2 × 20%	=	$0.40
Market effect = $1 − 0.40	=	$0.60
Total		$1.00

Fas 33 called the inflation effect "the effect of general price-level change," and the market effect "increase in current cost net of inflation." It did not require comprehensive constant dollar adjustments to be applied to the current cost information, only adjustments to the increase or decrease in current cost amounts of inventory and property, plant and equipment. This limitation, however, was predicated on the fact that the statement also required constant dollar information, including the purchasing power gain or loss on net monetary items.

Not considered in FAS 33 was the conceptual problem of combining two different kinds of unit of measurement: money dollars, which the FASB calls *nominal dollars*, and constant dollars, which are hypothetical units of identical purchasing power. This problem, which can be likened to adding quarters to subway tokens, may not be capable of producing a meaningful result.

THE OBJECTIVES OF ACCOUNTING FOR CHANGING PRICES

The basic objective of FAS 33 was to provide information on the most significant effects of changing prices on business enterprises:

> If those effects are not recognized, poor decisions may be made in all sectors of society. Investors may lack important information for decisions on how much to invest, in which enterprises to invest, and on what terms; creditors may have a weak basis for decisions on the granting and pricing of credit. Consequently, the cost of capital may be too high or too low for individual enterprises; resources may be allocated inefficiently. Furthermore, people in government who participate in decisions on economic policy may not obtain the most relevant information on which to base their decisions. (Para. 92)

It was argued that these effects could not be adequately understood until they were directly reflected in financial reports. They influenced different firms differently; their understanding necessitated widespread discussion in terms that explicitly incorporated changing prices effects; and statements about those effects by managers and others would acquire greater credibility if such information were published. Accounting for changing prices was consistent with the objectives of financial reporting laid down in SFAC 1, namely, to provide information

1. to help users to assess the amounts, timing, and uncertainty of prospective cash flows to the enterprise.

2. about resources and claims to those resources, and about transactions, events, and circumstances that change them.

3. about an enterprise's performance, provided by measures of earnings and its components.

ACCOUNTING MEASUREMENT MODELS

The traditional measurement model used by accountants is based on realized, arms-length transactions. Representing the enterprise as a system of inputs and outputs, the prices placed on the inputs at the time of acquisition remain valid for all events occurring after the point of input. At the output phase, realized exit prices are substituted for input prices, permitting income (profit) measurement through the comparison of outputs (revenues) with inputs (costs).

There are, of course, both problems in the application of this basic rule and exceptions to it. Problems arise when divisible inputs are divided up over separate activities, as occurs in the consumption and sale of inventories during and after the manufacturing process, and in the utilization of fixed assets for production. We speak of an allocation of inputs over operations "based upon" the acquisition prices of the inputs. Similarly, the loss of value over time that accompanies the use of fixed assets is measured by an allocation, called depreciation, depletion, or amortization, that is "based upon" the acquisition prices of the assets. These allocations undermine the apparent simplicity of the historical cost model.[8]

The exceptions concern writing off part or all of the input value of an asset when it has become permanently impaired through obsolescence, physical damage or deterioration, or other unfavorable circumstance. This is believed to arise from the operation of the principle of conservatism, but may equally be ascribed to realism in accounting. The converse side of realism, writing up the input value of an asset when circumstances indicate an increase, is virtually never encountered; it is said that opposition to write-ups in the United States is an historical survival of the experiences of the economic crash that led to the Great Depression of the 1930s, and is policed by the SEC in the hope of avoiding a recurrence of that tragedy. It may be observed that liabilities are not written down until due process of law has reduced the legal obligation they represent, nor are they written up when interest rates decline and their present value increases.

This measurement model is sometimes referred to as the "cost principle" and is said to utilize a *stable dollar assumption*. Abstracting from the question of ascertaining quantities, the measurement issue can be expressed as: What price best represents a given quantity in its various uses as data for accounting measurements? Two principal alternatives have been proposed and have obtained substantial support.

Constant Dollar Accounting

Technically, constant dollar accounting differs from historical cost accounting in only one respect: Data are expressed in units of the same (uniform) purchasing power. This is effected by multiplying each accounting item by a coefficient, the numerator of which is the purchasing power index into which historical costs are being translated, and the denominator, the same index at the date the item entered the accounting system. (In principle, each entry should be so translated, but in practice only monthly or yearly aggregates and end-of-period balances are affected.)

The effect of this translation, however, is to restate items at different prices than those used in the historical cost accounts. For the purpose of constant dollar accounting, accounts are divided into two classes, monetary and nonmonetary. Monetary items are accounts containing entries that are fixed in terms of the monetary unit, whose face value is also their money value. (This explains the FASB's use of the phrase "nominal dollars" for money dollars.) The balances of monetary accounts, of course, do not appear in the income statement, but in the statement of financial position. Nonmonetary items are accounts containing entries that are not fixed in terms of the monetary unit, whose prices can change while they are in the possession of the firm. The movements of nonmonetary items appear in the income statement; their balances at the end of a period are not expressed in units of end-of-period purchasing power.

In effect, by restating income statement items into average-of-period dollars, and nonmonetary balance sheet items into average or end-of-period dollars, the accounts are adjusted for the effect of changing prices. The effect is not *found*, however, but *assumed*. This can be demonstrated by an example.

A firm owns equipment that cost $900 in 19X0, when the price index was 120 (1967 = 100). If the average price level for 19X4 was 200, this equipment will appear in constant dollar net assets at C$1,500 gross (less accumulated depreciation). The constant dollar income statement will show depreciation expense, assuming straight-line depreciation over five years, of C$300, as compared to historical cost depreciation of $180. Thus, whether or not this item of equipment increased in price during the time it was owned by the firm, its book value will be translated into a different value on the assumption that its price increased at the same rate as did prices generally, as reflected in the price index used.

Current Cost Accounting

There are substantial variations in the methods of current cost (or current value) accounting; here we shall restrict ourselves to the FASB method.

In this form of accounting, expenses and assets are expressed in terms of their prices at the date of use or sale, or at the balance sheet date, with assets at their recoverable amount if it is lower. The prices are the specific prices of the quantities reflected in the expense or asset accounts, and not prices in general, or units of the same purchasing power. However, adjustment is limited to cost of goods sold, inventories, depreciation, depletion, and amortization expense, and property, plant, and equipment. (Firms that adopt the alternative of presenting comprehensive current cost financial statements are permitted to use constant dollar adjustments for all other income statement items and certain specified balance sheet items, but not current cost.)

FAS 33 allowed firms to find the current cost of a new item of inventory by finding the current cost to purchase or manufacture. The current cost of a used item of property, plant, and equipment (the normal case) is the cost of acquiring the same service potential and may be found:

a. by measuring the current cost of a new asset with the same service potential as the asset had when new, and reducing this amount by depreciation

b. by measuring the current cost of a used asset of the same age, description, and condition

c. by measuring the current cost of a new asset with a different service potential and adjusting the amount for the difference in service potential

In practice, the indexation method is widely used, with a current cost price index being found for the specific asset or a group of like assets.

For example, a firm owns equipment that cost $900 in 1970, and a building that cost $2,000 in 1975. Similar equipment, having the same productive capacity, costs $2,000 today, and the construction cost index stands at 200 (1975 = 100). The current cost amounts will be $2,000 for the equipment and $4,000 for the building, less accumulated depreciation for the period since acquisition in each case, assuming that the recoverable amounts are higher. Depreciation expense will be calculated on the average current cost amounts for the current fiscal year.

It will be seen that the method of current cost accounting differs from the method of constant dollar accounting in that the effect of changing prices is found, and not assumed. The accuracy of this observation diminishes as inventory and property, plant and equipment are aggregated and restated as a class rather than individual items, but is not altogether eliminated.

Lower Recoverable Amounts

In order to avoid the restatement of assets, under both constant dollar accounting and current cost accounting, at unrealistically high values, the statement called for a reduction to "recoverable amount" if this were known to be lower than the restated amount. "The value to the business of an asset cannot exceed the maximum sum that an enterprise would be willing to pay to acquire the asset" (para. 193). This "value in use" was defined as net realizable amount if the asset in question is about to be sold, or net [sic] present value of future cash flows from other assets.[9] Reduction to lower recoverable amount is consistent with the characteristics of current cost methods of accounting for the effect of changing prices, but not with the constant dollar method, which makes no pretense of reflecting real world conditions other than changes in the purchasing power of money.

CAPITAL MAINTENANCE AND MEASUREMENT MODELS

The origin of the concept of capital maintenance can be traced to corporation law, where it is found in the form of the "capital impairment rule" or "profits test." This feature of corporation law prohibits the payment of dividends other than out of profits. In order to ascertain the amount available for dividend, a corporation must provide for any diminution of capital during the period in which the dividend is to be paid, that is, it must ensure that its capital is maintained. The definition of capital is found in the corporation law, and is often simply the number of shares at issue multiplied by their par values. Thus, it suffices to compare this figure with net assets in order to see if capital has been maintained or not.

The transition from a legalistic to an economic view of accounting has directed accountants' attention to economic, rather than legal, capital. As long as the primary purpose of accounting was seen as the discharge of a legal or equitable obligation, a legal concept of capital maintenance was satisfactory; the adoption of an objective of providing information useful for economic decisions has rendered this concept too narrow. The FASB's choice of constant dollar and current cost methods of measurement was explicitly related to the need to maintain capital. What does "capital" mean in this context?

It is tempting to assume that "capital" means "economic capital," but this is not necessarily the case. Para. 100 of FAS 33 stated that "Capital is maintained when revenues are at least equal to all costs and expenses," and the appropriate measurement of costs and expenses depends on the concept of capital maintenance adopted. The first proposition rules out economic capital. The economic capital of a firm can be represented as the present value of future net cash flows to the firm, and if revenues and expenses are equal, there will be no future net cash flows. Capital, in this case, is zero, and therefore capital maintenance is not a meaningful concept. Other evidence, however, points to a definition of capital that equates it with net assets, or assets minus liabilities, so that capital maintenance means that some specified measure of resources would still be available to the firm even if all the income of the period were distributed in the form of dividends.

Starting with the basic equation

$$\text{assets} = \text{liabilities} + \text{equity}$$

and recognizing the fact that assets become expenses and create revenues, we arrive at the expanded equation

$$\text{assets} + \text{expenses} = \text{liabilities} + \text{revenues} + \text{beginning equity}$$

It is the "beginning equity" concept of capital that the FASB wanted to see maintained. Obviously, the issue of capital maintenance is bound up with the measurement of income, since the valuation of assets determines both expenses and the valuation of beginning equity (net assets).

The literature on accounting for changing prices discloses three categories of capital maintenance. One of these is said to be equivalent to the concept of economic capital; it is the maintenance of the capital invested in the firm by its owners. This may be measured either in nominal dollars or in units of uniform purchasing power. Not only is this not the concept referred to in FAS 33; it is also irrelevant, because the firm cannot account for the capital of its owners. The value to its owner of an investment in a quoted corporation is the market price per share multiplied by the number of shares held.

The other two categories are discussed in para. 100 of FAS 33.

Financial capital maintenance. The firm's capital (net assets) may be maintained in either nominal dollars or units of purchasing power. Suppose that the firm's net assets at the beginning of a period amounted to $10, and at the end of the period to $12, both measured in historical cost terms. Then, assuming no capital contributed or withdrawn, an income measurement of $2 would show that the capital of $10 was being maintained. Assume, however, that the beginning capital reflected ten units of product at $1 each, and that the capital at the end of the period was represented by eight units of product at $1.50 each. Then clearly, although the capital was being maintained in money terms, it was not being maintained in real terms. Constant dollar accounting would adjust the figures on the assumption that the principal effect was attributable to the general level of prices. If this had increased by 20 percent during the period, we could adjust the historical cost figures as follows:

Beginning capital, in end-of-period units of purchasing power	C$12
Ending capital, in end-of-period units of purchasing power	$12
Income	C$ 0

Physical capital maintenance. The above example reveals that twelve end-of-period dollars would not in fact maintain the firm's real capital, because the specific price of its assets had increased by 50 percent, not 20 percent. In order to compute income under the physical capital maintenance approach, we would need to adjust the figures in respect of the specific price change. This would produce:

Beginning capital, at end-of-year prices	$15
Ending capital, at end-of-year prices	$12
Loss	$ 3

The FASB asserted that the use of current cost accounting assures the maintenance of physical *operating capability.* More precisely, it permits the measurement of income or loss as the increase or decrease in net assets during a period, in real terms. We shall see later that a complex business organization presents certain problems when the concept of physical capital maintenance is applied.

Although the problem of capital maintenance is usually discussed as a problem of income measurement, in many cases there is an explicit or implied reference to the impact of income taxation. If income taxes are levied on historical cost income, and prices have increased, then the real capital of the firm is being reduced through taxation. In the previous example, a tax of 50 percent on the money income of $2 would reduce the operating capability of the firm, but no tax would be imposed if taxable income were computed in constant dollars. If, however, there were a real loss of $3, and taxable income were computed on the same basis, this would result in a government subsidy to the firm in the amount of any income tax refund obtained.

FAS 33 required both constant dollar and current cost adjustments to historical cost financial statements for the measurement of income from continuing operations and net assets under each of the two methods. The statement also suggested (para. 56) that some enterprises may wish to present comprehensive current cost/constant dollar supplementary statements, but there is no evidence that this suggestion has been taken up.

CONSTANT DOLLAR AND CURRENT COST ACCOUNTING COMPARED

It may be helpful to present at this point an overview of the principal characteristics of the two systems. Table 9.1 presents these characteristics.

Neither system of accounting comes to grips with all aspects of current values in financial reporting. For example, neither in constant dollar accounting nor in current cost accounting has it been proposed to mark monetary assets to market when, for example, interest rates change, or adjust monetary liabilities for such

Table 9.1
Constant Dollar—Current Cost

Unit of account	Units of uniform purchasing power	Nominal (money) dollars
Price level	General, usually represented by a Consumer Price Index	Specific, usually represented by the price index of a particular commodity or type of product
Classification of accounts	Monetary and nonmonetary	Monetary and nonmonetary
Differences arising	a. Beginning of period – assets and liabilities restated in constant dollars, equity (net assets) being the difference. Thus, the increase in amounts is concealed in the "rolling forward" of historical cost to constant b. During period - differences on restatement of monetary items isolated as "purchasing power gain or loss on net monetary items."	Nonmonetary items only. Increase (or decrease) in carrying amount (usually called a "holding gain or loss") isolated when historical cost translated into current cost. dollars.
Disposition of differences	Purchasing power gain or loss only-often regarded as an element of economic income, but FAS 33 required separate disclosure outside the income statement	Holding gain or loss often regarded as an element of current cost income, but FAS 33 required separate disclosure outside the income statement.
Capital maintenance concept differences	Financial capital	Physical capital

market effects. Indeed, the problem of accounting for liabilities during a period of changing prices has been given little attention throughout the debate between supporters of the two systems. A Price Waterhouse publication of 1977 contained a suggestion for avoiding the issue entirely, by defining "capital" to include long-term debt, deferred taxes, and possible minority interests and unfunded retirement benefits.[10]

Supporters of constant dollar accounting point to the following advantages:

—Use of the same unit of measurement through the financial statements.

—Improvement of interperiod comparability.

—That it is not a departure from historical cost. "The technique changes the measuring unit, not the attribute—historical cost—being measured. It follows therefore that most of the familiar accounting conventions are unchanged."[11]

—Disclosure of the loss or gain in purchasing power during a period of changing prices.

Opponents of constant dollar accounting respond that:

—The unit of measurement is derived from a consumer price index. It is (1) not relevant to productive entities, and (2) distorted by the known errors such indices contain.

—If the restated amounts reflect the average experience of the economy rather than the experience of the entity, comparability is not improved.

—Failure to depart from historical cost is not an advantage, accountants being well aware of the weakness of this conventional basis of accounting.

It may also be noted that constant dollar accounting modifies historical cost accounting in unpredictable ways, modifications that are often concealed by the practice of adjusting only aggregates and balances. The purchasing power loss or gain is a meaningless figure in the context of a financial statement, even a supplementary one. Expressed as it is in "units of uniform purchasing power," which either relate to some base year long gone, or else change from year to year, the loss or gain may not be construed as an element of "economic income" however that construct is defined. Users of financial statements being accustomed to interpret them in terms of money dollars can be expected to have great difficulty in making the transition to an essentially nonmonetary unit of account that looks like money but is not.

Supporters of current cost accounting point to the following advantages.

—Use of a consistent valuation framework throughout the financial statements (value to the business).

—Recognition of specific effects on the entity. For example, the effect of changing prices on a computer manufacturer may result in lower current cost expenses and asset values during a period when the general level of prices rises.

—Use of money dollars means that adjusted income (or loss) has the same meaning as in historical cost financial statements, that is, it represents the distributable amount (assuming capital maintenance) abstracting from the need to finance fixed assets, credit, and inventories.

—Restatement of assets at current cost amounts permits the balance sheet to demonstrate operating capability in end-of-period dollars.

—The increase or decrease in assets from holding resources during a period in which their prices change is disclosed.

Opponents of current cost accounting point out that:

—It falls short of current value accounting in that only certain items are restated (intangible assets, investments in other companies, and liabilities are excluded).

—There is a substantial departure from historical cost accounting principles, requiring a considerable effort to comprehend on the part of financial statement users.

—It assumes that assets will need to be replaced in order to maintain operating capability, when the replacement decision may be many years in the future.

—The so-called holding gains and losses are normal incidents of profit-seeking activities, and should be reflected in the financial statements only when realized.

—The impact on the net monetary position is not disclosed, either in respect of the purchasing power gain or loss, or the extent to which increased costs fall upon lenders rather than equity-holders.

—The nature of the "unrealized holding gain or loss" is unclear, and there is no agreement on whether it should be included in income.

Observe that we are here discussing supplementary financial statements to disclose the effects of changing prices. If we were to consider the need to replace historical cost financial statements by either constant dollar or current cost accounting, a different set of objections would arise to both. In some countries there are legal obligations surrounding financial reporting, which this type of financial statement would probably contravene. In this respect we may note that in Europe, a section of the European Community's Fourth Directive on Company Law permits departure from historical cost for specific balance sheet items under certain conditions, and allows either the replacement value method (widely used in The Netherlands) or other current values. This directive must be applied to each member country by national legislation, and, at the time of writing, only The Netherlands had legislation permitting accounts to be prepared on a current value basis if necessary for the presentation of a true and fair view of financial position and results.

Another legal aspect of changing the basis of accounting relates to the contractual arrangements of the firm. Such contracts as bank term loans, debenture trust deeds, and management remuneration arrangements would need to be rewritten or reinterpreted in the light of the different valuation rules applied.

Finally, the area of government regulation of business enterprises raises a host of questions that would have to be answered in changing from the historical cost basis. The most important of these questions undoubtedly is the definition of taxable income for income tax purposes, and it should be observed that the taxation authorities have proved virtually unmovable on the issue of allowing another basis than historical cost to be used in the determination of business profits, not only in the United States but in many other countries of the world, including The Netherlands where current cost accounting is well understood.

CURRENT COST/CONSTANT DOLLAR ACCOUNTING

It might be thought that some of the other objections to each of these methods of preparing supplementary information on the effects of changing prices could be overcome by combining them in the form of current cost/constant dollar accounting. Paras. 138–44 of FAS 33 contain the FASB's reasons for believing that such accounting "can provide a useful basis for users' assessments of whether an enterprise has maintained the purchasing power of their investments" (para. 137).

This argument takes the following form.

1. The objective of investment is to earn a return that ultimately becomes available in cash to meet personal expenditures.

2. Investors are also concerned about the purchasing power of the cash they will receive.

3. Thus, investors will be interested in knowing the maximum amount they can spend in a given year without expecting a decline in future purchasing power.

4. This requires the use of a constant dollar measuring unit.

5. By using constant dollars, the investor will be able to know how much to save out of current cash receipts in order to compensate for the effects of inflation.

6. The same arguments can be applied to measurements of the performance of a business enterprise.

7. "The application of constant dollar accounting to information prepared on a current cost basis can be regarded as an adjustment for changes in the general purchasing power represented by the worth of the enterprise insofar as that worth is recognized under current cost accounting" (para. 142).

8. Current cost income from continuing operations is measured (under FAS 33) approximately in average-of-the-year units of purchasing power. The increase or decrease in current cost (of assets) during the year, however, reflects the difference between measures in end-of-year dollars and beginning-of-year dollars. Calculation and disclosure of the inflation effect restore consistency with the statement of income from continuing operations.

We have observed the inconsistency of combining two essentially distinct measurement methods and performing arithmetic operations on the result. Here we note further that the FASB assumed that the capital maintenance concept relevant for an individual investor was also relevant to a business enterprise; we have tried to show that it is not. The expenditure patterns of a business enterprise are different from those of an individual, since they relate to a specific category of producer goods and not the general universe of consumer goods. Finally, the assumption that the information required by FAS 33 is useful in helping the user of financial statements to assess future net cash flows in terms of amount, timing, and relative certainty is very questionable.

The following comments from the Sandilands report are also relevant to this subject.[12] They have particular force in that the Sandilands Committee was perhaps the most representative body of accountants, business executives, attorneys, and civil servants ever to conduct a sustained examination of the alternative methods of accounting for inflation.

> It has been suggested to us that a particular price increase consists of a certain amount due to inflation and the remainder due to other factors. In our view such a distinction is meaningless. It would only be of use if there were an identifiable and quantifiable phenomenon of inflation independent of individual price changes, but in our view such an independent phenomenon does not exist. It is misleading to assume that the movement in some wide-ranging specific [retail] index can approximate to the rate of inflation in the abstract and, for example, that if the price of a commodity increases by 100 percent during a period when the [retail] index increases by 20 percent, that 20 percent of the price increase is due to inflation and 80 percent is due to other factors.

A NOTE ON THE INDEX NUMBER PROBLEM

In order to convert historical amounts into units of the same purchasing power, economic statisticians prefer to use the price index of a base year, say, 1967. This "deflates" the monetary amounts for the effects of inflation, and has the additional advantage of reducing the number of computations from year to year. Prior years' calculations do not need to be "rolled forward" into the purchasing power units of a subsequent period, and new graphs need not be drawn every year. Thus, the gross national product is usually expressed in *base period constant dollars*.

Accountants have taken the view that base period constant dollars are not informative, because the purchasing power of the past period is not relevant. They have consistently advocated use of the purchasing power of the latest period for which figures are presented, known as *current period constant dollars*. Last period's constant dollar figures must therefore be "rolled forward" or updated if presented in comparative statements.

In its wisdom, the FASB adopted *average of the current year constant dollars,* which it called current dollars. This was believed to save some computation, because most income statement transactions could be assumed to occur at an even rate during the year, and thus no transformation would be required for them. On the other hand, the rule could produce strange results, for example, end-of-year monetary assets presented at lower amounts in current dollars than in nominal dollars. Because the data required by FAS 33 were partial, these results were not apparent.

CONCLUSION

This chapter has drawn attention to the unsettled state of accounting for changing prices that resulted from the promulgation and suspension of FAS 33. That statement was viewed as an attempt to implement the objectives of SFAC 1, by extending the range of financial reporting to the effects of changing prices. The FASB was unable to distinguish the usefulness of constant dollar and current cost accounting for this purpose, and therefore adopted both, and even a combination of the two. The discussion of the conceptual bases of the two methods in this chapter has drawn attention to the principal differences between them, differences that have led some commentators to see them as serving different purposes. Whereas constant dollar accounting is viewed as simply changing the unit of measurement, current cost accounting is seen as a move toward value accounting.

Views on the use and usefulness of FAS 33 disclosures were strongly negative, with some comments supporting the continuance of this statement solely on the grounds that more time was needed for its evaluation. Yet the historical trend of accounting and financial reporting can be seen as a movement toward incorporating the effects of changing prices. This is supported by evidence that some management accounting systems incorporate such effects, and the controllers of the companies concerned believe that what is useful to managers will also be useful to investors, creditors, and others, albeit in aggregated form.

NOTES

1. This phrase denotes accounting for changing prices in an inflationary environment, and may usually be interpreted as "inflation accounting."
2. Stephen A. Zeff, ed., *Asset Appreciation, Business Income and Price-Level Accounting, 1918–35* (New York: Arno Press, 1976).
3. "Should Accounts Reflect the Changing Value of the Dollar?" *Journal of Accountancy*, February 1918.
4. "Depreciation, Appreciation and Productive Capacity," *Journal of Accountancy*, February 1918.
5. 169 U.S. 466 (1898).
6. 212 U.S. 1 (1909).
7. Henry W. Sweeney, *Stabilized Accounting* (New York: Harper and Bros., 1936).
8. See Arthur L. Thomas, "The Allocation Problem in Accounting Theory," *Studies in Accounting Research No. 3* (Evanston, Ill.: American Accounting Association, 1969).

9. "Present value of future net cash flows" is indicated; net present value is this amount less the cost of the asset in question, and shows the profitability of investing.

10. Price Waterhouse & Co., *Accounting in the Face of Inflation*, January 1977, p. 15.

11. Ibid., p. 25.

12. *Inflation Accounting: Report of the Inflation Accounting Committee*, London, Her Majesty's Stationery Office, CMND. 6225, June 1975, para. 47 (known as the Sandilands report, after the chairman of the committee).

CHAPTER 10

CURRENT COST ACCOUNTING

"Value" can be defined as the representation of an object as a sum of money. Historical cost accounting is an amalgam of valuation methods, only some of which are related to acquisition (input) prices. They depart from such prices in several ways; manufactured inventory results from a series of allocation procedures, and fixed assets are reported at "cost less accumulated depreciation." Accounts receivable from sales are exit (or proceeds) values, and inventories and marketable equity securities must be reported at the lower of cost or market. Some long-term receivables and leased assets and obligations are valued at present values (discounted cash flows method). The basis of some balance sheet and income statement items defies rational explanation. It is clear that we are observing a gradual departure from historical cost, and present-day accounting theory is in search of a logically consistent substitute. Current cost accounting provides this; it is referred to elsewhere as "the state of the art."[1]

EXIT PRICES

One alternative is the use of exit prices for all items and elements of an accounting system. Exit prices are *net realizable value* (net, that is, of disposal costs). This solution appeals to economists, who attempt to trace economic movements through selling market prices, and who therefore value inventory changes in the national income accounts at market prices. Although usually illustrated as end-of-period adjustments to historical costs, an operating system would continuously update accounts to the prices at which the objects concerned could be sold (in the case of liabilities, purchased?) on the open market.[2]

There are practical problems with exit prices. Some inventories (particularly work in process) and specialized equipment have no ascertainable selling prices, and the assumption that all assets could be liquidated and liabilities settled in an orderly manner at current prices is at least debatable. Nor is exit price without its own defects. If a manager purchases a good for $10 that he regularly sells for $15, and immediately reports a $5 gain, why bother to sell it? Why not buy as much as possible? Or borrow to pay the dividend from the not yet realized profit?

The principal problem, however, lies in the purpose that accounting information must serve, that of accountability. Reporting assets and liabilities in exit prices assumes that which should be demonstrated, the effects of the firm's inputs on its outputs. Insurers require evidence of cost before making good a casualty loss. Shareholders require evidence of realization before agreeing that a profit has been earned. The income tax authority, on the other hand, would be overjoyed to impose a tax as soon as an increase in value is recorded, but would balk at the prospect of allowing a deduction if the change is a value decrease.

The argument against exit values was well stated by Edgar O. Edwards:

1. They necessitate anomalous revaluations on acquisition.

2. The value of an object to its possessor is greater than its value to another by, at a minimum, location-specific costs such as freight and installation.

3. Net realizable value at one point in time says nothing about the price that will be realized subsequently.

4. Abandoning entry (input) prices renders difficult the process of tracing a set of factors of production during the process whereby value is added.[3]

Another candidate for replacing historical cost is present value (of forecast future net cash flows). This method was devised by the SEC for the oil and gas reserves of petroleum companies, under the name Reserve Recognition Accounting, and subsequently specified as required supplementary information by FAS 69. It necessitates heroic assumptions not only about future cash flows, but also about their timing and the rate of discount.

The Sandilands Committee in its report (see Chapter 9) stated that current (replacement) cost is the preferred alternative to historical cost. Using RC for replacement value, RV for net realizable value, and PV for present value (of expected future net cash flows), it presented the following six alternatives, in which value to the firm is marked with an asterisk.

1	2	3	4	5	6
PV	RC	RC	PV	RV	RV
>	>	>	>	>	>
RC*	PV*	RV*	RV	PV	RC*
>	>	>	>	>	>
RV	RV	PV	RC*	RC*	PV

Current (replacement) cost represents value to the firm in all but two cases, in one of which presumably the asset would have been sold. The other case involves present value, which requires projections of future cash flows and their timing *and* the selection of a discount rate.

CURRENT VALUE AS REPLACEMENT COST

The relevance of replacement cost was brought to the attention of economists in the last century by the Austrian Eugen Böhm-Bawerk. Stopping at a Viennese coffee house on his way home from work one winter's night, he found his overcoat missing when he got up to continue his journey. The measure of his loss, he reasoned, was what it would cost him to replace it. Bonbright applied this reasoning to business enterprises, and arrived at the concept of "deprival value."[4] He defined deprival value as the lower of sales value and replacement cost, otherwise known as "value in use."

Replacement value theory, which presents us with a fully developed accounting system using current cost, was the work of Theo Limperg during the period 1912–18. Limperg was both a practicing accountant and professor of managerial economics at the University of Amsterdam in The Netherlands, and well aware of the limitations of marginal cost that, then as now, dominated economic theory. (Attempts were made in the 1920s by some Anglo-American economic theorists to challenge reliance on marginal cost, but failed to attract the support of their colleagues.) Shortly stated, many assumptions are necessary in order to support propositions based on marginal cost, and virtually all of them are absent from real-world situations. One of the most critical is the problem of time. In John Barth's novel *Giles, Goat Boy*, an allegory of the American university, the economics faculty is satirized in a chapter in which Giles is given a task to do "in no time." He accomplishes it by climbing the campus tower and stopping the clock.

Students of Limperg, and his successor Abram Mey, introduced current cost accounting (called "replacement value accounting" or RVA) in a number of Dutch businesses during the 1930s. (Note that this was a time of declining prices; one of the virtues of RVA is that it is useful in all phases of the business cycle.) About thirty public companies quoted on the Amsterdam stock exchange report on this basis, including the electrical and electronic multinational Philips NV. The underlying philosophy was influential on the Sandilands Committee in the United Kingdom, but has met with little interest in the United States. We shall consider why this is so after having described it.

The purposes of managerial accounting are said to be score-keeping, attention-directing, and problem-solving. Replacement value accounting starts from the proposition that the function of accounting is to provide these kinds of information for decisions, so that financial accounting is viewed as a subset of managerial accounting. To make rational decisions, the manager must calculate what it costs to make and/or sell, and the accounting system serves to validate these decisions, both to the manager and to the investor. This requires continuous updating of the accounting records from historical to current values.

BASIC PROPOSITIONS OF REPLACEMENT VALUE THEORY

The following assumptions underlie replacement value accounting:

1. An object can have only one value at the same place at the same time. This results in the rejection of historical cost values if prices change, for any cause.
2. For any object that can be replaced, and will be in the normal course of business, value cannot exceed replacement value.
3. Replacement value is the technically necessary and economically unavoidable sacrifice involved in replacing an object held, used, or sold *on the measurement date*. This differs from replacement cost, which is the sacrifice measured on the date of replacement.
4. For any object that cannot or will not be replaced, replacement value is net realizable value, in The Netherlands called "proceeds value."
5. For any business decision, cost is calculated in replacement values.

We will examine each of these assumptions in more detail.

One Value

The use of different values for the same object is confusing and deceptive. It is confusing because it forces the manager to confront a false problem: Which of two otherwise identical but differently valued objects shall I use or sell? If they are identical, it makes no difference. It is deceptive because it tempts the manager to play accounting games, either for the supposed benefit of the firm, or in some cases, for personal gain. This is generally acknowledged in discussions of the LIFO method of inventory valuation, which recognize its profit manipulation possibilities, but the problem presents itself in all cases other than those where uniform values are used. Besides replacement value, these are weighted average and standard cost.

Replacement

The replacement assumption is often referred to in the Anglo-American literature as the physical capital maintenance assumption. If a goldsmith is to maintain a certain activity level, he must end every day with the same quantity of gold in inventory. Since the price of gold fluctuates, sale of any item costs the goldsmith in raw materials what he must pay to replace it. This simple fact is difficult to observe in a complex manufacturing situation, but it applies equally to the production of bread, wedding gowns, automobiles, or any good or service for which there is a continuing demand.

Measurement

Textbooks invariably define "cost" in terms of a sacrifice of factors of production for the attainment of a given object. They omit the important words "technically necessary and economically unavoidable" before "sacrifice." To understand this, we must see all costs as quantities multiplied by prices.

The phrase "technically necessary" reflects the fact that costs are first and foremost sacrifices of quantities of resources. If the sacrifice exceeds (or even falls short of) the technically necessary, because of waste, inefficiency, or a fortuitous substitution opportunity, then the difference represents a loss (or a gain), not a cost. This assumption underlies standard costing, where the difference is part of the variances, not of cost.

Similarly, the price of the factor of production used must be economically unavoidable. Firms find themselves in the position of over- or underpaying for factors of production for a variety of reasons—shortages due to forecasting errors, bargain purchase opportunities, necessity to substitute one type of material or labor for another. These are historical accidents, having no normative significance, and the manager/investor cannot rely on the same conditions reappearing in the future. Again, standard costing proceeds from the same assumption, leading to the calculation and reporting of price variances.

We must also emphasize the significance of the measurement date. Factors of production are acquired in accordance with exogenous conditions of input markets and endogenous treasury circumstances, underlying the concept of an economic lot size or order quantity. These influence the calculation of replacement value, but do not determine it. The updating process permits changes in input markets and financial position to affect carrying amounts (abstracting from the question of tolerances) as they occur, and not when replacement takes place.

Proceeds Value

Not all goods and services held, used, or sold by a firm will be replaced. For example, items are placed on sale by a department store when they become obsolete, or the line is discontinued. Both historical cost and replacement cost are irrelevant in this case. A more difficult example relates to mines of minerals, such as petroleum. We refer to such a mine as a "wasting asset," by which we mean that the capital invested is recovered through exploitation and sale, and this underlies the so-called successful efforts approach to accounting for oil and gas wells. Each well is a separate investment; if it is economically viable, costs of acquisition and development are capitalized and amortized by depletion. If not, they are written off. A number of oil and gas producers do not accept this premise, regarding their investments as resulting from the need to replace oil and gas produced. They use the alternative "full cost" method of accounting for preproduction costs, under which all costs of acquisition and development are capitalized, and amortized by depletion.

Otherwise stated, the distinction between replacement goods and nonreplacement goods is often a matter of policy rather than observable facts, as indeed is the decision which items to put on sale in a department store. The classical case is that of the U.S. steel companies. The open-hearth, or Bessemer, process of producing steel was rendered obsolete in the 1940s by the oxygen-enriching LD process, which drastically reduced the time required to produce a ton of steel. U.S. steel companies refused to accept the fact that their furnaces had no replacement value, and during the 1950s and 1960s insisted on attempting to recover the cost of using them from their customers. The latter found that foreign steel was cheaper and of better quality, so that the domestic market was flooded with imports. (The U.S. companies even attempted to persuade the Internal Revenue Service to permit them to deduct depreciation based on the reproduction cost of the obsolete facilities.) Had the U.S. companies recognized that their plant was not replaceable, and that its proceeds value was zero, they would have been better able to price their products so as to compete with the imports.

Cost as Replacement Value

If managers use replacement value (where relevant, proceeds value) in decisions concerning use and sale of factors of production, then operating statements and financial reports that are used to evaluate business results and managerial performance must do likewise. Otherwise, reported results will be an amalgam of operating results and the impact of exogenous factors, impossible to analyze.

We will now consider the implications of these assumptions for financial reporting.

THE HOLDING GAIN OR LOSS

An asset or a liability of any firm is removed from the market on which such assets and liabilities are traded. It is *in suspense* from the perspective of the economy as a whole. If such an object changes in value during this period, in all forms of current cost accounting the carrying amount is written up or down by the amount of the change (quantity × price). This difference is called a holding gain or loss, because it is attributed to the act of holding rather than that of purchase, use, or sale.

Two conflicting views of the holding gain or loss have emerged in the accounting literature. One view, referable to the all-inclusive income approach, is that the gain or loss or enters into and forms part of the determination of income, that is, should be credited or debited to the income statement. The other, the remeasurement view, is that the loss or gain simply restates capital by repricing it in current costs, and therefore does not constitute a part of income. The FASB's rules for reporting current cost data, being partial in nature, avoid confronting this issue directly, but exclude the "increase or decrease in the current cost amounts of inventory and property, plant, and equipment" from the determination of "income from continuing operations." It is reported as a separate item on current cost income statements, but not incorporated in net income.

The Dutch system of replacement value accounting is more complex and also more unequivocal. Part of the holding gain or loss is attributed to interest during the holding period which, in contrast to FAS 34, is calculated on assets and not allocated from liabilities. The remaining difference is reduced (or increased) in respect of the tax effect, and the balance is added to or deducted from stockholders' equity, as a revaluation account. Losses are debited against the revaluation account, but conservatism dictates that once this is reduced to zero, any further losses are charged against income.

The Gearing Adjustment

An article in *The Times* (London) dated October 1, 1975, argued that a holding gain consisted of two components, one financed by creditors and the other by stockholders. Only the first represents a gain (to stockholders), the other being a restatement of capital. This concept was adopted by the U.K. standard on accounting for changing prices (SSAP 16) under the name of "gearing adjustment." During a period of rising prices, it permits firms to modify the impact of increased current costs (as compared with historical costs) in the current cost income statement. The gearing adjustment is total current cost adjustments × loan capital/total capital employed.

Assume a company with the following balance sheets:

| | December 31 | |
	19X0	**19X1**
Assets	500	600
Loans	200	200
Equity	300	400

The increase in assets (100) is due entirely to the increase in the current cost of assets.

In order to maintain their 19X0 capital, stockholders would have needed an equity of 60 percent of assets at the end of 19X1, or 360. The holders of the loan capital had claim on 40 percent of the 19X0 assets, and 40 percent of the 19X1 assets amounts to 240. Since the liability is fixed at 200, there has been a transfer of 40 to stockholders. This 40 is credited to the income statement, and partly offsets the increased current cost of sales and depreciation.

The Canadian standard on accounting for changing prices also adopted a form of gearing adjustment, there called the "financing adjustment."

Criticisms of the Gearing Adjustment

The gearing (financing, leverage) adjustment differs significantly from the purchasing power gain or loss on monetary items. It is expressed in money dollars, not hypothetical units of uniform purchasing power. Critics have addressed themselves to its calculation and presentation, not to the concept.

First, since firms cannot maintain an optimal financial structure, the amount of the adjustment will fluctuate from year to year in part due to increases and decreases in borrowings. (The Canadian standard calls for the use of the average amount of loans during the period, to reduce the effect of such fluctuation within a period.)

Second, the adjustment increases income, which signals that borrowing is a benefit regardless of interest and risk factors. (Some commentators remark that the gearing adjustment compensates for higher interest rates during an inflationary period.)

Third, because the type of asset held affects the amount borrowed, the gearing adjustment reflects the composition of assets as much as the effect of changing prices.

Christine Drummond and Alan Stickler demonstrate two methods of calculating the (Canadian) financing adjustment, which received extended treatment in Appendix B, "Illustrations and Guidance," to the Canadian Standard, "Reporting the Effects of Changing Prices," (1982).[5]

BACKLOG DEPRECIATION

The FASB also chose to disregard the current cost issue of "backlog depreciation." This results from year-to-year increases in replacement cost; the current year's depreciation expense will be based on current cost, but prior years' charges turn out to have been too low to provide sufficient accumulated depreciation.

In Figure 10.1 we see a machine that cost $500 at time 0, has a five-year useful life, and no salvage. Using the straight-line method, historical cost depreciation expense will be $100 each year. Assume that the current cost of the asset increases by 10 percent annually. If depreciation expense increases at the same rate, accumulated depreciation will amount to only $610 at the end of Year 5, whereas replacement value will be $731. The area above the solid line and below the dotted line represents the backlog depreciation, a total difference of $121 between the depreciation expense charged in Years 1 through 5, and the replacement cost of $731 in Year 5.

The backlog depreciation must be charged to expense each year, in addition

Figure 10.1
Backlog Depreciation

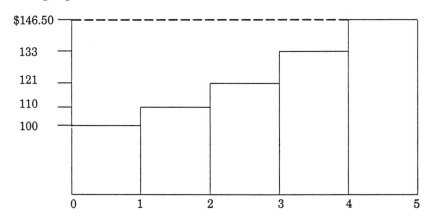

to that year's depreciation expense as calculated under FAS 89; either that or debit stockholders' equity each year for a prior period adjustment. In the former case, depreciation expense will be:

	Year 1	Year 2	Year 3	Year 4	Year 5
Regular	$100	$110	$121	$133	$146
Backlog	$ 0	$ 10	$ 21	$ 36	$ 54
Total	$100	$120	$142	$169	$200

Backlog depreciation is automatically excluded from FAS 89 current cost supplementary information. For example, the information for Years 4 and 5 would show:

	End Year 4	End Year 5
Adjusted historical cost	$665.00	$732.50
Adjusted accumulated depreciation	$532.00	$732.50
Net carrying amount	$133.00	$ 0

The carrying amount of $133.00 at the end of Year 4 is increased by restatement to Year 5 current cost ($67.50) and decreased by restatement of the depreciation ($54.00) to $146.50, charged to expense as current cost depreciation for Year 5.

FAS 89, "FINANCIAL REPORTING AND CHANGING PRICES"

This statement recommended that firms preparing U.S. dollar financial statements in accordance with GAAP disclose supplementary information on the effects of changing prices.

The minimum disclosure recommended was:

1. For the current year, the difference between the amount in the primary statements and the current cost amounts of cost of goods sold and depreciation, depletion, and amortization expense.

2. For each of the five most recent years:

   a. Net sales and other operating revenues

   b. Income from continuing operations on a current cost basis

   c. Purchasing power gain or loss on net monetary items

   d. Increase or decrease in the current cost or lower recoverable amount of inventory and property, plant, and equipment, net of inflation

   e. The aggregate foreign currency translation adjustment on a current cost basis if applicable

   f. Net assets at year-end on a current cost basis

   g. Income per common share from continuing operations on a current cost basis

   h. Cash dividends declared per common share

   i. Market price per share at year-end

3. The principal types of information used to calculate current cost, and differences between methods and useful lives used in calculating depreciation in the primary financial statements.

The information should be stated in either average-for-the-year or base period constant dollars. The index to be used is that of the U.S. Bureau of Labor Statistics Consumer Price Index for All Urban Consumers (the CPI-U). For foreign operations consolidated, either the "restate/translate" or the "translate/restate" method may be used. In the former case, an appropriate index in the foreign country would be selected for restating.

THE WORKING CAPITAL PROBLEM

The conventional wisdom is that the effects of inflation are reflected in the loss of purchasing power that occurs through holding cash. As we saw in Chapter 9, they also affect other monetary assets, such as accounts receivable, and are compensated by gains through owing money, both short- and long-term debt, in an inflationary period. This preoccupation with cash and other monetary assets and liabilities diverts attention from the order position, which also implies losses and gains. For example, accepting sales orders at fixed prices commits the firm to receive cash having a lower purchasing power at a future date; placing purchase orders at fixed prices has the opposite effect. This is an additional argument for extending the accounting threshhold to embrace commitments as well as contracts. The observation draws attention to the problem of working capital generally.

Financing a business involves raising money for fixed assets and working capital. Working capital must support a projected level of activity, represented by investments in current assets (cash, receivables, inventory, and various prepayments) to the extent that spontaneous financing through supplier (and employee) credit is not available (current liabilities.)

Monetary working capital is represented by those current assets and current liabilities that are fixed in money amount (for most people, working capital minus inventories). If monetary working capital is positive, the firm loses purchasing power through inflation; if negative, the opposite. Some firms argue that inventories should be regarded as a monetary asset, however, because competition prevents them from passing price increases on to customers. Because working capital is usually (not invariably) positive, it follows that such firms lose during inflation.

In times of inflation, working capital requirements increase, while working capital does not. Firms attempt to maintain the same gross profit percent, and are lucky if they can at least maintain the same gross profit amount. This implies a decline in activity and profitability. Suppose a firm requires $600,000 of working capital to employ twelve workers. Now let the price level increase so that it takes $60,000 per worker to maintain the same activity level. Without an increase in working capital the firm can only afford to employ ten workers.

This problem can be highlighted by means of the return on working capital (ROWC) ratio, defined as

$$\frac{\text{operating income}}{\text{sales}} \times \frac{\text{sales}}{\text{working capital}}$$

Only after the firm earns a return on working capital can there be any question of remunerating fixed capital. Given the "profitless prosperity" that characterizes the operations of many large corporations in the United States, this ratio would draw attention to working capital issues that are critical to profitability in a time of increasing prices.

This problem, to which the FASB made inconclusive reference in paras. 121–29 of FAS 33, was addressed by the United Kingdom *Statement of Standard Accounting Practice No. 16*. SSAP 16 contains a requirement for a *monetary working capital adjustment* (MWCA) to be charged or credited in arriving at restated (current cost) operating income, in contrast to the gearing adjustment, which is added to operating income to arrive at distributable income. The Accounting Standards Committee also issued *Guidance Notes on SSAP 16*, which provided detailed instructions on the composition of monetary working capital, but continuing problems were identified in an article on the subject published in 1980.[6] These observations lend force to the proposition that the issue concerns working capital as a whole, and not just "monetary" working capital.

WHY DO ACCOUNTANTS RESIST THE INEVITABLE?

Current cost (value) accounting (not necessarily expressed in constant dollars) is the state of the art. Financial reports contain information, and current cost accounting adds information about the effects of changing prices without reducing in any way the value of traditional financial statements. From a commercial point of view, it is hard to understand the reluctance of accountants to market a new and improved product. Why is this idea whose time has come so slow to impose itself on the business community?

One explanation lies in the role that financial statements play in income taxation. Assessment is based on historical cost financial statements, and the tax authorities have proved immovable on this point. There have been some concessions that go part of the way toward meeting the objection that, in times of inflation, an income tax on historical accounting profit taxes capital, but this is only a part of the story.

The LIFO Method of Inventory Valuation

In times of rising prices, LIFO tends to protect capital in a similar manner to replacement cost, by charging current cost of goods sold against revenues from sales. Yet this effect is not inevitable, and if inventory is reduced the opposite effect occurs. Further, the last price paid is not the same as the replacement price, and may at times be lower than earlier prices paid. In spite of these and other, particularly control, problems, LIFO has shielded large amounts of paper profits from the taxman's shovel.

Accelerated Depreciation

Although the methods accepted by the Internal Revenue Service result in only the historical cost of fixed assets being charged to expense, it is believed that the ability to charge higher amounts in early years of useful life permits a degree of tax deferral. This belief is questionable for two main reasons. First, accelerated depreciation is an economically justifiable way of determining the expense of holding depreciable assets in a wide range of circumstances, regardless of the income tax regulations. This is particularly true in the case of high technology industries, which must recover the cost of investment from their customers over a relatively short period. Second, firms in most industries tend to overstate useful lives, which acts as a brake on modernization and thus reduces their competitiveness.

The SEC

Another restraining factor is the SEC, which has consistently set its face against upward restatement of asset values, taking the view that such procedures contributed to the collapse of share prices in the 1930s. The SEC's insistence on partial disclosure of replacement costs and values that preceded FAS 33 made the information supplementary only, and because it was not revived when FAS 33 was suspended by FAS 89 it may be assumed that ASR 190 reflected the views of the then chief accountant, John Burton, rather than those of the commissioners. The commissioners and staff of the SEC are mainly lawyers, whose thinking can be expected to be dominated by legal rather than economic factors, and historical cost has enormous importance under statute and case law.

Standard Costing

Firms might be expected to demonstrate more interest in current cost accounting for internal management reports, and indeed, some corporations (GE, FMC in the United States, and oil companies in the United Kingdom) are known to utilize current cost data in this context. Some U.K. companies report current cost profit in addition to historical cost income, even though this is no longer required under U.K. GAAP. One factor that may have delayed this movement is the use of standard costing in the United States and the United Kingdom. Standard costs reflect replacement costs, and in their purest forms, replacement values, for direct labor and direct materials, which often make up the lion's share of total cost. Although the overhead component of standard cost rarely (if ever) reflects current cost depreciation, or the replacement cost of other components, it may be surmised that managers accept the fact that overhead cost allocations are very approximate, and believe that improving the measurement of overheads would not affect unit costs to a material extent.

Legal Liability

It is widely believed that departing from historical cost would expose public accountants to additional liability. Given the state of high anxiety under which the profession lives, this is a major constraint. Yet one must wonder to what extent such fears result from competent legal advice, because even lawyers know that prices have risen, and it is only a matter of time before the courts begin to question whether financial reports are entitled to ignore this fact. One has even seen corporate advertising that draws attention to the deceptive nature of net income in a period of inflation.

CONCLUSION

The rate of inflation in the United States declined during the 1980s, and its immediate impact on financial statements was thereby lessened. Nevertheless, its continuing impact is considerable, evidenced by the fact that the consumer price index now stands at three and one half times what it was a generation ago. A ''modest'' inflation rate of 5 percent a year results in a doubling of prices over fifteen years. Further, some prices go up (and some go down) at a faster rate than is reflected in the general price level, and markets and technology render assets obsolete and cause a sudden decline in their value that is not reflected in systematic depreciation.

Indeed, as these words are written in 1992, at a time of worldwide recession and significantly lower interest rates, we can foresee the probability of substantial price declines in the years to come. If the effects of changing prices are not reflected in internal operating and external financial statements, it is clear that managers and investors will be seriously misinformed about the profitability of their investments.

NOTES

1. ''Current Value Accounting—The State of the Art,'' *World Accounting Report*, January 1983, pp. 1–2.

2. Raymond J. Chambers, *Accounting Evaluation and Economic Behavior* (Englewood Cliffs, N.J.: Prentice-Hall, 1966); and Robert R. Sterling, *Theory of the Measurement of Enterprise Income* (Lawrence, Kans.: University Press of Kansas, 1970). The fact that Sterling was unaware of Chambers's work speaks to the insularity of accounting academics in the United States.

3. Edgar O. Edwards, ''The State of Current Value Accounting,'' *The Accounting Review*, April 1975, pp. 235–45.

4. J. C. Bonbright, *Valuation of Property* (New York: McGraw-Hill, 1937).

5. Christine S. R. Drummond and Alan D. Stickler, *Current Cost Accounting* (Toronto: Methuen, 1983), p. 117.

6. Mike Wright and Ivy Papps, ''The Use of a Monetary Working Capital Adjustment,'' *Accountancy*, September 1980, pp. 55–57.

CHAPTER 11

THE FINANCIAL STATEMENTS

What are financial statements? How do they serve the information objective of financial reporting? Are there any constraints upon their form and content? How should financial statement information be displayed? In this chapter we will attempt to answer these and other questions, which are often taken for granted by accountants.

Additional problems presented by consolidated financial statements, particularly those that consolidate or equity-account translated foreign currency statements will not be examined. The more significant of them are discussed in Chapter 16 of my *Accounting Theory*. Suffice it to say that the issues raised here apply to them also.

BASIC FINANCIAL STATEMENTS

In accounting textbooks we frequently encounter the phrase "basic (or required) financial statements." Unfortunately, not all textbooks agree on what is covered by the phrase, and the FASB does not accept the proposition that some financial statements are basic. In the view of its chairman, financial statements are what the FASB says they are. (More recently, the term "primary financial statements" has begun to appear, but the problem remains.)

If we examine the financial statements of a business enterprise anywhere in the world we will find that they consist of a balance sheet and an income statement (the latter usually called a profit and loss account). Accounting scholars in the United States agree that "basic financial statements" include a balance sheet, an income statement, and (since 1987) a statement of cash flows. They are divided on whether another basic statement is the statement of changes in stockholders' equity or the statement of retained earnings. Some commentators (including the FASB, in SFAC 5) evade the issue by referring to a "full" set of financial statements, which would include, in addition to the three enumerated above, a statement of "investments by and distributions to owners during the period." The FASB has also flown a kite for a statement of comprehensive income, to rectify its own errors in permitting some gains and losses to bypass the income statement.

Chapter 3 pointed out that the accounting model permits the business entity to be represented as an accounting entity by a balance sheet, an income statement, and a statement of other changes in assets and liabilities (than net income) during a period. This last was made explicit in APBO 19, since replaced. None of the sources consulted listed the notes to the financial statements, although many published balance sheets and income statements say explicitly that "The notes . . . form part of these statements." Perhaps it is too often assumed that everyone expects statistical tables to be annotated, yet the notes go beyond the clarification of accounting methods. Finally, a set of financial statements must include an auditor's report: The unexamined life may sometimes be worth living, but the unaudited financial statements are rarely worth reading.

It is clear that in the United States there is no prescribed form for the financial statements. SEC Rule 4–01 merely states, under "Form, Order and Terminology," that financial statements may be filed in such form and order, and should use such generally accepted terminology as will best indicate their significance and character.

THE BALANCE SHEET

Although writers have attempted to substitute the name "statement of financial position," financial statements usually call the statement in question a balance sheet. Indeed, there are real obstacles in the way of accepting a balance sheet as portraying financial position. Defining assets, liabilities, and equity as observations recognized, measured, and classified in accordance with GAAP, the U.S. balance sheet conforms to the equation: assets = liabilities + equity. This is in fact the basic double-entry equation, but Figure 3.1 suggests an alternative: capital = fixed assets + working capital. The latter form of balance sheet, which conforms to the basic propositions of corporation finance, has established itself in the United Kingdom.

The balance sheet has recovered its primacy in recent years as the FASB has begun to acknowledge an "asset and liability" view in resolving accounting questions. For example, FAS 96 and 109 specifically adopted this view for the purpose of income tax deferral. All accounting begins and ends with a balance sheet, according to Charles Sprague, in his *Philosophy of Accounts,* "the origin and terminus for every account."[1] Thus, the balance sheet provides a framework for the financial statements.

Different objectives have been identified for the balance sheet.

Resources and Obligations

The view that the purpose of the balance sheet was to display resources and obligations was examined by W.A. Paton more than sixty years ago. He pointed out that the classes "asset" and "economic resource" were not identical; some assets are not recognized by economists as resources, notably intangibles, and some economic resources (for example, human capital) only appear as assets under very restrictive conditions. Similarly, many obligations are not recognized as liabilities. Nevertheless, the tradition of official studies aimed at expounding a conceptual framework has been to rely on the concepts of resources and obligations. The FASB in SFAC 6 defined assets as probable future economic benefits, and liabilities as probable future sacrifices of economic benefits. It was then forced to admit that something more is required before such resources and obligations are reported as assets and liabilities, namely, measurement, relevance, and reliability. Further, it defined equity not in terms of obligation, but as a residual interest (assets − liabilities.)

What Is Owned and What Is Owed

Perhaps the most common definition of assets pre-APB was "things of value owned by a business." Indeed, this is probably the layperson's concept of asset, but the context of a business enterprise renders it unusable, although banks in particular would love such a restricted concept. It can be extended to cover not just property but also "valuable rights" (but again, not all such rights are included). For example, self-generated intangibles such as goodwill and brand names are not reported as assets, even though the business possesses rights in respect of them.

In FAS 19 the FASB laid down rules for reporting expenditures incurred for finding and developing oil and gas reserves. These rules provided that such expenditures should be capitalized until it is determined whether the field or well contains economically exploitable reserves; at that point, alternatives are permitted (the successful efforts and full-cost methods). It is clear that such an asset is difficult to associate with the legal concept of ownership.

Turning to liabilities, the "own versus owe" concept views equity as a residual, another indication that we are looking at a now obsolete concept of the balance sheet. Even if we restrict our attention to debt, however, the equation fails. The fact that, in practice, some legal debts (for example, pensions) are omitted may be disregarded as indicative of poor accounting, but the fact that many other obligations than debts are included in liabilities cannot be ignored. The accrual system is based on recognizing obligations before they become enforceable debts, or even commitments, and the FASB has implemented this view in a number of statements, most notably in FAS 5, "Accounting for Contingencies," but also in the statements covering accounting for income taxes, pensions, and other postemployment benefits.

Transactions in Suspense

The view that the balance sheet represents simply a step between two income statements, a list of leftovers remaining after the preparation of an income statement, is ascribed to the *matching principle* that reflects the point of view that the income statement is the prime statement of interest, because it reflects earning power. It is argued that revenues and expenses are period concepts, and assets and liabilities are not, so that the prime task of the accountant is to match expenses against revenues. Unfortunately, this does not help us to find out what goes into the balance sheet, only what goes out.

Nevertheless, this proposition that a balance sheet contains evidence of transactions, other events, and circumstances that are "in suspense" at a certain moment has considerable explanatory power. Every accountant knows that a suspense account is opened for an observation that cannot be explained, an undocumented receipt or payment, a missing piece of equipment, a claim to be investigated. It is possible to generalize this observation in respect of assets, liabilities, and owners' equity. To the extent that they possess a common feature it is that the entity has not yet finally resolved them; they are carried forward as balances in a balance sheet because future events will determine their disposition. In this respect, every balance sheet item is executory and uncertain.

The Cash Concept

Some writers, basing their views on the economist's theory of the firm, propose to restrict the balance sheet to "current cash equivalents" (Chambers) and to thus convert it into a true statement of financial position, where "financial" means "amount of cash." Some go further and argue that all parties are interested in the generation and use of cash, as a basis of predicting future net cash flows, and thus valuing the enterprise at the (discounted) present value of expected future net cash flows. Some real estate development firms have published supplementary statements that purport to disclose assets and liabilities on this basis, but real estate is an example of a wasting asset, and most analysts regard cash flow as the primary object of interest for such entities. Even so, enthusiasm for the practice waned in the late 1980s when real estate values turned sharply down.

Nevertheless, subjective evaluations are necessary even for cash flow-based asset and liability valuations. In the last analysis, the present value of the excess of future net cash flows over a normal return on the type of investment in question is just as much an asset, in this framework, as is any other source of receipts. Economists call it "subjective goodwill."

Balance Sheet Display Questions

Although balance sheets are found in every country, they differ in form and content. Even in the United States, balance sheets can look very different, quite apart from the fact that GAAP-mandated disclosures are both relatively few and ambiguous.

We have pointed out that a balance sheet may correspond to either equation: assets = liabilities + equity, or capital = fixed assets (capital) + working capital. This draws attention to the problem of classification. In the United States a classified balance sheet is one that groups separately current assets and current liabilities, thus permitting the calculation of working capital. It corresponds to the equation: current assets + noncurrent assets = current liabilities + noncurrent liabilities + equity. In many countries, however, classification means something different.

Because of the convenient assumption that accountants have solved the classification problem there has been little attention paid to this issue in the accounting literature. (Nor to the associated question of terminology, which is far from standardized.) Classification is based upon problem-solving. In the formulation of Descartes, one must divide every problem to be solved into as many parts as are necessary, and the calculation of working capital is only one such problem. There is the question of liquidity, for example, which in many countries is reflected in a definition of current assets that excludes inventory. There is also the important question of solvency, which suggests a grouping of liabilities with or without a subgroup of current liabilities. The common U.S. practice of reporting intangible assets separately from property, plant, and equipment contrasts with the practice in most other countries, of including all long-term investments in one category of fixed assets.

We also observe the same issue with respect to the ordering of assets and liabilities. Most companies in the United States attempt to order assets in accordance with diminishing liquidity and liabilities in the order in which they will be met, followed by equity. This is far from standard, however, and utilities generally follow the opposite ordering, which is almost universally the case outside the United States. Placing the most insignificant asset, cash, in first place on the balance sheet conforms with only one logic: It is the asset most likely to be understood by bankers, whose influence dominates the U.S. balance sheet in a number of ways.

On the other hand, the issue of liquidity is usually disregarded in ordering assets. A striking example is the piece of equipment that is taken out of service and put up for sale. ARB 43 prohibits reporting it as a current asset. Further, a retail store's inventory can, and often will, be turned into cash long before its receivables are collected, and what used to be referred to as cash equivalents (a term now restricted to one type of commercial paper) and are reported immediately after cash are often held for many years without being liquidated. A company in financial difficulties will often find that receivables are hard to collect, because customers no longer need retain its goodwill.

On the liabilities side, some short-term bank loans are in fact revolving credits that could not be paid off without liquidating the reporting entity. Some long-term debt may have call provisions that result in its repayment at short notice, and some may be equity in substance and carry voting rights and other privileges of ownership. Indeed, the problem of off-balance sheet financing strikes at the roots of the liquidity question, but in different ways. Some contractual arrangements may call for the firm to make payments, but others, such as bank credit facilities, may eliminate the need for de facto liquidity, as a bank credit card eliminates the need to carry cash or even have a bank checking account.

If the concept of the balance sheet as consisting of items in suspense is accepted, then an alternative system of classification is suggested, namely, one that corresponds to the stages of the investment and operating cycles. This seems to have been in the minds of the authors of ARB 43, Ch. 3A, when they defined working capital through their definitions of current assets and current liabilities:

Current Assets

Cash and other assets or resources commonly identified as those that are reasonably expected to be realized in cash or sold and consumed during the normal operating cycle of the business.

Current Liabilities

Obligations whose liquidation is reasonably expected to require the use of existing resources properly classifiable as current assets or the creation of other current liabilities. They include obligations for items that have entered the operating cycle.

The operating cycle was defined as the average time between acquiring materials or services and the final cash realization. This is, of course, a definition of the liquidity cycle, not the operating cycle. References to the ''operating cycle,'' however, imply a distinction between capacity and activity that might have been built upon by subsequent standard-setting. It would have resulted in this primary classification of assets, with liquidity as a subclassification. Similarly, it would have drawn attention to the need to display the capital of the enterprise, rather than a miscellaneous accumulation of credit balances.

The Distinction between Liabilities and Equity

We have criticized the assumption of the FASB's conceptual framework (and of other institutional studies) that equity is a residual. This assumption has been called in question by a 1990 discussion memorandum of the FASB on the distinction between liabilities and equity, resulting from the observation that many financial instruments have characteristics of both.

The basic distinction is that equity is a form of ownership, whereas liabilities are debts. The obligations differ in respect of rights and duties; a creditor can sue for payment of interest and repayment of principal on maturity, whereas a proprietor can only vote at meetings of the company. The issue of dual financial instruments arises out of the behavioral observation, that individuals may wish to be both proprietors and creditors, the former in the hope of achieving high returns, the latter in order to assure themselves of some returns. New forms of security have been issued, such as convertible debt and preferred stock, which permit individuals to achieve their different objectives with the same investment. More innovative financial instruments have offered the possibility of refining these objectives further, to achieve a predetermined return with a specified degree of risk. Income tax considerations also enter into the merging of the two categories. The discussion memorandum discusses the problem of accounting for and reporting these dual characteristic securities.

The definitions in SFAC 6, we shall not be surprised to find, are of no assistance in answering such questions. Further, the issue is overladen with the question of form versus substance. For example, many corporations have issued mandatorily redeemable preferred stock instead of debt, mainly because intercorporate dividends are sheltered from double taxation. In substance, the corporation is borrowing money that must be repaid, and the SEC has expressed concern that such securities might be excluded from debt in the measurement of solvency by calculation of debt/equity ratios. For this reason, the SEC has ruled that mandatorily redeemable preferred stock will not be combined with other elements of stockholders' equity, but reported separately therefrom. A similar problem arises in respect of common stock issues that stipulate that the issuer must reacquire the stock at the holder's election in certain circumstances.

The question that most concerned the FASB, however, was accounting for stock compensation. If the conventional distinction between liabilities and equity is maintained, then the accounting treatment of settlements under stock option and similar plans differs according to whether the payout is in stock or in cash. The discussion memorandum also discusses certain transactions with owners, such as purchases and reissuance of equity securities (treasury stock, for instance). The basic issue, however, which concerns compound financial instruments, may force the FASB to revisit the definitions in SFAC 6.

THE INCOME (EARNINGS) STATEMENT

The term ''income statement'' has been a more successful innovation than ''statement of financial position,'' even though most accountants still refer to it as the ''P&L.'' Variations include statement of earnings (or earnings statement), a terminology that conceals one of the most critical display problems. This is the distinction between net income and results from operations, which the U.S. audit report asserts are the same thing, but which everyone except the auditor knows are not.

The three burning issues in income statement presentation are:

1. The distinction between operating results and net income
2. The format of the statement
3. The items reported in the statement

Operating Results and Net Income

The interest of investors and financial analysts in *future maintainable income* results from their desire to use this figure in order to value the firm, or a share in it. Whether the algorithm is a simple "number of years purchase" or a sophisticated multiple regression analysis, the future earnings stream is a necessary element, and to the uninformed the best indicator of the future is the past. This was recognized by the FASB in SFAC 6, which provided a definition of comprehensive income as the change in equity from nonowner sources, and also mentioned another term, earnings, left undefined.

The thrust of accounting standard-setting until the 1980s was toward an all-inclusive income statement, producing the so-called clean surplus. This is now attributed to a revenue-expense approach, derived from the view that the income statement was primary, in recognition of the importance of share valuation models based on earnings per share. Because of the liquidity and solvency problems of many U.S. corporations, and in partial recognition of the impact of inflation on the balance sheet, in recent years the FASB has turned to an asset-liability approach, emphasizing balance sheet effects rather than income statement objectives. Nevertheless, the all-inclusive income statement is based on the assumption that there is no other resting place for realized revenues/gains or expired expenses/losses between the income statement and the equity section of the balance sheet. On the other hand, many items that enter into the determination of net income are exceptional in that they may not be expected to affect the firm in future years.

In the past, and even today in some other countries, this problem was resolved by means of a two- or three-part profit and loss account. The first part demonstrated the substitution of revenues for expenses and resulted in "trading" or "operating" profit. The second part adjusted this profit for exceptional and extraordinary items, prior period items, and accounting adjustments, and perhaps showed the income tax expense for the period, ending with net profit. A third section would include profit-related items such as profit-sharing bonuses, dividends, and, if not shown above, income tax expense, and the balance would be added to or deducted from stockholders' equity as the change in retained earnings.

This solution was not elegant enough for U.S. accountants, but the problem remained, and has been dealt with in a number of ways. Dividends are excluded from the income statement, and are a direct debit to retained earnings; the basic statements are therefore articulated on not one figure but two (net income and distributions to owners). The income statement itself is divided into two sections, the first resulting in income from continuing operations. This figure begins the second, which contains certain obviously nonrecurring items on an after-tax basis (results of discontinued operations; extraordinary items; cumulative effect of change in accounting principle) resulting in net income. Prior period adjustments have been virtually defined out of existence; the rare cases of error correction and certain tax adjustments are taken directly to retained earnings, bypassing the income statement altogether. It is important to note, however, that many true prior period items are normally reported as part of current income statement items, either above or below income from continuing operations. Similarly, because of a narrow definition of extraordinary items in APBO 30 (and apart from a few special cases subsequently provided for) many nonrecurring items are reported as parts of revenues and expenses. On the other hand, the FASB requires some changes in accounting principles resulting from new standards to be reported like prior period adjustments. Finally, there is no clear distinction between revenues and gains, and expenses and losses, so that this potential means of distinguishing nonoperating results is not being used.

This confused picture has been altered for the worse by FASB statements of accounting standards that prescribe certain transactions, other events, and circumstances besides contributions from and distributions to owners to bypass the income statement. These include unrealized losses (and in some cases gains) on noncurrent portfolios of marketable equity securities, effects of translating foreign operations into U.S. dollars and other currencies, and one case in pension accounting, which are reported as changes in stockholders' equity. Proposed rules requiring financial institutions to mark securities to market also contain provision for the resulting gains and losses to go directly to equity.

The FASB's contribution to the resolution of this problem came in SFAC 5, where it was proposed that earnings might replace net income, differing by excluding the cumulative effect of a change in accounting principle. Earnings would become comprehensive income through a new statement that would sweep up such changes, prior period adjustments, and the other items that are now taken directly to stockholders' equity. Not the least of the concealed uses of this statement would be to provide a resting place for gains and losses resulting from accounting for the effects of changing prices which, as pointed out in Chapters 9 and 10, have provided accountants with an insoluble reporting problem. It is interesting to see that we are slowly, painfully, and expensively returning to the old idea of a two- or three-part profit and loss account. The change would be more rapid if accountants were not obsessed with promulgated accounting standards.

Income Statement Formats

The debit/credit form of income statement has disappeared, and the report form is universal. This is a function of the influence of printers, who abhor empty space on the pages of annual reports. Because the typical firm will have many income statement debits and few credits, their objections affect this statement in particular. It has led to the erroneous assumption on the part of textbook writers, that an income summary is somehow not the same as an income statement.

The conventional distinction between single- and multistep formats has become obsolete because of the GAAP treatment of discontinued operations, extraordinary items, and cumulative effect of a change in accounting principle. In effect, a minimum of two steps is always required if any of these three items is present. Some corporations report gross margin as sales minus cost of goods sold, but even others break at income from continuing operations before tax, in order to highlight income tax expense. One seeks but does not find any distinction between gains and revenues other than sales, or between losses and nonoperating expenses. The treatment of interest and other financing expenses is also variable.

Perhaps more serious for the analysis of results is the frequency with which bastard classifications are found. It is rare to find expenses listed purely by nature, but very common to find "cost of goods sold" followed by "interest expense" and even "depreciation." The problem results in part from the capitalization of expenses in inventory, and sometimes in own manufacture of fixed assets. German accountants solve this problem by means of a value-added statement. In this form of income statement, expenditures are reported unaffected by the amounts capitalized in inventories. General Electric experimented with a similar format some years ago, but gave it up, possibly because the public was not yet ready for such an innovation. A simplified form is given in Table 11.1.

Table 11.1
Value-Added Form of Income Statement

Sales revenues

+ or − Net change in inventories

+ Production of own equipment

= Total output

− Purchases of goods and services

= Total value-added

− Other expenditures (analyzed by type)

= Net income

Income Statement Items

APBO 30 prescribes the following items:

Income from continuing operations before income taxes

Provision for income taxes

Income from continuing operations

Income/loss from discontinued operations

Extraordinary items

Effect of change in accounting principle

Net income

APBO 15 requires certain earnings per share data to be shown on the face of the income statement. In addition, APBO 20 states that, in the event of a change in accounting principle, earnings per share computed on a pro forma basis will be shown on the face of the income statements for all periods presented as if the newly adopted accounting principle had been applied. Neither specifies an income statement *item*, and earnings per share need not be reported for nonpublic companies. Thus, with the exception of APBO 30 disclosures, firms have complete discretion regarding which items they will show in the income statement.

A great deal of income statement information is required by GAAP, but not necessarily in the income statement. Recall that the elements of the income statement are defined in SFAC 6, and statements of financial accounting concepts are not GAAP. Such items as sales revenues, income from other sources, gains, losses, cost of goods sold, depreciation expense, research and development expenditure expenses during a period, interest expense, pension cost, and many more may be disclosed in the notes to the financial statements. This is an additional reason for regarding notes as part of the basic statements. It appears as though the prime influence on the conventional content of the income statement is the corporate income tax return; disclosure in the statement correlates highly with the Internal Revenue Service Form 1120. Nevertheless, variability is as striking here as in the balance sheet.

THE STATEMENT OF CASH FLOWS

During the period 1860–1960 the statement of changes in financial position (SCFP) under various names became accepted as a third basic financial statement, and APBO 19 required one whenever financial statements that purported to be in accordance with GAAP were presented. Its functions were clearly specified by APBO 19: to summarize financing and investing activities, and to complete the disclosure of changes in financial position during the period. From the latter viewpoint, one change is disclosed in the income statement, namely, the increase or decrease of net assets due to net income or loss, and another, distributions to owners, in a statement of retained earnings. Other significant changes, however, such as sales and purchases of assets, are difficult to ascertain from a comparison of balance sheets.

Dissatisfaction with the SCFP centered on both concept and readability:

1. It was a "new" statement, and strange to some financial statement users; textbook writers relegated it to an inferior position in their works.

2. It was generally presented using a reconciliation format, rather than a direct "sources and uses of funds" format, which some users found confusing.

3. Variability of form and content made comparative use difficult.

4. Many firms, following the emphasis of APBO 19, highlighted change

in working capital, whereas many critics argued that change in cash was more important.

5. Inclusion of other events and circumstances, as well as transactions, obscured the cash effects of operations, financing, and investing.

6. A number of unresolved technical issues, themselves a function of the constantly changing business environment, seemed to prevent any movement toward a standard form of SCFP.

In the 1970s, however, the SCFP became the subject of particular criticisms arising out of a new preoccupation with cash flows. The Trueblood report, which became the foundation for SFAC 1, "Objectives of Financial Reporting by Business Enterprises," postulated that financial statements should assist users in assessing future net cash flows in terms of amount, timing, and uncertainty. Although it was acknowledged that accruals and deferrals were helpful, they nevertheless conflicted with the ideology of cash flows. Voices emanating from financial markets called for cash flow statements. Analysts trained as economists think in terms of cash flows, and regard all past expenditures as sunk costs. Bankers understand only cash (we have noted their influence on the classification of assets) and believe that the regularities that underlie their own cash flows must also characterize those of business enterprises generally. All of these critics believed that knowledge of past cash flows would help them to predict future cash flows.

One of the interesting features of this period was a study of the W. T. Grant Company, a bankrupt retail firm, which showed that its cash flows from operations declined and became negative long before its working capital decreased.[2] From this one observation it was inferred that cash flow information is more useful than working capital change information! The case was influential in moving the FASB toward a cash flow statement, as the 1980 discussion memorandum, "Reporting Funds Flows, Liquidity, and Financial Flexibility," revealed. In 1981 the Financial Executives Institute urged its members to emphasize cash flows in the SCFP, but reaffirmed its view that the SCFP should continue to be a required financial statement. This recommendation resulted in many corporations changing from the working capital to the cash basis during the 1980s, and there was a considerable move toward standardizing the form of the SCFP during this period. FAS 95, effectively replacing the SCFP with the SCF, was issued in 1987, by which time it was probably no longer necessary.

Defects of FAS 95

FAS 95 permits financial statement preparers to choose between the direct and the indirect (reconciliation) formats. The FASB explained this choice on the grounds that corporations did not collect cash flow information in the form that the direct method requires. This was a variant on one of the three classical responses of accountants to suggestions that they improve financial statements: The information is not available, or would prove too costly to obtain, or would give competitors an unfair advantage. Every business prepares a cash budget, which specifies planned receipts and disbursements in great detail, and which is converted from a planned to an actual basis as the fiscal year unfolds. By the end of the year it is a statement of actual receipts and payments, and the proposition that the items in this statement cannot be rearranged in the form laid down by FAS 95 is clearly not supportable. The reason why the great majority of firms are using the reconciliation format for the SCF is probably the same as the reason why they used it for the SCFP. It shows how a profit or a loss during a period relates to changes in the cash balance at the end, and why a profit does not necessarily cause an increase in cash, or a loss a decrease. FAS 95 requires a schedule showing a reconciliation between net income and cash from operations to be provided even if the direct method is used, and firms may see little advantage therefore in this method.

FAS 95 requires cash flows to be classified into operating, investing, and financing. (A fourth category reveals the effects of changes in foreign exchange rates on foreign currencies consolidated.) This format became popular during the 1980s, but is not the only possible scheme. Another classifies cash inflows into *external* and *internal* (the French call the latter *autofinancement*, which in English sounds too much like a car loan) and outflows into fixed assets and working capital. Not only does this avoid Byzantine argument about what is or is not operating, which FAS 95 had to define as anything except investing and financing, but it reports the proceeds of a sale of fixed assets as finance and not negative investment. Of course, economists prefer the latter approach, because it mirrors the macroeconomic concept "net investment."

FAS 95 requires the net change in cash to be designated "for the period" and not "of the period." It is deceptive to report receipts from accounts receivable, for example, whether directly or indirectly, as cash from operations during the period covered by the SCF. Some of the receipts derive from the operations of the prior period, and some of the operations of the period have not provided any cash receipts. This observation applies to every item in the SCF, and if the stated objective is correct—to assist users in predicting future cash flows—then failure to make them aware of this is a serious defect.

The Problem of Cash Flows

One of the arguments of the promoters of the SCF was that cash is an empirical observation, whereas some of the components of working capital are based on subjective estimates. Thus, the problems presented by the SCFP could be avoided in a SCF. Cash was defined by FAS 95 to include cash on hand, or on demand at a financial institution, or highly liquid investments that have original maturities of three months or less and are therefore not subject to price fluctuations arising from interest rate changes.

The introduction of a statement of cash flows in the United States in 1987 was preceded by Canada and New Zealand, and followed by South Africa, the United Kingdom, the Republic of Ireland, and other countries. The International Accounting Standards Committee also started to formulate an international accounting standard on the subject. Comparison of these standards and proposed standards reveals that what appeared to be unequivocal in fact contained a large number of ambiguities. A 1991 study examining the conceptual and practical differences revealed that these concerned:

1. *Applicability.* Different entities were affected.

2. *Status.* The SCF is not always a financial statement.

3. *Objective.* Sometimes cash flows, sometimes reconciliation of change in cash with net or operating income (direct versus indirect method).

4. *Concept of cash and cash equivalents.* Treatment of bank overdrafts, in particular. This point was confirmed in a 1992 study.[3]

5. *Classification.* What constitutes operating? financing? investing? Interest is a critical problem.

6. *Treatment of income taxes.* To allocate or not to allocate?

7. *Treatment of leases.* Is the principal component of the payment financing or investing?

8. *Disclosures required.*[4]

Among the omissions the authors mention government subsidies, probably a result of an ideological denial of the role of the firm as welfare recipient.

We can accept the proposition that a statement of cash flows helps to understand past cash flows, and to depict the relationship between them and past net income or loss. Apart from the case of institutions whose operations imply a certain regularity of cash flows, such as banks, there is no evidence that past cash flows aid in the assessment of future cash flows. Further, the view that the quality of earnings (the reliability of the net income figure) can be measured by the extent to which it correlates with operating cash flows is too simplistic to be useful for any but the most superficial analysis. A growth firm that must extend credit can have a permanent operating cash flow problem, whereas a firm that is on the road to bankruptcy and is liquidating assets can have a positive cash flow from operations.

THE FOOTNOTES

Even though the notes are parts of the financial statements, and many GAAP-mandated disclosures appear there, surprisingly little has been written on the subject of what in fact belongs. Analysis of their contents reveals that they contain three kinds of information:

1. Mandated disclosures, such as research and development expenditures, contingent liabilities, and interest and taxation payments that are not shown on the statement of cash flows. Many corporations, however, omit some GAAP-mandated disclosures altogether.

2. Schedules and exhibits that might have been presented in the balance sheet or income statement, or as separate statements, but have been included in the notes instead. Examples are the analysis of inventories, details of property, plant, and equipment, and the summary financial statements of the finance subsidiaries of manufacturing firms. The statement of changes in financial position started life in the notes before being given its own separate page in the report.

3. Explanations of items appearing in the balance sheet and income statement. The first footnote is usually the description of accounting policies for items where GAAP allows alternatives, although one often finds comments on matters where no alternative is permitted, such as research and development costs and foreign currency translation. Methods of asset valuation, impact of leases on future years, and the effects of stock options, pensions, and other employee benefit arrangements commonly call forth detailed notes.

Supplementary financial statements (not to be confused with SEC-required supplementary schedules) such as segment reporting under FAS 14, and the data on the effects of changing prices formerly published under FAS 33, may be found among the footnotes, but the FASB required the reporting of oil and gas reserves under FAS 19 and 25 outside the footnotes. The FASB has indicated that much of the qualitative information on risk and uncertainty that analysts are calling for will be presented in the footnotes.

Regrettably, the footnotes have become a substitute for disclosure in the body of the balance sheet or income statement, which avoids the necessity of making an accounting decision. For example, footnoting the market value of investments that are carried in the balance sheet at cost obviously does not assist the balance sheet to perform its functions. The LIFO method of inventory valuation produces surprising and often unforeseen effects on both balance sheet and income statement, which can sometimes be discovered from data provided in the footnotes. (The U.S. income tax LIFO regulations prohibit the use of another inventory method on the income statement, but not on the balance sheet; accountants have shown remarkably little ingenuity in circumventing these rules, compared to their tax avoidance skills.)

It is time for the role and scope of the footnotes to be reexamined, and a degree of standard practice introduced. Their number and size have increased in recent years, partly because of GAAP and partly because of a perceived need for "due diligence" protection. Most footnotes fail to provide the intended information, because the complexities of business practices cannot be contained in a short note, and a long one will go unread. Table 11.2, taken from SFAC 5, is indicative of the FASB's longstanding failure to grasp this issue and deal with it satisfactorily.

CONCLUSION

In this chapter we have remarked on the chaotic state of current practice with respect to the financial statements. In spite of the vast amount of GAAP promulgated by the FASB, little or nothing has been done to confront this problem, and what has been done has often aggravated it. The abstract models presented in accounting textbooks, while no doubt useful tools for introductory studies, fail to prepare the student to handle the complexities of real life.

The problem is confounded by the differences between financial statements filed with the SEC, and those contained in published annual reports. In principle, all the disclosure requirements of Regulation S-X, other than the so-called supplementary schedules, should be included in the annual report. These include many not mandated by GAAP.[5] Because of the increase in the amount of disclosure mandated both by the SEC and the FASB, annual reports have tended to omit some material, becoming "summary annual reports." Several years ago, General Motors challenged the SEC to rule on this practice, and the SEC made it known that, providing the reports indicated where the omitted matter could be found (the 10-K form) and providing the auditor was prepared to report that the statements fairly present in accordance with GAAP, there was no objection. Thus, in recent years we have seen a slight reduction in the number of pages of the typical annual report, and a major dilution of the scope of GAAP.

NOTES

1. Charles E. Sprague, *The Philosophy of Accounts* (New York: The Ronald Press, 1907).

2. James A. Largay and Clyde P. Stickney, "Cash Flows, Ratio Analysis and the W. T. Grant Company Bankruptcy," *Financial Analysts Journal*, August 1980, pp. 51–54.

3. R. S. Olusegun-Wallace and Paul A. Collier, "The "Cash" in Cash Flow Statements: A Multi-Country Comparison," *Accounting Horizons*, December 1991, pp. 44–52.

4. Herve Stolowy and Sylvie Walser-Prochazka, *The American Influence in Accounting: Myth or Reality? The Statement of Cash Flows Example* (Paris: Ernst & Young, 1991).

5. Robert S. Kay and D. Gerald Searfoss, eds. *Deloitte and Touche Professors Handbook* (Boston: Warren, Gorham & Lamont, 1989), 4–4.

Table 11.2
Types of Information

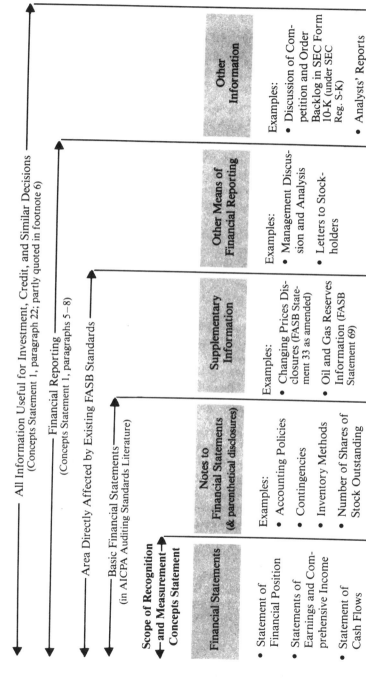

—— All Information Useful for Investment, Credit, and Similar Decisions ——
(Concepts Statement 1, paragraph 22; partly quoted in footnote 6)

—— Financial Reporting ——
(Concepts Statement 1, paragraphs 5–8)

—— Area Directly Affected by Existing FASB Standards ——

—— Basic Financial Statements ——
(in AICPA Auditing Standards Literature)

Scope of Recognition and Measurement Concepts Statement

Financial Statements	Notes to Financial Statements (& parenthetical disclosures)	Supplementary Information	Other Means of Financial Reporting	Other Information
• Statement of Financial Position • Statements of Earnings and Comprehensive Income • Statement of Cash Flows • Statement of Investments by and Distributions to Owners	Examples: • Accounting Policies • Contingencies • Inventory Methods • Number of Shares of Stock Outstanding • Alternative Measures (market values of items carried at historical cost)	Examples: • Changing Prices Disclosures (FASB Statement 33 as amended) • Oil and Gas Reserves Information (FASB Statement 69)	Examples: • Management Discussion and Analysis • Letters to Stockholders	Examples: • Discussion of Competition and Order Backlog in SEC Form 10-K (under SEC Reg. S-K) • Analysts' Reports • Economic Statistics • News Articles about Company

Source: FASB *Statement of Financial Accounting Concepts No. 5.*

CHAPTER 12

IMPROVING THE FINANCIAL STATEMENTS

The previous chapter drew attention to some of the more obvious deficiencies in the form and content of published financial statements. Before proceeding to discuss possible improvements, it is advisable to explain what is covered by this phrase. A complete set of financial statements consists of a balance sheet, an income statement, a statement of cash flows, footnotes, and an audit report. Supplementary statements, such as a statement of retained earnings, or of changes in stockholders' equity, or a segment report, simply analyze financial statement information. They can be viewed as unnumbered footnotes that have been given their own separate pages.

WHY STANDARDIZE FINANCIAL STATEMENTS?

It should not be necessary to argue the case for uniformity of financial statements. SFAC 2 adopts representational faithfulness, comparability, and consistency as primary qualitative characteristics of accounting information. This implies that phenomena common to all entities should be reported the same way. Indeed, the standard-setting function exemplified by the FASB assumes that variability should be eliminated and alternatives admitted only when justified by real differences of transaction, other event, or circumstance.

Yet the work of the FASB and its predecessors demonstrates no move toward uniformity of presentation. Even where display is prescribed, as in FAS 95 for the statement of cash flows, alternatives exist. More common are standards such as APBO 17 (Intangible Assets) that contain not one word about how, when, or where information should be displayed. Indeed, the issue of display, which featured prominently in the FASB's proposals for a conceptual framework, has been consistently avoided. One can have sympathy with the FASB, given the propensity of accountants to acknowledge their own genius. Accounting textbook writers have, for more than a generation, tried to persuade practitioners to substitute "Statement of Financial Position" for the more usual and easily understood "Balance Sheet" and one can imagine the conflicts that standardization of display will engender! It has even been alleged that public accountants oppose uniformity because of a fear that it will reduce their fee-earning capacity, a viewpoint that conflicts sharply with the prevailing view that the financial statements are assertions of management.

Nevertheless, the time for decision has arrived. The global marketplace is upon us, with worldwide, twenty-four-hour-a-day trading of stocks and bonds. The countries of the European Community have adopted uniform financial statements in their legislation implementing the EC's Fourth Directive. True, the recognition and measurement standards of the EC countries differ widely, but differences of form have been minimized, to the apparent satisfaction of financial analysts.

Again, the growth of computerized databases is an irresistible force leading to uniformity of presentation. In his authoritative study of financial statement analysis, George Foster points out that a database may exclude data sought for some or all firms, classify financial statement information inconsistently across firms, and even contain errors that are, in part at least, a function of the need for data processing clerks to make judgments.[1] The existence of on-line databases provides analysts with the opportunity to both access and modify financial statements; they may wish to eliminate goodwill from assets, for example, or adjust income statement items for the effects of inflation. The SEC's EDGAR System of electronic filing will permit users to draw off account and other data and format their own financial aggregations. These modifications are enormously facilitated by uniformity of financial statements.

Finally, new developments in business, resulting from changing social, economic, and political conditions, lead inexorably to the need for uniform financial statements. The growth of countertrade, which now accounts for the greater part of the commercial exchanges in the world, cannot be permitted to inspire differential reporting practices. The ubiquity of the joint venture, particularly in former communist countries, poses a need for financial statements that are uniform among countries, aggravated when more than one foreign partner is involved. At least one should not have to deal with a variety of forms from the same country. Political changes associated with the expansion of capitalism necessarily rely on the creation of economic business statistics derived from financial reports, and on the use of financial statements as a basis for income and other forms of taxation. The global economy is increasingly dominated by large transnational enterprises that are able to transcend the idiosyncracies of nations.

It should be obvious from the evidence in Chapter 11, or indeed, from any attempt to use U.S. financial statements, that they demonstrate a degree of nonuniformity that constitutes a real barrier to the financial analyst, and a significant cost factor in the accounting and auditing process. Indeed, this variability may contribute to the credibility problem and the growth of litigation based on alleged audit failure.

RECENT DEVELOPMENTS IN THE UNITED KINGDOM

Whereas the U.K. legislation implementing the European Community's Fourth Directive has led to a significant standardization of U.K. balance sheets, profit and loss accounts and income statements there is still wide variability. For this reason, and presumably as a step toward uniformity, the Accounting Standards Board issued two exposure drafts in December 1991.

Statement of Principles, Chapter 6, "Presentation of Financial Information" stated that financial statements comprise "primary financial statements" and supporting notes, and "in some cases, supplementary information." Primary financial statements consist of:

—a profit and loss account

—a statement of total recognized gains and losses (explained below)

—a balance sheet

—a cash flow statement

This was followed by an inconclusive philosophical discussion, adequately represented by the following quotation: "The decision as to the degree of aggregation will depend on the extent to which the benefit of disclosing is offset by the cost . . . of preparing and disclosing . . . [and] of using more detailed information."

Financial Reporting Exposure Draft No. 1, "The Structure of Financial Statements—Reporting of Financial Performance" (FRED 1) appears to be intended to give U.K. preparers guidance similar to that contained in APBO 30. Its objective was to move from a simple performance indicator (the bottom line) to highlighting a range of important components of financial performance. As a minimum, the profit and loss account should show the analysis of turnover (sales), exceptional items, and operating profit, together with comparative figures for the same items. Statutorily required data between turnover and operating profit should be given in a note.

Because under the companies acts only realized gains and losses may be included in the profit and loss account, FRED 1 calls for "an additional primary financial statement of financial performance" to include all gains and losses recognized in the period, such as holding gains and losses resulting from revaluations. This parallels the FASB's intention to distinguish earnings from comprehensive income, albeit without the clear basis for the distinction arising out of the U.K. legal system.

FRED 1 also calls for reporting separately the results of discontinued opera tions, here defined in more commercial and less abstract terms than in APBO 30. Thus, the sequence of disclosure is to be:

Results of continuing operations, including those of acquisitions during the period

Results of discontinued operations

Exceptional transactions and events, distinguishing those arising out of discontinued operations "analyzed on the face of the profit and loss account"

Extraordinary items

Profit for the period

"Material profit or loss on sale or termination of an operation should always be shown on the face of the profit and loss account." Apart from these meager instructions nothing more was said. An example of a complete profit and loss account was illustrated "for guidance" and explicitly stated not to form part of FRED 1. Although there is no joy to be obtained from a study of this document, it does at least demonstrate a recognition of the problem with which this chapter is concerned.

STANDARDIZATION OF FORM

Two alternative approaches to uniformity, representing the polarity of the subject, will be explored in this chapter. One essentially accepts the prevailing method of promulgating GAAP, with its gaps and inconsistencies, but attempts to standardize the form of the financial statements. The other is a comprehensive proposal for a new approach to establishing accounting standards.

In a 1969 article I presented some ideas for two new financial statements; one provided a model for what later became the statement of cash flows, the other, for the SEC-mandated supplementary information on reserve recognition accounting by the petroleum industry.[2] The principal innovation discussed, however, has never received attention.

I argued that a substantial degree of uniformity in financial statement presentation was both desirable and feasible. Financial reporting essentially tracked the liquidity cycle of the firm (often erroneously referred to as the operating cycle in the accounting literature), and this cycle was common to all business enterprises. Thus, many countries have adopted standard forms of balance sheet, income statement, and statement of cash flows that are used by all reporting entities. Unfortunately, these forms differ from country to country, but such differences are gradually being eliminated both through international cooperation and through the efforts of transnational corporations.

The key assumption made in my 1969 article was that the items in the financial statements are part of the same system. A system is an object viewed as a set of interrelated parts; in a closed system, such as an accounting system, virtually all parts and relationships are specified. As pointed out in previous chapters, many critics of accounting, and the FASB, seem to have in mind an open system of financial reporting, in which some relationships are left undefined. This does not presuppose that the closed system underlying the financial statements must be jettisoned, however; indeed, the control aspects of double-entry bookkeeping are so important that it is extremely difficult to believe that managers will agree to be deprived of it.

An integrated financial statement would in effect combine the income statement, statement of cash flows, and balance sheet. This statement, a simplified version of which is illustrated in Table 12.1, was derived from a statement that I developed when in practice forty years ago. A client was very confused when the income statement showed a profit, but there was no money in the bank, or reported a loss at a time when the bank balance increased. By integrating these observations I discovered a means of responding to the inevitable questions.

The one-piece financial statement was designed to serve four main functions:

1. To demonstrate the relationship between value flows represented in the income statement, and their state at a point in time, represented in the balance sheet. The effect of changes in assets and liabilities on the cash balance is included as one item in the financial statement, but a separate schedule of cash flows is illustrated. A separate statement of changes in stockholders' equity is also desirable.

2. To integrate the funds (cash) flow statement. There is evidence that this relatively new financial statement has presented analysts with some difficulties; integration is designed to clarify its function. On this point, my original proposal contemplated a funds flow statement similar to a statement of changes in financial position—cash basis, that is, one prepared using all significant financial events, cash or noncash. The narrow cash flow emphasis of the new statement detracts from its informational content.

3. To facilitate comparisons of financial ratios, whether vertical, horizontal, or against predetermined standards.

4. To solve the problem of the "clean surplus" in the manner advocated at the time by the AICPA (but since disavowed by the FASB).

Note that the data in Table 12.1, provided to add a note of realism to the illustration, also make use of the concept of the statistically significant digit. If an income statement reports sales of $100,481 and depreciation expense of $5,142 in arriving at net income of $9,493, and depreciation is a crude (although necessary) estimate, it is clear that the result is not meaningful beyond, at best, the thousands figure. Many financial statements now make use of this concept, at least in form.

The following comments will also aid in the comprehension of Table 12.1.

Table 12.1
Combination Income Statement, Statement of Cash Flows, and Balance Sheet

All figures in U.S. $ Millions.

FOR THE YEAR ENDED ..... AND AT ......

#	Item	Value
1	Sales of goods & services	1000
2	Distribution costs	50
3	Net proceeds of sales	950
4	Manufacturing cost of sales	800
5	Gross margin	150
6	Administration costs	14
7	Income from operations	136
8	Nonoperating income	4
9	Nonoperating expenses	3
10	Income before interest and taxes	137
11	Interest expense	2
12	Income before taxes	135
13	Income tax expense	35
14	Net income	100
15	Prior years' items	2
16	Available for distribution	102
17	Dividends	52
18	Retained for the year	50
19	Cash flow (see schedule)	-41
20	Cash and cash equivalents	9
21	Accounts receivable	271
22	Liquid assets	280
23	Inventories	330
24	Current assets	610
25	Fixed assets in use - net	97
26	Total operating assets	707
27	Long-term investments	5
28	Fixed assets not in use	0
29	Total assets	712
30	Current liabilities	204
31	Medium-term liabilities	40
32	Long-term liabilities	0
33	Total liabilities	244
34	Stockholders' equity	468
35	Total equities	712

Statement of Cash Flows

#	Item	Value
	From operations:	
36	Accounts receivable	30
37	Inventories	-40
38	Accounts payable	2
39	Other accruals	2
40	Depreciation, amortization	17
41	Total from operations	11
	From investing:	
42	Equipment sales	5
43	Other asset sales	0
44	Equipment purchases	-47
45	Other asset purchases	0
46	Total from investing	-42
	From financing:	
47	Medium-term liabilities	8
48	Long-term liabilities	-18
49	Stockholders' equity	0
50	Total from financing	-10
51	Net cash flow	-41
	Beginning cash balance	102
	Dividends	-52
	Net cash flow	-41
	Ending cash balance	9

Selection of Items

The data set consists of the statements specified in the heading. Although a separate statement of cash flows has been provided, this could also be integrated into the body of the combined statement, instead of being inserted through a single number. The items selected for display can be found in diverse sets of financial statements, and are believed to be universal. Costs are classified by function, which is presumably the preferred method of large corporations; a classification by nature for small firms is easily accommodated. A classified balance sheet is assumed. Regrettably, because some U.S. corporations list their assets and liabilities in order of increasing liquidity and reverse order of maturity (as do most foreign corporations), an alternative model would be required for them.

Conformity with GAAP

The form is believed not to conflict with any existing GAAP. "Income from operations" can be interpreted to mean "continuing" operations, and results of discontinued operations would be included in "nonoperating income" or "nonoperating expense," together with extraordinary items and the cumulative effect of a change in accounting principle. Details would be appropriately provided in the footnotes.

Treatment of Dividends

The conventional treatment of dividends is anomalous; they are the only direct debit to retained earnings permitted under GAAP (apart from expenses, gains, and losses arising out of the issue, repurchase, and redemption of stock). The combined statement maintains this anomaly, and extends it to the statement of cash flows. For this reason, dividends do not appear in the SCF, being deducted directly from the income retention for the year. The treatment of prior year items, as a modification of net income, is consistent with APBO 30 and FAS 16.

Numbering

The practice of numbering the items in financial statements is found in many other countries. A uniform alphanumeric system was adopted by EC countries following the provisions of the Fourth Directive. This is not only an aid to comparability; it also facilitates financial statement preparation and reduces the cost of, and probability of error in, the production of data sources. Further, it can be of major assistance in calculating financial numbers, including ratios, in a consistent manner, as we shall now demonstrate, using the numbers in Table 12.1. (To calculate *working capital*, deduct line 30 from line 24.)

Liquidity ratios. Current ratio $= {}^{24}\!/\!{}_{30}$. Acid-test ratio $= {}^{22}\!/\!{}_{30}$.

Solvency ratios. Debt/equity ratio $= {}^{33}\!/\!{}_{34}$. Times interest earned $= {}^{10}\!/\!{}_{11}$.

Profitability ratios. Gross margin $= 5 \times {}^{100}\!/\!{}_{1}$. Net margin $= 14 \times {}^{100}\!/\!{}_{1}$. Return on total assets $= 14 \times {}^{100}\!/\!{}_{29}$. Effective tax rate $= 13 \times {}^{100}\!/\!{}_{12}$.

Turnover ratios. Inventory $= {}^{4}\!/\!{}_{23}$. Any other asset, divide into 1.

Not illustrated, but implicit, is the ability to expand the numbering system to three or more places. For example, a company operating in different markets could use the numerals 1.1 through 1.9 for subclasses of sales. Fixed assets in use could be analyzed by using 25.1 for land, 25.2 for buildings, and so on, and classes 25.6 through 25.9 for depreciation, depletion, and amortization. (If the numbers 1 through 9 are replaced by 01 through 09, the decimal point can be omitted.)

Financial analysts would be particularly appreciative of this convenience. They are believed to prefer that annual reports not present financial ratios, ostensibly because they see this as one of their functions, but providing them with a simple numerical framework of this kind would certainly be an enormous benefit.

THE FRENCH STANDARDIZED ACCOUNTING PLAN

One alternative, then, is to retain the tattered patchwork of promulgated and nonpromulgated GAAP, and simply standardize the form and content of the financial statements. The other, more radical, solution is along the lines of the uniform chart of accounts, the nature and function of which was explained in Chapter 3. Because the emphasis here is on practice rather than theory, we shall continue the discussion with reference to the French *Plan Comptable Général* (standardized accounting plan). This has had great influence on accounting and financial reporting in a number of European, African, and Asian countries, and has certainly demonstrated a capacity to handle the demands that users place on financial reports.[3]

The original idea for a standardized national accounting system came from a German accountant, Eugen Schmalenbach, and the National Socialist government introduced a uniform chart of accounts in the 1930s to aid its control over the economy. (The mandatory feature was eliminated after World War II, when the German economy was liberated from many wartime controls; however, the German chart is still in widespread use there, on a voluntary basis.) The Germans occupied France from 1942 through 1944, and required French industrial firms working to support the German war machine to use the same chart.

After the liberation of Paris in August 1944, a number of measures were taken by the interim government to assist reconstruction and eventually economic development. One of them consisted of nationalization of many industries: coal mining, banking, insurance, gas and electricity, air transportation, and even specific companies, such as Renault automobiles, which had collaborated with the Germans. Another was the adoption of centralized economic planning; it should be recalled that both socialists and communists were influential members of the interim government. Economic statistics were in short supply, and in order to improve those coming from the business sector a *Commission de Normalization de Comptabilies* (Accounting Standards Commission) was established. The commission started with the 1942 chart of accounts that the Vichy government had introduced on orders from the German occupier, but considerable modifications were made by the practitioners and textbook writers who cooperated in the task of producing a new chart, published in 1947.

THE 1947 PLAN COMPTABLE GENERAL

The first order of business was to produce a chart of accounts that would be imposed on very large industrial undertakings, all defense contractors, and the nationalized industries. In spite of this, the 1947 plan was so flexible that many accountants welcomed its usefulness; more than 45,000 copies of the official government-printed edition were sold, together with many more privately printed editions. Even small firms applied it, on a voluntary basis, and it eventually established itself throughout the economy.

Besides its logical structure, what lay behind this rapid acceptance of what was, in fact, a new approach to accounting and financial reporting? The plan consisted of a comprehensive set of accounting principles and practices; a conceptual framework together with most of its potential applications. It provided:

1. A set of definitions of financial and cost accounting terms.

2. A classified and decimally coded list of accounts, including control and subsidiary accounts and contra accounts.

3. A description of the procedures whereby transactions, other events, and circumstances were to be entered in these accounts, using the principles of double-entry bookkeeping (which account to debit, and which to credit).

4. Valuation rules for assets and liabilities, including depreciation, accruals and deferrals, and adjusting and reversing entries.

5. A section containing cost accounts, distinguishing between fixed and variable costs, with principles of cost ascertainment and the use of the perpetual inventory method.

6. Model financial statements (balance sheet and two-part profit and loss account).

7. A separate section for statistical data.

Because of this comprehensive approach the plan was able to serve its primary purposes of aiding business managers, facilitating interfirm comparisons, and providing national income statistics for the business sector. In addition, it was quickly adopted by instructors in high schools and colleges, who discovered that the plan simplified the task of teaching accounting.

Between 1947 and 1957 some eighty adaptations of the plan were prepared for particular trades and industries, by committees of accountants and managers from those industries. This permitted the French government to extend the mandatory use of the plan to all but the smallest firms in these industries, and the process still continues.

BASIC STRUCTURE OF THE FRENCH PLAN

The 1947 plan adopted a basic stucture resembling the international chart of accounts demonstrated in Chapter 3 (not surprising since they had a common origin).

Class 1. Capital accounts (owners' equity plus long-term liabilities).

Class 2. Fixed assets and other noncurrent assets.

Class 3. Inventories.

Class 4. Personal accounts receivable and payable.

Class 5. Cash and short-term investments.

Class 6. Expenses, by nature.

Class 7. Revenues, by nature.

Class 8. Profit and loss (income) accounts.

Class 9. Cost accounts.

Class 0. Statistical (nonmonetary) accounts.

The balance sheet was prepared from classes 1 through 5, and the profit and loss account from 6 and 7. Subsidiary accounts within a class were given two-digit numbers beginning with the class number; subsubsidiary accounts, three-digit numbers; and so on. For example, within class 2, account 20 was prescribed for ''preliminary expenses'' (organization costs) but could equally have been labeled ''intangible assets,'' in which case organization costs might bear the number 200. This change was in fact made in 1982, and capitalized research and development costs were given account number 203.

An interesting feature of the plan was the use of contra accounts for the reclassification of expenses by nature into costs by function. Through this device, operating statements and budgetary comparisons could be prepared according to either classification or both. Many other features of the plan commend themselves to any accountant who has ever had the task of developing a chart of accounts for an enterprise.

CHANGES TO THE PLAN SINCE 1957

The plan was revised in 1979, 1982, and 1987, the last revision to conform its content to the Fourth Directive of the European Community. Among other innovations, the 1987 plan provides alternative forms of financial statement (vertical or horizontal) but utilizes the standard EC itemization scheme and its alphanumerical index. The plan provides model schedules to the financial statements. Class 8 is now designated "special accounts" so that it can be used for other summaries besides the profit and loss account and balance sheet. The latest versions of the plan have abandoned the concept of "output" rather than "revenue" under which the income statement would show own construction of plant and equipment and other nonexteriorized production as outputs of the firm. However, it includes two special accounts for contingent liabilities under guarantees and endorsements and the corresponding asset (receivable).

One of the innovations that the Fourth Directive brought to the plan was the concept of "true and fair" presentation. The comparable French expression *reguliérs et sincères* speaks more to compliance with legal rules than to fair presentation, and adoption of the true and fair view has directed attention to the need for footnotes and analyses of significant items. The latest version of the plan includes three draft forms of financial statements: the EC version, a set that goes beyond the disclosure requirements of the EC, and a shorter set for small businesses.

WHAT CAN BE DONE?

We have presented a basic choice, between a standard form for financial statements unaccompanied by any radical change in GAAP, and the replacement of GAAP by a comprehensive accounting plan on the French model. No enthusiasm can be detected in the English-speaking world for either model; accountants, and presumably the managers who employ them, do not want to be denied the opportunity to express their individual personalities, or more mundanely, to paint their own pictures.

Nevertheless, the time is coming when accountants will have to face this issue, as the U.K. experience demonstrates. In addition to the factors spelled out earlier in this chapter, the confusion surrounding preparing and auditing financial statements that purport to correspond with another comprehensive basis of accounting (than GAAP) points to a need for a flexible framework that can be expanded or contracted in accordance with the needs of the situation. For example, regulated firms such as banks and insurance companies have to prepare financial statements in accordance with federal or state requirements that conflict in certain respects with GAAP. The accounting profession is currently struggling with this issue, which has produced a separate body of "preferred accounting principles" and with the related one of cash basis or income tax basis financial statements. The French plan is flexible enough to be adapted to these different needs.

SOME PROBLEMS NEVER GO AWAY

The adoption of a uniform accounting system and a standard format for financial reporting is the first measure that an acquiring company takes after assuming control over another company. It is evident that rational decision-making requires consistent and comparable information, and form is important in this regard.

It is not so clear, however, that content is so readily standardized. In the first place, bona fide differences must be permitted to appear, rather than be swept into a preconceived classification. The French plan is flexible enough to accommodate such differences. The main problem is one of valuation, and the associated one of allocation. Chapter 10 recommended current value historical accounting, because it drastically reduces the area of controversy in the field of valuation. Allocation problems arising out of different business policies and strategies are not so easily eliminated, even in groups of companies whose policies and strategies are supposed to be the same throughout. This issue, which has been documented with respect to oil and gas companies by the American Petroleum Institute, cries out for more general accounting research.

But even in the narrow context of form, who will assert a responsibility to change the status quo? Not the public accounting profession, which has a demonstrated ability to oppose innovation. Will accountants in trade and industry voluntarily accommodate their varying needs in the United States as they have in France? The profession of management accountant is in equal disarray at the present time. The SEC's lawyers are neither interested nor qualified, and the FASB has missed the boat. The federal government lacks the power to legislate for corporations generally, and the states are just not interested. Even academics can be expected to continue to ignore this issue, obsessed as they are with research in information economics that presupposes its solution. Nevertheless, one is encouraged by the fact that communism collapsed under the pressures of social needs.

NOTES

1. George Foster, *Financial Statement Analysis*, 2d ed. (Englewood Cliffs, N.J.: Prentice-Hall, 1986), pp. 80–83.

2. Kenneth S. Most, "Two Forms of Experimental Accounts," *The Accounting Review*, January 1969, pp. 145–52.

3. Anne Fortin, "The 1947 French Accounting Plan: Origins and Influences on Subsequent Practice," *The Accounting Historians Journal*, December 1991, pp. 1–25.

CHAPTER 13

THE FUTURE OF AUDITING

Chapter 5 examined the condition of auditing practice in the United States, and found it wanting. Fundamental weaknesses include the lack of a supportive legal framework, excessive commercialization, and a defective educational system. This chapter will continue to document the problems, and point to more specific measures that the accounting profession must take if it is to reduce the "expectation gap." Great encouragement in this endeavor has been provided by a recent book authored by Felix Pomeranz, whose auditing experience and expertise are unquestioned.[1] He focuses on the need to use technology to reduce audit risk exposure as an integral part of the audit process. The following paragraphs draw freely on his ideas, but the emphasis on auditing in a global environment is my own.

THE STATE OF THE PROFESSION OF AUDITOR

The practice of auditing is the scene of intense competition, and the profession's response has been price-cutting to ensure market share, and diversification for profitability. For these reasons large firms have grown at the expense of the medium-sized, and the supply of talent has diminished so that starting salaries have escalated. In spite of the megamergers of the last few years, however, partner salaries even in large firms lag behind comparable remuneration of actuaries, lawyers, and financial specialists. The proportion of audit fees to total fees is now barely above 50 percent.

There have been a large number of well-publicized cases of business failure that have been characterized also as audit failures. Some of these involved companies failing within days of the issue of an unqualified audit opinion. Others revealed auditors showing poor judgment, or making obvious errors that suggested incompetence, or failing to discover management's errors. In a very few cases auditors have displayed uncharacteristic venality, cooperating in management fraud and taking bribes or receiving inappropriate loans. There have been many documented cases of failure to follow generally accepted auditing standards, few of which have led to disciplinary action, much less decertification.

Auditors have displayed lack of a knowledge of the industry of the audited firm, an obvious prerequisite to the performance of an audit and one that is recognized by those firms which advertise their industry specializations. Attention was drawn to this through the failure of a large number of savings and loan associations, where novel financial instruments seem to have perplexed the auditors unduly. Such ignorance is not confined to this area, however, and the loss of hundreds of millions of dollars by Volkswagen A.G. through foreign currency speculation was believed to have been aided by the fact that the company's auditors did not fully understand foreign exchange transactions. The nature of professional education, particularly in the United States, makes it unlikely that professionals will receive such technical training at school, so that knowledge depends upon the fortuitous accidents of a business career.

The response of the public accounting profession has been an amalgam of mea culpas, disclaimer of guilt, an emphasis on the limitations of an audit ("no auditor can be expected to discover elaborate management frauds"), and issuing additional audit standards in spite of the fact that existing ones have been disregarded. Research has pointed to the problem of overload in respect to both accounting and auditing standards, and we have pointed out in previous chapters the undue complexity and pervasive ambiguity of U.S. GAAP, which undoubtedly contributes to audit errors.

Another response, favored by the Treadway Commission and the SEC, is the audit committee consisting of one or more outside directors of a corporation. There is no indication that such committees do in fact support and improve the external (or internal) audit function; outside directors are usually appointed by the company's chief executive either because they are friends or to satisfy some perceived social need, such as representation of women or minorities. In neither case is there an effort to ensure that the directors are minimally qualified to understand the work of the board of directors, and those who are tend to be lawyers. A recent study confirmed these observations.[2]

SPECIFIC AUDITOR DEFICIENCIES

Pomeranz lists a number of specific defects that these responses have done nothing to eradicate:

—Auditors are confused about their social function, and about the internal auditor's mission.

—There are frequent violations of basic standards of fieldwork, such as planning and supervision, studying internal control, and collecting evidence.

—Auditors lack proper skepticism and will accept any explanations, particularly management's representations.

—There is violation of professional rules, such as those calling for contact with a predecessor auditor.

—Auditors do not understand the record-keeping process itself.

—Auditors are insensitive to the state of the economy, or the industry.

—Auditors do not understand their client's business.

—Auditors lack knowledge of the backgrounds of client executives, of the control environment of top management, of the operating environment with its pressures to perform, and of physical production and distribution systems.

—Auditors fail to dig into files, which usually contain reports on problems.

—There is an unjustified reliance on statistical procedures. "Coarse analytical procedures" have proved more effective in uncovering fraud.

—Peer review adds to nonchargeable time but does not necessarily improve quality.

—"Keeping current" with professional pronouncements reduces auditor productivity.

—The functional organization of accounting firms (audit, tax, consultancy) is too inflexible to adapt to modern matrix management.

WHAT POMERANZ PROPOSES

As the title of his book suggests, Pomeranz is mainly concerned with improving the effectiveness and efficiency of the audit. He agrees that the general objective of an audit is the expression of an opinion on fair presentation, but more specific areas of exposure can be identified, such as protection of assets, control over computer access, and management representations, which may relate to existence or occurrence (of capital or revenue items), completeness of records, rights, duties, and obligations, valuation or allocation, and presentation and disclosure (display).

In respect of the existence of assets, for example, he points out that maintenance records can be used for verification of new acquisitions, and emphasizes the fact that management fraud that overrides controls precedes the creation of an unadjusted trial balance. It is mainly with respect to the use of databases as an audit tool, however, that Pomeranz sees improvements in audit technology. His updated and expanded audit risk model involves search for information from four sources:

—client's industry and business

—client's key executives

—the operating environment (pressures on executives to perform)

—the legal and regulatory environment

He proposes the creation of a "master tracking sheet" for threats and risks.

THE NEED FOR AN AUDIT

In the United States it is widely believed that nonpublic companies and other social entities do not require auditing, and that the cost of an audit would be greater than its benefit. This viewpoint is gaining wide currency around the world, because of the deterioration in audit productivity to which Pomeranz draws attention. He points out that an increase in audit effectiveness implies doing more, yet increased productivity implies doing less. In many countries the choice seems to be, do less.

On the other hand, apart from a de minimis exception, it is hard to argue the case for exempting entities from an audit obligation. Some countries, such as Canada, provide in their company laws that nonpublic companies may dispense with the obligation by resolution of all, or a majority of, stockholders. Yet I would not like to be an elderly widow, dependent for my income on a one-third interest in my late husband's business, if its management, even though they might consist of my children, were not subject to an external audit.

Some years ago Turgut Var told the story of two charitable trusts that were established in the Middle Ages, to administer hospitals in Turkey and Venice. The Turkish one endured for over four centuries, and terminated only after an earthquake destroyed the subject property. The Venetian one lasted less than a century before becoming bankrupt. The difference? The Turkish trust was subject to annual audit under the Ottoman legal system, whereas the Venetian trust operated virtually without any social control.[3]

KREUGER, CORNFELD, AND DUQUE

Three relatively modern scandals illustrate these points precisely. Perhaps the best recent instance of an accounting problem that became a social problem was the Kreuger case of the early 1930s. Much has been written about the principal character involved, the late Ivar Kreuger, and about the financial transactions of the Kreuger and Toll Company that resulted in losses to investors on at least two continents. A major factor contributing to the success of the pyramid scheme conducted by Kreuger was his consistent refusal to have his holding company audited, and the failure of banks and other financial institutions that peddled his paper to insist on audited financial statements as a basis for their collaboration. According to a recent study, the Kreuger scandal was directly responsible for the passage of the U.S. securities laws of 1933 and 1934, the second of which established the SEC to oversee corporate accountability, as well as for the New York Stock Exchange's 1932 rule requiring new listees to agree to audits in subsequent years.[4] Kreuger and Toll was audited only after the company had gone bankrupt.

History may be said to have repeated itself thirty-seven years later, with Investors Overseas Services, Ltd. (IOS), often referred to as the Bernie Cornfeld or Vesco affair, after its founder and principal predator, respectively. Bernie Cornfeld started selling mutual fund investments in Europe in the 1950s, and discovered large amounts of U.S. dollars available for investment. He therefore formed IOS, a mutual fund that controlled International Investment Trust (IIT), itself controlled by IIT management. Both were incorporated in the Duchy of Luxembourg, which provides a tax haven and other forms of protection for companies. IOS was first a Canadian and then a Panamanian company, and its operations were structured to avoid regulation.

At the height of its prosperity in the late 1960s and early 1970s, IIT had assets totaling $375 million, about 40 percent of which were U.S. securities. Some of these securities were the products of John M. King, through King Resources Company (KRC), a public corporation, and the Colorado Company (TCC), a nonpublic company. Both KRC and TCC bought and sold natural resource properties as tax shelter investments, and some of the transactions passed through a wholly owned Netherlands Antilles subsidiary. Although some of these companies were audited (and the auditors concerned came in for severe criticism when the affair reached the courts), there was no audit of the entire operation.

The bankruptcy of King and the failure of his companies precipitated a crisis at IOS, and Robert Vesco was brought into the latter company ostensibly to save it. He proceeded to loot it of the valuable securities, about $300 million, without any objection from the banks, public accounting firms, and underwriters associated with the company. (Vesco has been reported to have since resided in several Caribbean countries, most recently Cuba, where he obviously has no difficulty in convincing Fidel Castro of the dangers of capitalism.)

An even more recent case, *U.S. v. Jose Castro*, is an example of the need for audit on a much smaller scale. It involved Alberto Duque, a Colombian national and the son of a successful coffee producer. After graduating from a U.S. military academy he attended university in Colombia, and in the early 1970s went to New York to seek his fortune. He worked as a messenger in his father's company and speculated in coffee futures.

Moving to Miami in 1977, Duque formed Domino Investments, Inc., a wholly owned Cayman Islands company, which held all of the stock of General Coffee Corporation, a coffee trader, as well as title to the very extensive list of personal assets he began to accumulate, including homes, cars, and jet aircraft. As a nonresident alien he had little difficulty in sheltering his dealings from U.S. tax and other regulations; he also formed a company for this purpose in Liechtenstein, another European tax haven.

In February 1981, Duque invested approximately $4 million as part of a group that acquired 51 percent of City National Bank Corporation, a holding company for a Miami bank. Shortly thereafter he acquired a controlling interest, paying his partners two and a half times what they had paid for their shares. He appointed himself chairman of the board, and named as vice chairmen two friends, one aged twenty-three, the other (by now president of General Coffee), aged twenty-five. Filings with the Federal Reserve Board in Atlanta stated that the funds came from Duque's personal resources and from a loan guaranteed by Domino Investments. In actual fact he borrowed $22 million from the Arab Banking Group in Bahrain, one-third owned by the government of Libya. Another $5 million loan came from Itka, a Panama-based company.

In charge at the bank, Duque borrowed $3 million from it to help General Coffee acquire Chase and Sanborn from Nabisco Foods. By this time he had obtained social status in Miami, cemented by the purchase of a 100-acre estate in North Carolina from one of its leading citizens. One of the most prominent local public relations firms accepted General Coffee and its subsidiaries as clients; the firm's procedures did not include a financial check, and when Duque eventually declared bankruptcy it was owed $17,000.

His financial problems seem to have started with his father, whose position in Colombia suffered for political reasons. They were certainly aggravated by his standard of living, which reputedly cost $1 million a month to maintain. In May 1983, Alberto Duque and four companies he controlled filed for protection under Chapter 11 of the U.S. Bankruptcy Code. He was subsequently indicted on charges of making false statements to banks with the intent of deceiving them into believing that his coffee and other inventories were much larger than they were. The jury found that he and his accomplices had misappropriated about $108 million from Miami banks by falsifying inventory data and other forgeries. Inflated receivables and fictitious aging reports were also used, and false invoices and computer reports prepared, known in-house as the "MM" (Mickey Mouse) books.

A striking feature of this case, especially following the McKesson and Robbins, De Angelis, and Billie Sol Estes cases, was the apparent ease with which large inventories can be fabricated as security for bank loans. Neither the Federal Reserve Board nor any of the banks that made these loans called for an audit, and the jurisdictions within which Duque operated had no statutory audit requirement. It is difficult to accept that established and reliable audit procedures would have failed to bring the frauds to light before they reached their eventual size.

AUDITING THE MULTINATIONAL CORPORATION

Each of these examples had an international dimension, and this feature was selected because of the pervasiveness of international operations in modern business. Even quite small firms are involved in transactions with foreign entities, and of course a multinational corporation by definition has investments, finance, production, and markets outside the country in which it is headquartered. Obviously this feature has major implications for the audit, because a supranational management can, to a large extent, effectively bypass the laws and regulations of the countries in which it operates.

Managers of multinationals look to their external (and internal) auditors to provide them with information about the effectiveness of their control systems. These assignments are made by top management, and it is only in the case where top management is corrupt, as in the Bank for Credit and Commerce International (BCCI) scandal uncovered in 1991, that such control systems are systematically perverted. BCCI's auditors have been accused of issuing clean opinions over a period during which the bank's depositors were being defrauded of billions of dollars. (Interestingly enough, Moslem banks have religious auditors in addition to secular ones, whose task it is, among others, to ensure that the firm is giving its correct share of profits to charity.) On the other hand, BCCI's auditors claimed that their eventual discovery of the frauds led to action by regulators. Indeed, the essential nature of the multinational's operations, which cut across the regulatory environment of nation states, makes the audit more difficult. An example will illustrate this point.

In an effort to achieve business success by exploiting resources globally, multinational corporations organize their own banking systems. Some create regional holding companies for this purpose, others establish finance companies in countries with favorable tax laws, such as Belgium and Ireland. The main purpose of these companies is cash management and reduction of exposure to foreign currency risks, by channeling funds from one country to another without the necessity to repatriate them first. At present, one of the basic procedures relied upon by the auditor is the bank confirmation. By direct communication with the client's banks, the auditor verifies balances and outstanding loans and other obligations, learns of the existence of safety deposit boxes and other repositories of cash and securities, and generally throws light on the existence and value of the client's assets and liabilities. What happens if the bank or banks are subsidiaries or affiliates of the client? The question is particularly telling when it is observed that most of the foreign subsidiaries of multinational corporations are not audited by the firm that audits the parent,[5] a situation that may be changing because it has proved costly.

These issues were the focus of my research report, *International Auditing*, published by the Canadian Certified General Accountants Research Foundation in 1988. This report identified a number of international banking problems, and pointed out that multinational corporations are also vulnerable through

—involvement in offshore insurance and reinsurance schemes.

—participation in bi- and multinational countertrade.

—utilization of letters of credit and foreign trade zone warehousing.

—political, social, and cultural diversity, reflected in different laws, customs, ethics, languages, and the characteristics of accounting and auditing practitioners in different countries.

It must be noted here that virtually no attention has been given to these problems by the accounting profession, and even the International Federation of Accountants has failed to issue any guidance.

THE LONG-FORM AUDIT REPORT

The form of the U.S. auditor's report has recently been changed in order to state more clearly what it represents, and for this purpose it is now longer than before. It is, however, still a "short-form" report. This phrase contrasts it with another kind of audit report, which is considerably longer. The long-form audit report may be of two kinds.

When I worked as an auditor for a U.S. public accounting firm in Europe, most of the engagements were to audit subsidiaries of U.S. or U.K. companies. For a number of reasons, it was the usual practice to accompany the audited financial statements with a report that enumerated problems of accounting systems or controls, or internal control, or decisions with regard to classification or display of items that might be controversial. This report was a work of art; it was not to unnecessarily alarm the engagement partner at headquarters, so that he would be impelled to arrive at our office and demand what was going on, or lead to offending the client's management through carping criticism, but it was to identify major problems clearly enough that we could avoid attack if something blew up in our faces. I claim to have refined any writing skills I possess on this hone. We called the report a long-form audit report, because we provided a short-form report on the financial statements themselves. To my knowledge it was and still is not the custom of most firms to provide management with this type of report and for this reason I shall call it an *internal* long-form report.

In several European countries, however, particularly Germany and the Scandinavian countries, the auditor provides the client with two audit reports. The short form states simply that the financial statements correspond with the company's books and with the relevant laws, which, because these are tax conformity countries, means tax laws as well as company laws. The long-form report, on the other hand, is an in-depth analysis of the financial statements and the results they display. These reports, which are not management audit reports, include:

—comments on the accounting system, which now embraces computer systems

—analyses of financial statement items that aggregate different data

—key financial ratios, with explanations of changes

—disclosure of hidden (secret) reserves that have been created through understatement of assets or overstatement of liabilities (This feature will be recognized by the U.S. accountant in relation to LIFO inventories, where the understatement is a consequence of income tax regulations. In tax conformity countries there are many such situations.)

—identification of other assets the market value of which differs significantly from their historical cost

—evaluation of significant contingencies

—a discussion of the business results in the light of the economic conditions that prevailed during the period

The reason for these *external* long-form reports is that the shares of most companies in these countries are voted by banks, either as owners or nominees, and bank officers accept a fiduciary responsibility in respect of them. The auditor is the eyes and ears of the bank officer. The objective of the audit extends beyond the submission of an opinion (the general objective, according to Pomeranz) and covers explicitly specific exposures, namely, protection of assets, control over computer access, and management representations. As more U.S. and U.K. auditors become involved in engagements on behalf of European parent companies, the external long-form audit report will become familiar to them and they will equip themselves with the necessary skills to provide such reports. This means eliminating the specific deficiencies to which Pomeranz has drawn attention.

WHERE DO WE GO FROM HERE?

During the nineteenth century, the work of the accounting profession gradually changed from accounting to auditing, and the incomes of practitioners depended on the quantity and quality of audit work performed. These individuals were part of the business community and often belonged to families engaged in commerce or manufacturing; sometimes they were investors in the companies they audited, even directors.

In the twentieth century the importance of auditing has declined, partly because public accounting firms have involved themselves in a variety of ancillary activities. This is indicated by the following list, which is not exhaustive, taken from an advertising publication of a large U.S. firm:

Business decision assistance

Finding financial sources

Audits, reviews, and compilations

Budgeting and business planning

Systems automation

Compensation and benefit planning

Cost control and containment

Risk management

Tax minimization

Business acquisition and sale

Accounting and reporting systems

Internal control development

Personal financial planning

Cash management

Importing and exporting

Product pricing

There is clear evidence that the failure to specialize on the audit, to develop new audit products, and to improve audit technology, have had a detrimental effect on the standard of auditing. Attempts to halt the decline by issuing generally accepted auditing standards have failed, because the standards themselves have avoided critical procedural detail, because they have been disregarded in practice, because disciplinary action against substandard auditors has been virtually non-existent, and because the very different operations of compilation and review have been allowed to confuse the public. It is widely acknowledged that fraud and other forms of corporate misconduct are rampant; a former chairman of the U.S. Federal Deposit Insurance Corporation, himself a CPA, stated that 40 percent of bank failures between 1980 and 1983 were attributable to fraud and insider abuse. The Treadway Commission accepted the existence of fraudulent financial reporting as a fact. The files of the SEC are replete with instances.

The decline in auditing has been accompanied by a decline in accounting. Nineteenth-century accountants bequeathed to us standard costing, consolidations, and the funds statement. Our generation can only claim the invention of the cash flow statement, which was the point of departure in an accountant's education fifty years ago. The massive documentation that constitutes generally accepted accounting principles is not responsible for the improvements that have taken place in financial reporting, which are a consequence of initiatives of the SEC and of corporate financial officers and their staffs. Public accountants have gone along with the standard-setting process in order not to be accused of rocking the boat.

Chapter 5 attributed the problems of the auditing profession in the United States to a failure of the system of professional education, to an abortive attempt to avoid liability under existing tort law, and to the commercialization of the audit function. This chapter has reinforced that view by:

1. enumerating specific auditor deficiencies, most of which point clearly to educational reform.

2. emphasizing the social importance of the audit, which supports the proposal in Chapter 5 for legislation that would both strengthen the auditor's position and reduce the opportunities available to tort lawyers.

3. proposing a return to accounting and auditing as the prime function of the public accountant, if necessary at the expense of the ancillary activities that seem more profitable at the present.

To the extent that the accounting profession is now grappling with educational reforms, under the guidance of the Accounting Education Change Commission, it is moving away from the acquisition of technical knowledge and toward improvements in communication skills and an emphasis on philosophical issues, such as ethics. The accounting profession is fixated on the audit of the public corporation, and has virtually abandoned lesser entities to the compilation or review; the likelihood that legislation will expand the duties and obligations of auditors is slim indeed. Even in the United Kingdom there is a movement in favor of abandoning the audit of small companies. And public accounting firms in the English-speaking countries are dedicated opponents of the laws and regulations that restrict their opposite numbers in France and other European countries to accounting and auditing.

THE AUDITOR'S TEN COMMANDMENTS

1. You shall not quote a fee for the audit of an entity before learning how it operates and how it is organized.

2. You shall not commence an audit without a written agreement specifying the entity to be audited and the fee.

3. You shall not commence a contractual audit without a written engagement letter, signed by the client, containing no scope restriction.

4. You shall accept no audit engagement where there exists any personal, moral, financial, or professional relationship that could influence the scope of the audit or the opinion submitted.

5. You shall not express an opinion without having obtained sufficient evidence to justify it to a reasonable and competent third party.

6. You shall prepare and maintain working papers that document the nature and scope of the audit, and its findings, and are capable of being read and understood by a reasonable and competent third party.

7. You shall not delegate any audit task to an employee, colleague, or associate without having satisfied yourself that this person possesses the same qualities that you would require were you to perform the work for yourself, and is willing to be supervised.

8. You shall not replace another auditor without having, through personal contact, ascertained from that individual the reason for the change.

9. If an opinion is given on financial statements, the report will clearly identify the statements in question and the opinion. A standard form of audit report will be given only if the auditor knows of no facts or circumstances that should be drawn to the attention of the user of the statements, that is not clearly apparent to a reasonable and competent user.

10. The auditor's report will be dated on the day when the audit work was completed, and all transactions, other events, and circumstances of which the auditor becomes aware up to and including that day are relevant to the opinion.

CONCLUSION

The auditor has only one thing to sell: a signature. Many individuals possess the same knowledge and comparable technical skills, but these do not make the public accountant. The expectation gap is at the same time a credibility gap, and restoration of the public's faith in the integrity of the profession is an essential element of its salvation. This, more than adding to the body of GAAS, is the way back.

NOTES

1. Felix Pomeranz, *The Successful Audit* (Homewood, Ill.: Business One Irwin, 1992).

2. Brenda S. Birkett, "The Recent History of Corporate Audit Committees," *The Accounting Historians Journal*, Fall 1986, pp. 109–24.

3. Turgut Var presented a paper on this subject at a meeting of the American Accounting Association in the early 1970s. He had previously described the accounting of the two trusts; see "Internal Control for Ottoman Foundations," *The Accounting Historians Journal*, Spring 1981, pp. 1–13.

4. Dale L. Flesher and Tonya K. Flesher, "Ivar Kreuger's Contribution to U.S. Financial Reporting," *The Accounting Review*, July 1986, pp. 421–34.

5. Vinod B. Bavishi and Harold E. Wyman, *Who Audits the World: Trends in the Worldwide Auditing Profession* (Storrs, Conn.: Center for Transnational Accounting and Financial Research, University of Connecticut, 1984).

CHAPTER 14

THE FUTURE OF FINANCIAL REPORTING

INTRODUCTION

The preceding chapters, following a careful historical survey of the development of accounting thought and a theoretical analysis of models and systems, contain the following proposals relating to the practice of accounting:

1. Fundamental changes are needed in U.S. federal and state laws governing corporations, to correct their lack of accounting and auditing provisions, perhaps the adoption of a uniform state corporation statute that will include such provisions (Chapter 5).

2. The accountancy profession should involve itself in educating people for the profession (Chapter 5).

3. The IASC should redirect its efforts toward establishing a logical basis for accounting standards, rather than trying to reach consensus on specific accounting practices (Chapter 6).

4. The U.S. system of regulating the accountability of public corporations needs renovating, including revising the SEC's Regulation S-X (Chapter 8).

5. Corporations should move to historical financial statements based on current (replacement) costs and exit values. A working capital adjustment is needed in a period of inflation (Chapter 10).

6. A study of the function of the notes to financial statements is long overdue (Chapter 11).

7. Simplification and standardization of the form and content of financial statements are urgently required (Chapter 11).

8. The United States economy would benefit from the creation of an accounting plan on the French model (Chapter 12).

9. The practice and economics of auditing call for a return to basic standards of performance and the elimination of the "expectation gap" (Chapter 13).

Some, if not all, of these recommendations can be found elsewhere in the finance and accounting literature. This chapter proposes something completely new. It takes as the point of departure the following quotation from George Benston's exposé of the failure of accounting and auditing regulation in the United States: "What role, then, should the SEC play with respect to accounting? I would hope that it would lead the profession in developing (but not requiring) methods that would make accounting statements relevant to investors."[1]

ACCOUNTING FOR THE FUTURE

The need for historical (not "historical cost") financial reporting is so basic that we may take it for granted. In Herzberg's terminology, it is an accounting hygiene factor but not a motivating factor. Assuming that it will continue to be satisfied by accountants and auditors, is that all there is? Can accountants provide no better services to society than to prepare and audit retrospective financial statements?

It is clear that society expects future-oriented information about the businesses on which it relies to produce wealth, in the form of dividends, interest, rents, wages, taxes, and capital formation. Much of the debate about accounting principles is based on this assumption, as is also the belief that moving from historical cost GAAP to current cost, or current cash equivalent, accounting principles will assist the assessment (= prediction) of future cash flows, and therefore the valuation of the firm and its securities. This was also one of the professed aims of changing from a statement of changes in financial position to a statement of cash flows.

Again, proposals for the reform of the system of corporate accountability proceed from the perceived need for future-oriented data. John C. Burton, when chief accountant of the SEC, saw a need for continuous, timely reporting as an alternative to periodic financial reports, presumably because it would assist users in modifying their projections more expeditiously. Borrowing from the example of management accounting, he suggested the use of exception reporting; companies would publish their projections and issue reports only when a change in expectations occurred. Much of the literature on the need for future-oriented data presupposes that the traditional accounting model is too restrictive for this function, and indeed, this assumption underlies the FASB's apparent unwillingness to adopt a more precise set of financial accounting concepts. In any case, non-accounting statistics may supplement GAAP-based data incorporated in traditional financial statements.

This preoccupation with making measurements of the past better suited to making predictions about the future proceeds from a basic fallacy: that the conceptual framework for evaluating the past is the same as that for predicting the future. This is not so, and indeed, it is difficult to accept the proposition that an investor or financial analyst is able to make such assessments, the data for which are obviously in the possession of management.

FINANCIAL AND MANAGERIAL ACCOUNTING

We are accustomed to describing the difference between financial and managerial accounting using the words "external" and "internal." Financial accounting deals with the interface between the firm and society; managerial accounting, with the internal structure and organization of the firm. A more basic distinction, however, is that the problems solved with the aid of the two kinds of accounting information are different. Financial accounting provides needed answers to questions concerning liquidity, solvency, and profitability, whereas managerial accounting serves the measurement of performance under the headings of efficiency, economy, and productivity. They appear to meet under the umbrella of return on investment (ROI), which at first glance depicts the relationship between profitability and productivity.

This is expressed in the equation:

$$ROI = \text{net income/sales} \times \text{sales/assets}$$

The net income/sales ratio represents the profitability of outputs, and the sales/assets ratio, the productivity of inputs.

The ratio provides only a gross approximation to the relationship between profitability and productivity because of the impact of the conflict between past and future. The assets of the firm, which are parts of uncompleted earnings cycles, have not earned any income in the period being analyzed, and the income of the period was earned on assets that have been liquidated, and which are obviously not included in the denominator.

More to the point, however, is the vital role played in managerial accounting by accounting for the future. This is clearly apparent from the use of budgets, which are planned financial statements for future periods extending from days, weeks, or months to, in some cases, a decade or more. What is useful to the manager is not the historical cost and management operating statements, but the budgetary comparisons showing how actual varied from budget. In this comparison, the budget is the norm; what actually happened has no normative significance.

Less clearly apparent is the future-oriented nature of cost and performance standards, which are the building blocks of the budget. Standard costs (in German, *Sollkosten*, what costs and outputs should be) must be discerned by a view of the future; otherwise they are worthless. They are quantities multiplied by prices, like any other accounting numbers, but of a special kind. The quantities represent factors of production or products that should be required for the production and distribution process, and the prices represent what should be paid, or received, for factor purchases and product sales, during the planned future period.

A common error of belief about the nature of budgets and standards is to treat them as forecasts rather than plans. To illustrate the difference, a demand curve for a product consists of forecasts of the quantities of likely sales at different prices; each point on the curve results from a forecast. A sales budget, however, expressed in quantities and prices, is one point on this curve that has been selected for the plan. It is not the *most likely* value for sales, based on statistical probabilities, although probability may be a factor entering into the act of choice. It is the *planned* value for sales based on a commitment of the individuals involved in the budgeting process, generally those who are capable of affecting outcomes by their actions.

THE BUSINESS PLAN

A business plan is a detailed description of the underlying assumptions, goals, objectives, and planned results that are involved in an initiative to start a new business. Such a plan will set forth the market research on which the business is based, describe the technology and personnel that will be employed, and specify the production and distribution processes. It will identify key personnel and other necessary elements, such as patents, franchises, and agreements with prospective suppliers and customers. Such a plan will conclude with a set of prospective financial statements that show hypothetical results for the first years of operation of the new business, called the "roll-out period." Venture capitalists and other informed investors require entrepreneurs to prepare such a business plan before they will consider investing in an enterprise, whether through loans or equity.[2] Such prospective financial statements resemble budgets, but are essentially different. They show what the business *can* do, rather than what it *should* do. This is obvious from the fact that the managers have not yet been employed whose commitment is necessary before a budget can be agreed. A real-life example will help to explain this distinction.

Many years ago I participated in setting up a business to utilize the then new technology for making products out of expanded polystyrene. The business plan was based on research that identified three markets: building materials, packaging, and jobbing operations using customer molds. It was assumed that the first year's sales would consist of these three product groups in the proportions 5:3:2. The cost estimates in the prospective financial statements reflected these proportions.

By the time the business started operations, the bottom had dropped out of the building construction market. Further, it proved longer and more complicated to move from design to mold to production of packaging for delicate products than had been envisioned. The production manager hired for the business had had previous experience in producing mannequins for retail stores in addition to his expertise with thermoplastic raw materials. He set up a production line for these items, and we were able to meet our sales target for the first year, but in the proportions 1:2:7. Naturally, the budget had to be radically revised, because the production of mannequins was much more labor-intensive than the extrusion of insulation board for the construction market, or the injection of plastic into molds.

Nevertheless, the prospective financial statements included in the business plan remained valid and did not require changing as a consequence of this short-term decision.[3] The assumed proportions of 5:3:2 were based on assumptions about the long-term production plan, and the economics of the firm were based on these assumptions. A buyer of shares in the company would be concerned with the achievement of these goals, and not with the temporary outcomes of a different production and sales plan.

After considerable SEC vacillation on the issue, prospectuses are now permitted to include prospective financial statements, and in some countries (for example, the U.K.) public accountants express their opinions on them.

WHAT IS "SYNTHETIC FINANCIAL REPORTING"?

I have used a synthetic approach to constructing financial statements, on the same basis as they are produced for a business plan, as expert witness in several legal cases involving the valuation of all or part of a business. Both of those described here involved small businesses, but a similar research-based approach to finding synthetic values could be used by a large firm.[4]

The Electronics Company

The problem was to value a company that had been acquired from its founder under duress. The predator (who was actually the plaintiff) was unable to operate the company profitably, and it experienced several years of losses following the acquisition. The defendant countersued for compensation, and the issue was how much the business was worth when he lost control.

I argued that the financial statements submitted by the plaintiff could not be relied on. Apart from the fact that they were unaudited, they had been prepared for income tax purposes and therefore reflected tax laws rather than business results. Further, to the extent that they reported losses, they represented management failures and not business value. Starting with the level (and composition) of sales for the two years preceding the takeover, and using the defendant's records as a check, I constructed a pro forma statement of maintainable profits, which provided a point of departure for my valuation algorithm. The court accepted this method, although it compromised on the valuation.

My work was relatively simple because the founder of the firm (the defendant) had contracted with a Japanese company to manufacture the product. The contract provided for financing through back-to-back letters of credit that effectively caused all costs, including interest for a total of 180 days from completing a production order to receiving payment from a U.S. customer, to be included in the contract price. Thus, constructing hypothetical, or synthetic, expenses was limited to selling and administration.

The Plumbing Supplies Wholesaler

This case involved a husband and wife business partnership with an agreement that provided, on a divorce, for one partner to buy out the other; the question was, at what price? Here the problem was to value a business that had been built with a capacity to grow, so that past results were only partially useful for arriving at a business value. For example, the assets included a purpose-built warehouse that was, perhaps, one-third larger than needed for current operations.

I ascertained sales per square foot data for the industry and the firm, and projected future sales using these data and past rate of growth. The gross margin percentage was fairly standard throughout the industry, and the operating cost structure was virtually fixed throughout the relevant range of activity levels. With these data I was able to project future profits, and arrive at a figure to be used in my valuation algorithm.

The parties accepted my valuation, and payments were made by the selling partner to the buying partner out of the subsequent cash flows. Several years later, a downturn in the construction industry rendered the projected profit impossible to maintain. This was not a factor at the time the valuation took place, however, and the business risk was reflected in the discount rate used.

A RESEARCH APPROACH TO DATA ACQUISITION

In the research reported in the article mentioned above my goal was to find an objective approach to the calculation of depreciation expense, one of the most subjective estimates in business financial statements. I surveyed the managers, not the accountants, of a sample of 100 companies in order to obtain their estimates of useful lives and residual values for selected categories of property, plant, and equipment. The results were compared with U.S. Treasury studies of asset lives for the same categories, derived from Internal Revenue Service sources, and the reasons for differences investigated. I assumed that straight-line depreciation was appropriate, although if evidence had presented itself to the contrary this assumption could have been varied. I was able to calculate how much depreciation expense should have been reported by each of the twenty companies in my sample, and I compared this figure with three depreciation amounts reported by those companies for the year in question: historical cost, constant dollar, and current cost. I found a significant understatement of depreciation expense by all companies except those in the electronics industry. The understatement was not eliminated by the constant dollar and current cost adjustments. I hypothesized that the calculation of asset lives is a matter of life and death to companies making computers and telecommunications equipment, which would explain why their estimates were compatible with mine. Other firms were perhaps understating depreciation through ignorance, or to improve their profit picture. The latter is indicated by a comparison of the ratio of depreciation expense to sales for older, struggling industries (steel, automobiles) and newer ones (electronics, pharmaceuticals, communications).

THE PROBLEM OF UNCERTAINTY

Such synthetic financial statements would contain mainly observations that are characterized by uncertainty. In actual fact, uncertainty characterizes many accounting data, which are dependent for their validity on what happens in the future. For example, fixed asset values in balance sheets are only credible on the assumption that the firm will recover the investment from its customers. The general form of this belief is called the "going concern" assumption; some commentators interpret it to mean that the firm will have an indefinite future life, but there is a consensus that it implies survival until capital has been recovered.

Another specific case was identified in FAS 5, where contingencies were classified into probable, reasonably possible, and remote. Different financial reporting treatment was laid down for each. FAS 109 introduced a new class in respect of deferred tax assets, "more likely than not." Canadian GAAP uses other terms, and the U.S. legal profession has voiced concern about a lack of precision in this regard because the American Bar Association has different definitions of probable and remote.

A spurious certainty pervades many accounting numbers that are in fact dependent on estimates. I first observed this phenomenon when checking inventory at a manufacturing plant many years ago. The count sheets included some odd lengths of steel rod which, by their rust-covered appearance, had obviously been on hand a long time. On inquiry I discovered that a past product called for a short length of such rod, say three feet of half-inch diameter. Of course, it was necessary to order the rod in lengths of eight feet; when the bookkeepers received a stores issue note for "3 ft. ½ in. steel rod" they simply credited inventory, and debited work in process, with three-eighths of the invoice cost, leaving the other five-eighths in inventory. I have a feeling that this type of situation is more common than is generally realized.

With respect to financial data, it has been observed that many accounting numbers are point estimates and would perhaps be better representations if given as ranges. For example, "Earnings, $1,444,782" suggests an unattainable accuracy; perhaps "Earnings, $1,000,000–$1,800,000" better suggests the estimating procedure. Approximating accounting numbers to the nearest significant digit would be one way to get around this problem. Some critics have proposed assigning probabilities to accounting numbers in order to arrive at expected values (in the statistical sense). Twenty-five years ago it was proposed to use a statistical measure of variance as a means of quantifying the degree of agreement among measurers (accountants).[5]

Again, the subject of financial instruments has redirected attention to the problems associated with valuing them for balance sheet purposes, whether as assets or liabilities. For example, accounts receivable are stated "net," which means at the probable recoverable amount, and an allowance procedure is used to arrive at the deduction from gross receivables necessary to reduce them to this amount. The values of other financial instruments are subject to market forces, such as fluctuations in interest rates, and this is by no means restricted to assets. The first (1977) edition of my *Accounting Theory* raised the question of marking liabilities to market, which had become a live issue in 1992.

There is also the view that uncertainties are properly dealt with in the notes to financial statements, or in other parts of the financial report such as management's discussion and analysis of the financial statements. To the extent that this is being done, we are confronted with the use of boiler-plate language that is meant to serve as a shield to protect the issuer from liability.

What is the significance of these questions where synthetic financial statements are concerned? Being essentially prospective, rather than retrospective, all the accounting numbers are estimates. There is no reason why these estimates should not be based on a variety of assumptions, producing several or many different outcomes, and a sensitivity analysis performed in order to arrive at a "best" value. Yet the accountant's skill lies in selecting such a "best" value, and presenting a smorgasbord of numbers from which the user is permitted to make a selection is an abdication of professional responsibility.

THE BENEFITS OF SYNTHETIC FINANCIAL REPORTING

The primary benefit of synthetic financial statements would be to provide users of financial reports with the future-oriented information that they seek, and that they need in order to make their decisions. For example, the valuation of a firm's securities, particularly its common stock, is normally a function of future earnings and cash flows, which are themselves a function of efficient activity utilizing existing and planned capacity. But there are also other benefits to be obtained:

1. Accountants would have an incentive to improve their understanding of business processes and organizations, in order to provide better and more informative financial statements.

2. Such statements would necessarily utilize replacement and exit values, resolving the conflicts presented by historical cost-based GAAP.

3. Being free from the incidence of historical accidents, such as arbitrary changes in tax rates and rules, and interest and foreign currency rate changes arising out of the supply and demand for money, ratio and

other statistical analyses using the accounting numbers would have normative significance. They would therefore be more useful for the three types of comparison: temporal, spatial, and with industry standards.

4. A new basis for rewarding top management performance would emerge: the extent to which the firm was able to achieve its potential.

SETTING STANDARDS FOR PROSPECTIVE FINANCIAL STATEMENTS

In the 1987 Centennial Issue of the *Journal of Accountancy*, Mednick and Previts pointed to the important role that public accountants were playing in the preparation of prospective financial statements.[5]

[W]e're on the brink of what could be an explosion of the basic attest function. In the past, the profession had generally limited that function to so-called financial information, or assertions, which were generally interpreted to include little, if anything, beyond historical financial statements . . . However, that narrow scope of practice has been expanding for a number of years to encompass a wide range of other financial information: financial forecasts and projections. (p. 234)

In 1985 the Auditing Standards Board of the American Institute of Certified Public Accountants issued a Statement on prospective financial information.[6] The Statement covers "financial forecasts" and "financial projections" and while the definitions of these terms fails to make a clear distinction between them, I interpret the first to mean perspective projections, and the latter, prospective projections. The International Federation of Accountants has also issued a statement, IAG 27, entitled "Examination of Prospective Financial Information."

The ASB publication assumes that accountants will be involved with this type of financial statement through compilation, examination, or applying agreed-upon procedures. Because required procedures for compilations are not extensive, the Statement suggests that the accountant should understand the process whereby the prospective financial information has been developed, and evaluate the preparation and the underlying assumptions of the financial statements. An examination should go further; the accountant should challenge the reasonableness and appropriateness of the underlying assumptions, and the Statement specifies certain procedures that should be undertaken and documented. The accountant's report on an examination should include:

—a statement that the examination was made in accordance with AICPA standards, and a brief description of the nature of such examination,

—the accountant's opinion that the prospective financial statements conform to AICPA presentation guidelines and that the underlying assumptions are reasonable,

—a caveat that the prospective results may not be achieved,

—a statement that the accountant assumes no responsibility to update the report for events and circumstances occurring after the date of the report.

The AICPA provided additional guidelines in *Statement of Position 90–1*, which adopted verbatim the contents of the 1985 Statement. These documents constitute a helpful start in the process of validating the role of the public accountant in providing an opinion on prospective financial statements issued to selected users or filed with the SEC in a prospectus. Much remains to be done, however, if such prospective statements are to become part of the corporate annual report.

ENVOI

The conventional approach to accounting theory identifies three phases of scholarly interest in the subject. Early writers were concerned with accounting measurement, arising perhaps out of the view that this was the responsibility that the SEC had placed upon the accounting profession.[7] This phase ended with the realization that "theory closure" could not be reached.[8] During the 1970s the profession's attention turned to decision usefulness and attempts were made to answer the question of what financial information is useful, relevant, and reliable. The FASB's conceptual framework project failed to find a satisfactory answer, based as it was on the dubious objective of aiding the assessment of future cash flows, and given its explicit historical viewpoint.

Contemporary with this second phase there emerged another movement, based on the proposition that information is a commodity and as such conforms to the laws of supply and demand. The ensuing research has targeted market (event) studies and includes behavioral experiments lumped together under the name "positive theory." Claiming to be empirical, this research has in fact contributed little or nothing to accounting practice; indeed, economic theory generally has had little or no effect on business practice. This chapter suggests that one theory may not be enough.

The problem of diversity in accounting measurement has been viewed as a problem of historical (not historical cost) financial statements. Prospective, or future-oriented financial statements need not be affected by this problem. Yet accounting theory and other financial accounting textbooks contain no mention of business plans, little reference to forecasts or budgets. Such future-oriented information is required by investors, creditors, and other users of financial statements, and the state of the art permits this need to be met. If such prospective financial statements have the same structure as retrospective financial statements, they can be produced to comparable reliability standards.[9]

Prospectives include prospective financial statements, and the SEC has accepted the involvement of public accountants with them by providing a "safe harbor" rule (SEC Release 33–6084 of June 1979.) The guidance that the AICPA has so far provided practitioners falls short of what is required if audited prospective financial statements are to be published in financial reports. No other innovation in accounting could be more exciting than this one.

NOTES

1. George J. Benston, "The Value of the SEC's Accounting Disclosure Requirements," *The Accounting Review*, July 1969, pp. 515–32.

2. David E. Gumpert, and Stanley R. Rich, *Business Plans That Win $* (New York: Harper & Row, 1985).

3. See also on this point Jeffry A. Timmons, "The Business Plan: A Step-by-Step Guide," in *The Portable MBA in Finance and Accounting*, ed. John Leslie Livingstone (New York: John Wiley & Sons, 1992), p. 167.

4. See Kenneth S. Most, "Depreciation Expense and the Effect of Inflation," *Journal of Accounting Research*, Autumn 1984, pp. 782–88.

5. Robert Mednick, and Gary John Previts, "The Scope of CPA Services: A View of the Future," *Journal of Accountancy*, May 1987, pp. 220–38.

6. Auditing Standards Board of the AICPA, *Statement on Standards for Accountants' Services on Prospective Financial Information*, "Financial Forecasts and Projections," American Institute of Certified Public Accountants, October 1985. *See also* AICPA Statements of Position (SOP) 89–3 and 90–1.

7. Robert Jaedicke, Yuji Ijiri, and Oswald Nielsen, eds., *Research in Accounting Measurement* (American Accounting Association, 1966).

8. Committee of the American Accounting Association, *Statement on Accounting Theory and Theory Acceptance* (Sarasota, Fla.: American Accounting Association, 1977).

9. The problems of financial reporting are being debated in many circles. A special commission established by the Institute of Chartered Accountants of Ireland has recently (1992) reported some sixty recommendations prepared in response to the question "Are published financial statements providing what users think they are providing or, more importantly, what they believe they need?" One of these recommendations is that the annual report should contain a statement of the company's objectives and strategic plan.

SELECTED BIBLIOGRAPHY

BOOKS

Accounting Standards Authority of Canada. *Conceptual Framework for Financial Reporting*. Vancouver, B.C., 1987.

Auditing Standards Board of the AICPA, *Statement on Standards for Accountants' Services on Prospective Financial Information*, "Financial Forecasts and Projections," American Institute of Certified Public Accountants, October 1985. See also AICPA Statements of Position (SOP) 89–3 and 90–1.

Bavishi, Vinod B., and Harold E. Wyman. *Who Audits the World: Trends in the Worldwide Auditing Profession*. Storrs, Conn.: Center for Transnational Accounting and Financial Research, University of Connecticut, 1984.

Beaver, William H. *Financial Reporting: An Accounting Revolution*. 2d ed. Englewood Cliffs, N.J.: Prentice-Hall, 1989.

Bonbright, J. C. *Valuation of Property*. New York: McGraw-Hill, 1937.

Briloff, Abraham J. *Unaccountable Accounting*. New York: Harper & Row, 1972.

———. *More Debits Than Credits: The Burnt Investor's Guide to Financial Statements*. New York: Harper & Row, 1976.

Carey, John. *The Rise of the Accounting Profession: From Technician to Professional 1896–1936*. New York: AICPA, 1969.

Chambers, Raymond J. *Accounting Evaluation and Economic Behavior*. Englewood Cliffs, N.J.: Prentice-Hall, 1966.

Chang, Lucia S., and Kenneth S. Most. *The Perceived Usefulness of Financial Statements for Investors' Decisions*. Gainesville: University Presses of Florida, 1985.

Chatfield, Michael. *A History of Accounting Thought*. New York: Robert E. Krieger, 1977.

Committee of the American Accounting Association. *A Statement of Basic Accounting Theory*. American Accounting Association, 1966.

———. *Statement on Accounting Theory and Theory Acceptance*. Sarasota: American Accounting Association, 1977.

Drummond, Christine S. R., and Alan D. Stickler. *Current Cost Accounting*. Toronto: Methuen, 1983.

Edwards, Edgar O., and Philip W. Bell. *The Theory and Measurement of Business Income*. Berkeley: University of California Press, 1961.

Financial Accounting Standards Board. *Scope and Implications of the Conceptual Framework Project*. Stamford, Conn.: Financial Accounting Standards Board, 1976.

———. "Objectives of Financial Reporting by Business Enterprises." *Statement of Financial Accounting Concepts No. 1*. Stamford, Conn.: Financial Accounting Standards Board, 1978.

———. "Qualitative Characteristics of Accounting Information." *Statement of Financial Accounting Concepts No. 2*. Stamford, Conn.: Financial Accounting Standards Board, 1980.

———. "Recognition and Measurement in Financial Statements of Business Enterprises." *Statement of Financial Accounting Concepts No. 5*. Stamford, Conn.: Financial Accounting Standards Board, 1984.

———. "Elements of Financial Statements." *Statement of Financial Accounting Concepts No. 6*. Stamford, Conn.: Financial Accounting Standards Board, 1985.

Flegm, Eugene H. *Accounting: How to Meet the Challenges of Relevance and Regulation*. New York: John Wiley and Sons, 1984.

Hopwood, Anthony G., ed. *International Pressures for Accounting Changes*. London: Prentice-Hall, 1989.

Inflation Accounting: Report of the Inflation Accounting Committee. London: Her Majesty's Stationery Office, CMND. 6225, 1975.

Jaedicke, Robert, Yuji Ijiri, and Oswald Nielsen, eds. *Research in Accounting Measurement*. American Accounting Association, 1966.

Kay, Robert S., and D. Gerald Searfoss, eds. *Deloitte and Touche Professors Handbook*. Boston: Warren, Gorham & Lamont, 1989.

Kellogg, Irving. *How to Find Negligence and Misrepresentations in Financial Statements*. New York: McGraw-Hill, 1983.

Lee, T. A. *Towards a Theory and Practice of Cash Flows*. New York: Garland, 1986.

Littleton, A. C. *Accounting Evolution to 1900*. New York: American Institute, 1933.

MacNeal, Kenneth. *Truth in Accounting*. Scholars Book Company (reprint), 1970.

Most, Kenneth S. *Accounting Theory*. 2d ed. Toronto: Holt, Rinehart and Winston of Canada, 1986.

Paton, W. A., and A. C. Littleton. *An Introduction to Corporate Accounting Standards*. American Accounting Association, 1940.

Pomeranz, Felix. *The Successful Audit*. Homewood, Ill., Business One Irwin, 1992.

Report of the National Commission on Fraudulent Financial Reporting. Washington, D.C.: AICPA, 1987.

Solomons, D. *Guidelines for Financial Reporting Standards*. London: Research Board of the Institute of Chartered Accountants in England and Wales, 1989.

Sombart, Werner. *The Quintessence of Modern Capitalism*. Trans. M. Epstein. New York: L. P. Dutton, 1915.

Stamp, Edward, and Maurice Moonitz. *International Auditing Standards*. Englewood Cliffs, N.J.: Prentice-Hall International, 1979.

Sterling, Robert R. *Theory of the Measurement of Enterprise Income*. Lawrence, Kans.: University Press of Kansas, 1970.

Stolowy, Herve, and Sylvie Walser-Prochazka. *The American Influence in Accounting:*

Myth or Reality? The Statement of Cash Flows Example. Paris: Ernst & Young, 1991.

Sweeney, Henry W. *Stabilized Accounting*. New York: Harper and Bros., 1936.

Thornton, D. B. "The Financial Reporting of Contingencies and Uncertainties." *Research Monograph No. 5*. Vancouver, B.C.: Canadian CGA Research Foundation, 1983.

ARTICLES

Barden, Horace G. "The Meaning of Auditing Standards." *Journal of Accountancy*, April 1958, pp. 50–56.

Benston, George H. "The Value of the SEC's Accounting Disclosure Requirements." *The Accounting Review*, July 1969, pp. 515–32.

———. "Required Disclosure and the Stock Market: An Evaluation of the Securities Act of 1934." *American Economic Review*, March 1973, pp. 132–55.

———. "The Market for Public Accounting Services: Demand, Supply, and Regulation." *Journal of Accounting and Public Policy*, Spring 1985, pp. 33–80.

Birkett, Brenda S. "The Recent History of Corporate Audit Committees." *The Accounting Historians Journal*, Fall 1986, pp. 109–24.

Brief, Richard P. "The Accountant's Responsibility in Historical Perspective." *The Accounting Review*, April 1975, pp. 285–97.

Edwards, Edgar O. "The State of Current Value Accounting." *The Accounting Review*, April 1975, pp. 235–45.

Flesher, Dale L. and Tonya K. Flesher. "Ivar Kreuger's Contribution to U.S. Financial Reporting." *The Accounting Review*, July 1986, pp. 421–34.

Fortin, Anne. "The 1947 French Accounting Plan: Origins and Influences on Subsequent Practice." *The Accounting Historians Journal*, December 1991, pp. 1–25.

Mason, Alister K. and Michael Gibbins. "Judgment and U.S. Accounting Standards." *Accounting Horizons*, June 1991, pp. 14–24.

Mednick, Robert. "Reinventing the Audit." *Journal of Accountancy*, August 1991, pp. 71–78.

Mednick, Robert and Gary John Previts. "The Scope of CPA Services: A View of the Future." *Journal of Accountancy*, May 1987, pp. 220–38.

Most, Kenneth S. "Problems in the Profession." *The Accountant*, April 16, 1966, pp. 462–63.

———. "The Great American Accounting Principles Controversy." *The Accountant*, March 23, 1968, pp. 377–81.

INDEX

AAA, publications, 5, 95
accountability, 112; growth of, 23–25
accountancy: art or science?, 32, 35, 110; education for, 73–74; impact of the legal system on, 73; marketing failure of, 200; rise of a profession, 24, 28; Uniform Accountancy Act, 68. *See also* accounting
accountants, regional organizations of, 77–78
accounting: accreditation, 73; as a closed system, 42, 104; and company laws, 27–28; and culture, 82; defined, 5–6, 95; economic consequences of, 7–8; financial, as a subset of managerial, 150; for the future, 205–7; harmonization, 79–84; history, 13–30; international, 11; measurement, 105, 134–35; perceived irrelevance of, 69; politicization of, 6; static and dynamic, 35–36; theory, 93–96, 212
Accounting Education Change Commission, 73, 201
accounting standards: anomaly of principles, 56; role of SEC, 6
accounts of Ancient Rome, 15–17
accrual accounting, 99
Age of Stagnation, 20–22

agency theories, 44, 122–23
AIA: Committee on Accounting Procedure, 53; Committee on Auditing Procedures, 64–65; special committee on cooperation with stock exchanges, 50
AICPA: and attracting better students, 75 n.6; Auditing Standards Board, 65, 213; function of, 2; history of, 61 n.1; practice sections, 66; prospective financial information, 211–12; publications, 5; Rules of Code of Professional Ethics, 58, 65, 72
Anderson Committee, 66–68
APB: demise of, 55; Opinions and Accounting Research Studies, 54; publications of, 5–6; *Statement No. 4*, 95–96
Aquinas, Thomas, 3
Arthur Andersen & Co. publications, 4, 63, 75 n.5
articulation, 104
ASB, *Statement on Auditing Standards No. 69*, 57
assets: defined, 101, 163; uselessness of definition, 109
assumptions, environmental, 98
"attribute" in accounting, 42, 100, 105

audit: certificate, 64; committee, 192; contrasted with investigation, 72; failure, 70, 191–92; long form report, 198–99; need for, 194; objective of, 71, 193; report, 1, 51, 64, 96, 117; standards, 64–66

audit expectation gap, 4, 10, 61, 74, 202

auditing: commercialization of, 74, 191; history of, 27–29; international, 88–89, 197–98; in the Middle Ages, 17; multinational corporation, 196–98; new approach to, 4; in the United States, 28–29

auditor: decline in importance of, 200; deficiencies of, 192–93; independence, 72; legal liability, 66, 70; responsibility for financial report, 117; state of the profession, 191–92; ten commandments, 201; value of signature, 202

backlog depreciation, 154–55

balance sheet: audit, 29; emphasis, 49; form of, 164–67; what is it?, 162–65

banks, influence of, 49

basic equation, 21, 104; expanded, 138; of finance, 39

BCCI, 68, 197

Benson, Henry, 78, 81

Benston, George H., 111, 204

Big Six, defined, 11 n.1

Blough, Carman, 52

Brief, Richard P., 4

Briloff, Abraham, 2

Böhm-Bawerk, Eugen, 3, 149

Burton, John C., 204

business plan, 206–8

Byrne, Gilbert, 51

Canada: conceptual framework, 107–8; GAAP, 59; regulation, 113

Canning, John, 3

CAP, Accounting Research Bulletins, 53

capital maintenance, 105, 129; and measurement models, 137–39

capitalism and accounting, 19–20

Carey, John, 61 n.1

cash: accounting, 3–4, 164, 172; different concepts of, 173–74

Chambers Development Co., 109

changes in financial position, 39, 119; and cash flows, 171–72

changing prices, 95; AICPA position, 125; current FASB position, 156; early literature, 129; general and specific, 132–33; legal aspects of, 142; monetary, 157; objectives of, 133–34; SEC position, 126; and working capital, 156–58

charts of accounts, 36

Church, Hamilton, 26

classification: of accounts, 36; bastard, 170; decimal coding, 35; defined, 165; French *Plan Comptable Général*, 188; need for, 34–35; Schmalenbach's, 35

clean surplus and comprehensive income, 104, 168

Coase, Roger, 94

commercialization of the profession, 4, 74, 200

company accounts, 27–28, 32; comparability of, 85, 90

compilation and review, 117

comprehensive income, 104, 168; defined, 102

conceptual framework, 42–43; Canadian, 46 n.3, 107–8; components of, 97; fails in it purpose, 109; global adoption of, 107–8

conservatism, 100

constant dollar accounting, 135; applied to current cost accounting, 143–44

constant value monetary unit, 34

Continental Vending, 60, 66, 71

contractual versus statutory audits, 29–30

Coopers and Lybrand, 78

corporations: annual reports, 117; governance of, 68–69; government control over, 81–82; impact on accounting, 21–22; lack of accounting and auditing laws in U.S., 29; model statute, 68

cost accounting, 23; and government contracts, 25

cost of accounting diversity, 80–81, 86, 180–81
criticism of accountants and accounting, 2–3
current cost accounting, 70, 136

decision models, 3
Dingell Commission, 2
disclosure, 114–15; differential, 121; and financial reporting, 120–22; how?, 119–21; legal significance of, 124; what?, 116–17; when?, 118–19; who?, 117–18
discounting obligations, 57
display: avoidance of issue, 179; balance sheet, 164–66
dividends, anomalous treatment of, 185
double-entry bookkeeping, 1, 13, 16; as a closed system, 18; history of, 19; relation to spreadsheets, 30
Duque, Alberto, 195–96

earnings, 102, 106
economic facts, 33
economic theory, 3, 94, 149
efficient financial markets, 44, 79–80, 118–19, 124 n.5
Elliott, Robert K., 4
entity assumption, 34
entity theory, 19, 34, 93–94
equity, defined, 101
Escott v. Barchris Construction Corporation, 122
European Community (EC), 28, 82–84; and auditor reciprocity, 89–90; Fourth Directive, 142, 180, 189
events (and circumstances), 32–33
exception reporting, 204
exit prices, 147–49
expenses, defined, 102

fair presentation, 1, 57
FASB: birth of, 55–56; changing prices, 127–28; conceptual framework project, 5, 42; Emerging Issues Task Force, 56; influence of SEC on, 6; international activities, 85; publications of, 6; purpose of, 1; productivity of, 56–57

Federal Reserve Board: influence of, 49; regulations, 60
Fells, J. M., 26
financial analysts, 3; influence of, 48, 80
financial and managerial accounting compared, 205–6
financial position, 36; statement of, 162
financial reports: comparability of, 85, 99; components of, 120; and financial statements, 5; measurement, recognition and display, 105; purpose of, 1, 7, 205; regulation in selected countries, 111–14; SEC requirements, 69; and tax conformity, 81–82
financial statements: basic, 161–62; consistency in, 100; defined, 96, 104, 106, 179; elements of, 101–5; form of, 162; integrated, 184; notes to, 105–6; objectives of, 99; primary, 181; SEC filings and annual reports, 114–16, 176; standard form of, 182–86; synthetic, 207–9; why standardize?, 179–81
Fisher, Irving, 3
Flegm, Eugene H., 61 n.1
footnotes, 105–6, 174–76
forecasts, distinguished from budgets, 206
Foreign Corrupt Practices Act, 7, 122; and Wyden Bill, 69
foreign currency translation, 8, 95
form versus substance, 167
fraudulent financial reporting, 7, 10, 44, 67–68; in Roman times, 16
French: auditing law, 72; National Accounting Council, 41, 88
Plan Comptable Général, 186–89

gains, defined, 102
Garcke, Emile, 26
gearing adjustment, 153–54
generally accepted accounting principles (GAAP): defects, 10, 61; hierarchy of, 57–58; history of, 48–57; importance of, 60; and the law, 60; required use of judgment, 59
generally accepted auditing standards (GAAS), history of, 63–65

Gibbins, Michael, 59
global financial markets, impact of, 180
going concern assumption, 34
government: accounting, 25;
    Governmental Accounting Standards
    Board, 57, 61 n.2

harmonization of accounting: basic
    issues, 88; in the EC, 83;
    internationally, 79–84; in the U.S., 80
Hess, Henry, 26
historical cost, 34, 147
holding gain (loss), 152–54
"House of GAAP," 57

impairment, 134
income statement: and earnings, 167–68;
    format, 169–70; GAAP requirements,
    170–71; U.K. proposed format, 182
income tax: accounting for, 61; influence
    on accounting, 24, 171
index number problem, 144–45
indexation, 128–29
inflation accounting. See changing prices
information, 42, 120–21; overload, 121;
    qualitative characteristics of, 99–101
Institute of Management Accountants, 26
Internal Revenue Service accounting
    requirements, 60
international: business, 196–97; chart of
    accounts, 37–39; financial reporting,
    44; profession, 77–78
International Accounting Standards
    Committee, 59, 78, 84–85; conceptual
    framework, 108; Exposure Draft 32,
    78; Standard No. 1, 100
International Federation of Accountants,
    77–78, 89, 198
inventory, fabrication of, 196
investment tax credit, accounting for, 55
Investors Overseas Services, 195
IOSCO, 80

journals, 20–21

Kellogg, Irving, 2
Kreuger, Ivar, 194–95
Kuhn, Thomas, 45

Lauzel, Pierre, 37
Lee, Geoffrey, 18
Lee, T. A., 4
legal theory of accounts, 33–34
legal liability of accountants, 2, 9, 159
legislation affecting accounting, 6–7
liabilities: defined, 108, 163;
    distinguished from equity, 166–67
LIFO, 31, 82, 150; and changing prices,
    130, 158; footnote disclosure, 175
Limperg, Theo, 149
liquidity, 165–66, 205
Littleton, A. C., 18, 95
long form audit report, 198–99
losses, defined, 102

MacNeal, Kenneth, 3
managerial revolution, 22; isolation of the
    accountant, 26
marking to market, 8, 139–40
Mason, Alister, 59
materiality, 101, 122
mathematical modeling, 26
May, G. O., 49–50
McKesson and Robbins, 64
measurement, defined, 135. See also
    accounting, measurement
medieval manorial accounting, 17
Mednick, Robert, 4, 69
Metcalf and Moss Committees, 7
multinational corporation, 196–98

net income (loss), as a substitution of
    revenues for costs, 41; unitary concept
    of, 49
Netherlands Institute of Accountants, 5
New York Stock Exchange: Committee
    on Stock List, 50–51; influence of, 48
Niebuhr, Bartholdt, 16
nominal accounts, 34

origins of writing, 14
other comprehensive basis of accounting,
    189
outside directors, 69

Pacioli, Luca, 13, 18–19, 31
Paton, W. A., 93–94, 129, 163

periodicity, 35
personal accounts, 34
personification theories, 33
Plan Comptable Général, 37, 80–81,
186–89; contents of, 187
planning model of the firm, 40
Plantin, Christopher, 21
Pomeranz, Felix, on auditing, 191–94
positive theory, 212
post-retirement benefits, 8
predictive information, 4, 70, 123, 204–
5. *See also* prospective financial
information
preferred accounting principles, 60
Price Waterhouse, 64, 91 n.2;
publications of, 140
principle: accounting, 54; proceeds value,
151–52; Webster definition of, 51. *See
also* exit prices
production time period, 32
professional schools, 73
profit and loss account, beginning of, 32.
See also income statement
proprietary theory, 19, 34, 93–94; hard to
kill, 46 n.1
prospective financial information, 116,
207–12; standards for, 211–12
public accounting and diversification,
199–200
purchasing power loss or gain, 141

railroad accounting, 23–24
ratios, 186; return on investment, 39,
206; return on working capital, 157
real accounts, 34
reciprocity, 90
recognition and realization, 106–7
regulation of financial reporting in the
U.S., 112–13
replacement cost: defined, 149;
explained, 150–51; legal decisions, 130
replacement value accounting, 149–53
*Report of the National Commission on
Fraudulent Financial Reporting*, 11
n.12
representational faithfulness, 100
research approach to accounting, 208

revenues, defined, 102
Rubin, Steven, 57

Sanders, Hatfield and Moore, 52
Sandilands Committee (report), 126, 144,
148–49
Schmalenbach, Eugen, 35–37, 46 n.2,
186
Schreiber, Heinrich (Grammateus), 31
scientific management, 26
SEC: annual reports, 69; ASR 4, 53;
ASR 150, 58; ASR 190, 126; changing
prices, 125, 159; disclosure, 114–16;
EDGAR system, 180; foreign filers,
86–87; oversight, 7; and prospectuses,
213; regulation by, 29, 81; Regulation
S-X, 52, 115, 176; Rule 144A, 87;
selective enforcement by, 113
securities legislation of 1933 and 1934,
52–53
Seidler, Lee J., 56
situational approach to accounting, 45
social issues, 9–10
soft data: need for, 116, 121; and open
systems, 183
Sombart, Werner, 18–20
South Sea Bubble, 27
sponsoring organizations, 56
standardized accounting, 79–81; financial
statements, 179–86, 190; in France,
186–89
standards overload, 56
A Statement of Basic Accounting Theory
(ASOBAT), 5
statement of cash flows, 43, 80, 99, 171–
74; alternative format, 173
*Statement of Financial Accounting
Concepts*: No. 1, 97–99; No. 2, 99–
101; No. 5, 105–7; No. 6, 101–5
stewardship theory, 17
stock exchange, origin of, 22
summary annual reports, 98, 115, 176
suspense, items in, 164
synthetic financial reporting, benefits of,
210–11
system defined, 182–83

tax conformity, 81–82
Taylor, F. W., 26

theory of accounts: legal, 32; continental
  European, 33
threshhold problem, 42
Treadway Commission, 10, 67, 192, 200
Trueblood Report, 55

U.K.: Accounting Standards Board, 114,
  181; changing prices, 126; FRED 1,
  181; No. 16, 126, 157–58; regulation,
  113–14; *Statementsof Standard
  Accounting Practice*, 59
*Ultramares Corporation v. Touche Niven
  and Company*, 64
uncertainty, 209–10
uniform accounting, 49; in France, 81,
  186–89; for railroads and utilities, 24
uniform financial reporting, 44; and
  countertrade and joint ventures, 180
unit of account, 15

United Nations Commission on
  Transnational Corporations, 82
U.S. v. Simon (Continental Vending), 60,
  66

valuation: allowances, 104–5; in
  accounting, 42
value, defined, 147
value added, 2–3, 39; form of income
  statement, 170
Var, Turgut, 194
von Bülow, Fritz, 3

W. T. Grant Company, 172
Wheat Committee Report, 55
Wilde, Oscar, 3
working capital: and cash flows, 172;
  effect of inflation, 156–58
Wyden Bill, 69, 119

About the Author

KENNETH S. MOST is Professor of Accounting at Florida International University in Miami, and has degrees in accounting, economics, and law. He was in practice as an international accountant and auditor for seventeen years before becoming an educator. Author of twenty books and research monographs, he has also published many articles in *Abacus*, *Accounting and Business Research*, *The Accounting Review*, *The Journal of Accountancy*, *The Journal of Accounting Research* and other leading professional publications in the United States and abroad.